PURITAN PAPERBACKS

An Ark for All God's Noahs

Thomas Brooks

1608–1680

Little is known about Thomas Brooks as a man, other than can be ascertained from his many writings. Born, probably of well-to-do parents, in 1608, Brooks entered Emmanuel College, Cambridge, in 1625. He was licensed as a preacher of the gospel by 1640 at the latest. Before that date he seems to have spent a number of years at sea, probably as a chaplain with the fleet. After the Civil War, Brooks became minister at Thomas Apostle's, London, and was sufficiently renowned to be chosen as preacher before the House of Commons on 26 December, 1648. Three or four years later he moved to St Margaret's, Fish-street Hill, London, but encountered considerable opposition as he refused baptism and the Lord's Supper to those clearly 'unworthy' of such privileges. The following years were filled with written as well as spoken ministry. In 1662 he fell victim to the notorious Act of Uniformity, but he appears to have remained in his parish and to have preached the word as opportunity offered. Treatises continued to flow from his agile pen. In 1677 or 1678 he married for the second time, 'she spring-young, he winter-old.' Two years later he went home to his Lord.

Thomas Brooks

An Ark for All God's Noahs

In a Gloomy Stormy Day,
or,
The Best Wine Reserved till Last,
or,
The Transcendent Excellency of a Believer's Portion
Above All Earthly Portions Whatsoever, etc.

The Lord is my portion, saith my soul;
therefore will I hope in him.
LAM. 3:24.

THE BANNER OF TRUTH TRUST

THE BANNER OF TRUTH TRUST

Head Office	*North America Office*
3 Murrayfield Road	PO Box 621
Edinburgh	Carlisle
EH12 6EL	PA 17310
UK	USA

banneroftruth.org

*

ISBN
Print: 978 1 84871 573 8
EPUB: 978 1 84871 585 1
Kindle: 978 1 84871 596 7

*

Typeset in 10/13 Minion Pro at
The Banner of Truth Trust, Edinburgh

Printed in the USA by
Versa Press Inc.,
East Peoria, IL.

Contents

Epistle Dedicatory

To all the merchants and tradesmen of England, especially these of the city of London, with all other sorts and ranks of persons that either have or would have God for their portion, grace, mercy, and peace be multiplied.

GENTLEMEN, – The wisest prince that ever sat upon a throne has told us, that 'a word fitly spoken is like apples of gold in pictures of silver,' or as the Hebrew has it, 'a word spoken, עַל־אָפְנָיו, upon his wheels,' that is, rightly ordered, placed, and circumstantiated. Such a word is, of all words, the most excellent, the most prevalent, and the most pleasant word that can be spoken; such a word is, indeed, a word that is like 'apples of gold in pictures of silver.' Of all words such a word is most precious, most sweet, most desirable, and most delectable. O sirs! to time a word, to set a word upon the wheels, to speak a word to purpose, is the project of this book. Though all truths are glorious, yet there is a double glory upon seasonable truths; and, therefore, I have made it my great business in this treatise to hold forth as seasonable a truth, and as weighty a truth, and as comfortable and encouraging a truth, as any I know in all the book of God. The mother of King Cyrus willed, that the words of those that spoke to her son should be in silk, but certainly seasonable words are always better than silken words.

Every prudent husbandman observes his fittest season to sow his seeds, and therefore some he sows in the autumn and fall of the leaf, and some in the spring and renewing of the year; some he sows in a dry season, and some he sows in a wet; some he sows in a moist clay, and some he sows in a sandy dry ground, as the Holy Spirit speaks, 'He soweth the fitches and the cummin, and casteth in wheat by measure,' Isa. 28:25. And so all spiritual husbandmen must wisely observe their fittest seasons for the sowing of that immortal seed that God has put into their hands; and such a thing as this is I have had in my eye, but whether I have hit the mark or missed it, let the Christian reader judge.

One speaking of the glory of heaven says, 'That the good things of eternal life are so many that they exceed number, so great that they exceed measure, and so precious that they are above all estimation,' *etc.* The same may I say concerning the saint's portion, for certainly the good things that are in their portion, in their God, are so many that they exceed number, so great that they exceed measure, and so precious that they are above all estimation.

The same author in one of his epistles has this remarkable relation, *viz.*, That the same day in which Jerome died, he was in his study, and had got pen, ink, and paper to write something of the glory of heaven to Jerome, and suddenly he saw a light breaking into his study, and smelt also a very sweet smell, and this voice he thought he heard: 'O Augustine, what are you doing? do you think to put the sea into a little bottle? When the heavens shall cease from their continual motion, then shall you be able to understand what the glory of heaven is, and not before, except you come to feel it as I now do.' Certainly, the glory of heaven is beyond all conception and all expression, and so is that portion that is a little hinted at in the following discourse. And, indeed, a full description of that God, that is the believer's portion, is a work too high for an Aaron when standing upon Mount Hor; or for a Moses, when standing on the top of Nebo after a Pisgah prospect; yea, it is a work too high and too hard for all those blessed seraphims that are still crying before the throne of God, 'Holy, holy, holy is the Lord of hosts.'[1] No finite being, though never so glorious, can ever be able fully to comprehend an infinite being. In the second verse of the sixth of Isaiah, we read that each seraphim had six wings, and that with twain[2] he covered the face of God, with twain his feet, and with twain he did fly, intimating, as one well observes upon the place, that with twain they covered his face, the face of God, not their own face, and with twain they covered his feet, not their own feet. They covered his face, his beginning being unknown; they covered his feet, his end being incomprehensible; only the middle are to be seen, the things which are, by which there may be some glimmering knowledge made out what God is. The wise man hit it, when he said, 'That which is afar off, and exceeding deep, who can find it out?' Eccles. 7:24.[3] Who can find out what God is? The knowledge of him *a priori* is so far off, that he whose arm is able to break even a bow of steel is not able to reach it; so far off, that he

[1] Num. 20:28; Deut. 32:49, and 34:1; Isa. 6:3.

[2] [That is, with two.]

[3] There are many depths in God which our shallow reason cannot fathom; and, indeed, it is the credit of our religion, and the glory of our God, that he is unsearchable.

who is able to make his nest with the eagle is not able to fly unto it; and so exceeding deep, that he who could follow the leviathan could not fathom it; that he who could set out the centre of the earth, is not able to find it out; and who then is able to reach it? In a word, so far off and so deep too, that 'the depth saith, It is not in me; and the sea saith, It is not in me.' It is such a deep to men and angels as far exceeds the capacity of both. Augustine speaking to that question, What God is? gives this answer: 'Surely such a one as he, who, when he is spoken of, cannot be spoken of; who, when he is considered, cannot be considered of; who, when he is compared to anything, cannot be compared; and when he is defined, grows greater by defining of him. If that great apostle, that learned his divinity among the angels, yea, to whom the Holy Spirit was an immediate tutor, did know but 'in part,' then certainly those that are most acute and judicious in divine knowledge may very well conclude, that they know but part of that part that was known to him.'[1] As for my own part, I dare pretend but to a spark of that knowledge that others have attained to, and yet who can tell but that God may turn this spark into such a flame as may warm the hearts of many of his dear and precious ones. Much is done many times by a spark.

O sirs! catch not at the present profits, pleasures, preferments, and honours of this world, but 'lay up a good foundation for the time to come,' provide for eternity, make sure your interest and propriety in God. It was an excellent

---

[1] Such are not only good scholars, but also great scholars, who have learned contentedly to be ignorant where God would not have them knowing.

saying of Lewis of Bavyer [Bavaria?], emperor of Germany: 'Such goods,' said he, 'are worth getting and owning, as will not sink or wash away if a shipwreck happen.' How many of you have lost your all by shipwrecks! and how has divine providence by your multiplied crosses and losses taught you that, that the good things and the great things of this world cannot be made sure! How many of you have had rich inheritances left you by your fathers, besides the great portions that you have had with your wives, and the vast estates that you have gained by trading; but what is become of all? Is not all buried in the deep, or in the grave of oblivion? Oh the inconstancy and the grand impostury of this world! Oh the flux and reflux of riches, greatness, honours, and preferments! How many men have we seen shining in their worldly pomp and glory like stars in the firmament, who are now vanished into smoke or comets! How has the moon of many great men's riches and honours been eclipsed at the full, and the sun of their pomp gone down at noon!

'It was,' says the historian [Justinian], 'a wonderful precedent of vanity and variety of human condition to see mighty Xerxes to float and fly away in a small vessel, who but a little before wanted sea-room for his navy.' The Dutch, to express the world's vanity and uncertainty, have very wittily pictured a man with a full blown bladder on his shoulders, and another standing by pricking the bladder with a pin, with this motto, *Quam subito*, How soon is all blown down! I am not willing to make the porch too wide, else I might have given you famous instances of the vanity and uncertainty of all worldly wealth, pomp, and glory, from the Assyrian, Chaldean, Persian, Grecian, and Roman kingdoms, whose glory now lies all in the dust. By all this it is most evident that earthly portions cannot be made sure, they 'make themselves wings, and they fly away,' Prov. 23:5.

Oh! but now God is a portion that may be made sure. In the time of the Marian persecution, there was a woman, who, being convened before bloody Bonner, then bishop of London, upon the trial of religion, he threatened her that he would take away her husband from her: says she, Christ is my husband. I will take away your child; Christ, says she, is better to me than ten sons. I will strip you, says he, of all your outward comforts; but Christ is mine, says she, and you cannot strip me of him.[1] A Christian may be stripped of anything but his God; he may be stripped of his estate, his friends, his relations, his liberty, his life, but he can never be stripped of his God. As God is a portion that none can give to a Christian but himself, so God is a portion that none can take from a Christian but himself; and, therefore, as ever you would have a sure portion, an abiding portion, a lasting portion, yea, an everlasting portion, make sure of God for your portion.

O Sirs! that you would judge that only worth much now, which will be found of much worth at last, when you shall lie upon a dying bed, and stand before a judgment-seat. Oh that men would prize and value all earthly portions now, as they will value them when they come to die, and when their souls shall sit upon their trembling lips, and when there shall be but a short step between them and eternity. Oh, at what a poor rate, at what a low rate do men value their earthly portions! then, certainly, it will be their very

[1] Mr Foxe, Acts and Monum. [See under Bonner.—G.]

great wisdom to value their earthly portions now as they would value them then. And oh that men would value this glorious, this matchless portion that is held forth in this treatise now, as they will value it and prize it when they come to die, and when they come to launch out into the ocean of eternity!

I have read of a stationer, who, being at a fair, hung out several pictures of men famous in their kinds, among which he had also the picture of Christ, upon which divers men bought according to their several fancies: the soldier buys his Caesar, the lawyer his Justinian, the physician his Galen, the philosopher his Aristotle, the poet his Virgil, the orator his Cicero, and the divine his Augustine; but all this while the picture of Christ hung by as a thing of no value, till a poor chapman, that had no more money than would purchase that, bought it, saying, Now every man has taken away his god, let me have mine too.

O Sirs! it would make any gracious, any serious, any ingenious, any conscientious heart to bleed, to see at what a high rate all sorts and ranks of men do value earthly portions, which at best are but counterfeit pictures, when this glorious portion, that is here treated on, hangs by as a thing of no value, of no price. Most men are mad upon the world, and so they may have much of that for their portion, they care not whether ever they have God for their portion or no. Give them but a palace in Paris, and then with that French duke [the Duke of Bourbon] they care not for a place in paradise; give them but a mess of pottage, and let who will take the birthright; give them but manna in a wilderness, and let who will take the land of Canaan; give them but ground which is pleasant and rich, and then with the Reubenites they will gladly take up their rest on this side of the Holy Land; give them but their bags full, and their barns full, and then with the rich fool in the Gospel they can think of nothing but of taking their ease, and of eating and drinking, and making merry, Luke 12:16-21. So brutish and foolish are they in their understandings, as if their precious and immortal souls were good for nothing but as salt to keep their bodies from rotting and stinking.

Oh that these men would seriously consider, that as a cup of pleasant wine, offered to a condemned man on the way to his execution, and as the feast of him who sat under a naked sword, hanging perpendicularly over his head by a slender thread, and as Adam's forbidden fruit, seconded by a flaming sword, and as Belshazzar's dainties, overlooked by an handwriting against the wall; such and only such are all earthly portions to those that have not God for their portion.

Well, gentlemen, remember this, there is no true happiness to be found in any earthly portions. Solomon, having made a critical inquiry after the excellency of all creature comforts, gives this in as the ultimate extraction from them all, 'Vanity of vanities, all is vanity.' If you should go to all the creatures round, they will tell you that happiness is not in them. If you should go to the earth, the earth will tell you that happiness grows not in the furrows of the field. If you go to the sea, the sea will tell you that happiness is not in the treasures of the deep. If you go to the beasts of the field, or to the birds of the air, they will tell you that happiness is not to be found on their backs, nor in their bowels. If you go to your bags, or heaps of gold and silver, they will tell you that happiness is not to be found in them. If you go to crowns and sceptres, they will tell you that happiness is too precious and too glorious a gem to be found in them.

As it is not the great cage that makes the bird sing, so it is not the great estate that makes the happy life, nor the great portion that makes the happy soul. There is no true comfort nor no true happiness to be drawn out of the standing pools of outward sufficiencies. All true comfort and happiness is only to be found in having an all-sufficient God for your portion: Psa. 144:15, 'Happy is that people, that is in such a case: yea, happy is that people, whose God is the Lord.' And therefore, as ever you would be happy in both worlds, it very highly concerns you to get an interest in God, and to be restless in your own souls till you come to enjoy God for your portion. A man that has God for his portion is a non-such;[1] he is the rarest and the happiest man in the world; he is like the morning star in the midst of the clouds; he is like the moon when it is at full; he is like the flower of the roses in the spring of the year; he is like the lilies by the springs of waters; he is like the branches of frankincense in the time of summer; he is like a vessel of massy[2] gold that is set about with all manner of precious stones.[3]

Nothing can make that man miserable that has God for his portion, nor nothing can make that man happy that wants God for his portion: the more rich, the more wretched; the more great, the more graceless; the more

---

[1] [Non-such = unequalled.]

[2] [That is, weighty, heavy.]

[3] This you will find fully cleared up in the following treatise.

honourable, the more miserable that man will be that has not God for his portion. The Sodomites were very wealthy, and who more wanton and wicked than they? The Egyptians and Babylonians were very rich, great, and potent in the world, and what greater oppressors and persecutors of the people of God than these? Oh the slavery, the captivity, and the woeful misery of the people of God under those cruel tyrants! Have not the Nimrods, the Nebuchadnezzars, the Belshazzars, the Alexanders, and the Caesars, *etc.*, been commonly the lords of the world, and who so abominably wicked as these? No men for wickedness have been able to match them or come near them.

It has been long since observed to my hand, that Daniel sets forth the several monarchies of the world by sundry sorts of cruel beasts, to show that as they were gotten by beastly subtlety and cruelty, so they were supported and maintained by brutish sensuality, craft, and tyranny.

I have read of a Lacedaemonian that said, that they well deserved death that did not quench tyranny, they should quite have consumed it with fire. But whether he hit the mark or missed it, let the reader judge. Well, Sirs! you may be the lords of this world, and yet you will certainly be miserable in another world, except you get God for your portion. The top of man's happiness in this world lies in his having God for his portion. He that has God for his portion enjoys all; and he that wants an interest and propriety in God enjoys nothing at all.

Gentlemen, I have read of a heathen who, seeing a sudden shipwreck of all his wealth, said, Well, fortune, I see now that you would have me to be a philosopher. Oh that you would say under all your heavy losses and crosses,

Well! we now see that God would have us 'lay up treasure in heaven,' Matt. 6:19, 20; we now see that God would have us look after a better portion than any this world affords; we now see that it highly concerns us to secure our interest and propriety in God; we now see that to enjoy God for our portion is the one thing necessary. Have not many of you said, nay sworn, that if you might but see and enjoy the delight of your eyes, that then you should have a sweeping trade, and abound in all plenty and prosperity, and grow rich and great and glorious in the world, and be eased of everything that did but look like a burden, *etc.* If it be indeed thus with you, why do you so complain, murmur, and repine? and why do many of you walk up and down the Exchange and streets with tears in your eyes, and with heaviness in your hearts, and with cracked credits, and threadbare coats, and empty purses? and why are so many of you broke, and so many prisoners, and so many hid, and so many fled? But if it be otherwise, and that you are sensible[1] that you have put a cheat upon yourselves, I say not upon others, and that as you have been self-flatterers, so you have been self-deceivers, the more highly it concerns you to do yourselves, your souls that right, as to make sure of God for your portion. For what else can make up those woful disappointments under which you are fallen?

It is a sad sight to see all the arrows that men shoot to fall upon their own heads, or to see them twist a cord to hang themselves, or to see men dig a pit for others and to fall into it themselves; and it is but justice that men should bake as they brew, and that they which brew mischief should have the first and largest draught of it themselves.

[1] That is, able to sense or feel.

Now the best way to prevent so sad a sight and so great a mischief, is to get God for your portion: for when once God comes to be a man's portion, then 'all things shall work together for his good,' Rom. 8:28, and then God will preserve him from such hurtful and mischievous actings. The whole world is a great bedlam, and multitudes there are that think madly, and that design madly, and that talk madly, and that act madly, and that walk madly. Now as you would not be found in the number of those bedlams, it highly concerns you to get God for your portion, that so you may be filled with that wisdom that may preserve you from the folly and madness of this mad world.

Gentlemen, the following sermons I preached in the year 1660, at Olave's, Bread Street, and God blessed them then to those Christians that attended on my ministry, and I hope he will bless them also to the internal and eternal welfare of your souls, to whom they are now dedicated. They are much enlarged; the profit will be yours, the labour has been mine. I judge them very seasonable and suitable to present dispensations, else they had not seen the light at this time. Curiosity is the spiritual adultery of the soul; curiosity is that green-sickness of the soul, by which it longs for novelties, and loathes sound and wholesome truths; it is the epidemical distemper of this age and hour.

And therefore, if any of you are troubled with this itch of curiosity, and love to be wise above what is written, and delight to scan the choice mysteries of religion by carnal reason, and affect elegant expressions and seraphical notions, and the flowers of rhetoric, more than sound and wholesome truths, then you may ease yourselves, if you please, of the trouble of reading this following treatise; only remember this, that the prudent husbandman looks more and delights more in the ripeness and soundness and goodness of the corn that is in his field, than he does at the beauty of the cockle; and remember, that no man can live more miserably than he that lives altogether upon sauces; and he that looks more at the handsomeness than he does at the wholesomeness of the dishes of meat that are set before him, may well pass for a fool.

Well, gentlemen, for a close, remember this, that as Noah was drunk with his own wine, and as Goliath was beheaded by his own sword, and as the rose is destroyed by the canker that it breeds in itself, and as Agrippina was killed by Nero, to whom she gave breath; so if ever you are eternally destroyed, you will be destroyed by yourselves; if ever you are undone, you will be undone by yourselves; if ever you are scourged to death, it will be by rods of your own making; and if ever the bitter cup of damnation be put into your hands, it will be found to be of your own preparing, mingling, and embittering.

Behold, I have set life and death, heaven and hell, glory and misery, before you in this treatise; and therefore, if you will needs choose death rather than life, hell rather than heaven, misery rather than glory, what can be more just than that you should perish to all eternity? If you will not have God for your portion, you shall be sure to have wrath for your portion, and hell for your portion, *etc.*

Well, sirs! remember this at last: every man shall only thank his own folly for his own bane, his own sin for his own everlasting shame, his own iniquity for his own endless misery.

I have now no more to do but to improve all the interest that I have in heaven, that this treatise may be blessed to all your souls, and that you all experience what it is to have God for your portion; for that will be my joy as well as yours, and my crown as well as yours, and my glorying as well as yours, in the great day of our Lord Jesus; and so 'I commend you to God, and to the word of his grace, which is able to build you up, and to give you an inheritance among them that are sanctified,' Acts 20:32; and rest, gentlemen, your souls' servant,

THOMAS BROOKS

A Matchless Portion

---

*The Lord is my portion, saith my soul; therefore will I
hope in him. –* Lamentations 3:24.

Introduction

Certainly if Ennius could pick out gold out of a dunghill,
I may, by divine assistance, much better pick out golden
matter out of such a golden mine as my text is, to enrich the
souls of men withal. The best of painters [Apelles], to draw
an exquisite Venus, had set before him a hundred choice
and selected beauties, to take from one an eye, another a lip,
a third a smile, a fourth a hand, and from each of them that
special lineament in which the most excelled; but I have no
need of any other scripture to be set before me to draw forth
the excellency of the saints' portion than that which I have
now pitched upon; for the beauty, excellency, and glory of a
hundred choice scriptures are epitomized in this one.

The Jewish doctors and other writers differ about the
time of Jeremiah's penning this book of the Lamentations;
but to be ignorant of the circumstance of time when this
book was made, is such a crime as I suppose will not be

charged upon any man's account in the great day of our Lord Jesus.

Doubtless this book of the Lamentations was composed by Jeremiah in the time of the Babylonian captivity. In this book the prophet sadly laments and bewails the grievous calamities and miseries that had befallen the Jews, *viz.*, the ruin of their state, the devastation of their land, the destruction of their glorious city and temple, which was the great wonder of the world, the profanation of all his holy things, the contemptible and deplorable condition of all sorts, ranks, and degrees of men; and then he complains of their sins as the procuring causes of all those calamities that God in his righteousness had inflicted upon them. He exhorts them also to patience under the mighty hand of God, and stirs them up to repent and reform, as they would have their sins pardoned, judgments removed, divine wrath pacified, their insulting enemies suppressed, and former acts and grants of favour and grace restored to them.

But to come to the words of my text,

Analysis of the Text and Topics

The Lord Jehovah, from *Havah*, *he was*. This name *Jehovah* is the most proper name of God, and it is never attributed to any but to God.

1. First, Jehovah sets out God's eternity, in that it contains all times, future, present, and past.[1]

2. Secondly, It sets out also God's self-existence, coming from *havah*, *to be*.

[1] The three syllables contain the notes of all times: *Je*, the time to come; *ho*, the time present; *vah*, the time past.

3. Thirdly, When either some special mercy is promised, or some extraordinary judgment is threatened, then the name of *Jehovah* is commonly annexed; to show that that God whose being is from himself, and who gives a being to all his creatures both on heaven and on earth, will certainly give a being to his promises and threatenings, and not fail to accomplish the words that are gone out of his mouth.

4. Fourthly, This name *Jehovah* consists only of quiescent letters, *i.e.* letters of rest, as the Hebrews call them, to show that there is no rest till we come to Jehovah, and that in him we may safely and securely rest, as the dove did in Noah's ark.

'Is my portion.' *Chelki*, from חלק, *chalak*; the Hebrew word signifies to divide. He alludes, as I take it, to the dividing of the land of Canaan amongst the Israelites by lot. 'The Lord,' says he, 'is my portion,' my part, my lot; and with this portion I rest fully satisfied, as the Israelites were to do with their parts and portions in that pleasant land. It is true, says Jeremiah, in the name of the church, I am thus and thus afflicted, and sorely distressed on all hands; but yet 'the Lord is my portion,' and that supports and bears up my spirits from fainting and sinking in this evil day.

'Saith my soul.' *Naphshi*, from נפש, *nephesh*; the Hebrew word has nine several senses or significations in the Scripture. But let this suffice, that by *soul* here in the text we are to understand the heart, the mind, the spirit, and the understanding of a man. Well, says the prophet, though I am in a sea of sorrow, and in a gulf of misery, yet my heart tells me that 'the Lord is my portion'; my mind tells me that 'the Lord is my portion'; my spirit tells me that 'the Lord is my portion'; and my understanding tells me that 'the Lord is my portion'; and therefore I will bear up bravely in the face of all calamities and miseries.

'Therefore will I hope in him.' The Hebrew word אוחיל, that is here rendered *hope*, is from יחל, *Jachal*, that signifies both hoping, expecting, and trusting; also it signifies a patient waiting upon the Lord.[1] The prophet Jeremiah had not only a witness above him, but also a witness within him, that the Lord was his portion; and therefore he resolves firmly to hope in the Lord, and sweetly to trust on the Lord, and quietly and patiently to wait upon the Lord, till God should turn his storm into a calm, and his sad winter into a blessed summer.

In my text there are three things observable:

First, An assertion or proposition in those words, 'The Lord is my portion.'

Secondly, A proof of it in those words, 'saith my soul.'

Thirdly, The use or inference from the premises in those words, 'Therefore will I hope in him.'

The words being thus opened, the proposition that I intend to insist upon is this, *viz*.:

Doct. That the Lord is the saints' portion, the Lord is the believers' portion.

I shall call in a few scriptures to witness to the truth of this proposition, and then I shall further open it to you: Psa. 16:5, 'The Lord is the portion of mine inheritance and of my cup: thou maintainest my lot'; Psa. 73:26, 'My flesh and my heart faileth: but God is the strength of my heart, and my portion for ever'; Psa. 119:57, 'Thou art my portion,

---

[1] Gen. 8:10; Isa. 42:4; Psa. 31:24.

O Lord: I have said that I would keep thy words'; Jer. 10:16, 'The portion of Jacob is not like them: for he is the former of all things; and Israel is the rod of his inheritance: the Lord of hosts is his name.'

Now for the further opening and clearing up of this great and glorious, this sweet and blessed truth, I shall endeavour to show you,

First, What a portion the Lord is to his saints, to his gracious ones; and,

Secondly, The reasons or grounds whereupon the saints have laid claim to God as their portion.

Part I
What a Portion God Is

I. For the first, *What a portion God is.* Now the excellency of this portion I shall show you by an induction of particulars, thus:

(1.) *First, God is a present portion.* He is a portion in hand, he is a portion in possession. All the scriptures that are cited to prove the doctrine, evidence this to be a truth, Psa. 48:14; Isa. 25:9. And so does Psa. 46:1, 'God is a very present help in trouble.' The Hebrew word *betsaroth* is in the plural number *troubles*, that is, God is a present help in *many troubles*, in great troubles, and in continued troubles. *Betsaroth* is from צור, *tsor*, that signifies to straiten, and closely to besiege. It notes the extremity of affliction and trouble.[1] When the people of God are in their greatest extremity, then God will be a present help, a present portion to them: Isa. 43:2, 'When thou passest through the waters, I will be with thee; and through the rivers, they shall not overflow thee: when thou walkest through the fire, thou shalt not be burned, neither shall the flame kindle upon thee.' God will be a present help, a present relief, a

---

[1] Maximilian, the emperor, was so delighted with that sentence of Paul, *Si Deus nobiscum*, if God be with us, who shall be against us? that he caused it to be written upon the walls in most rooms of his palace.

present support, a present comfort, a present portion to his people, in all those great and various trials that they may be exercised under: Psa. 142:5, 'I cried unto thee, O Lord: I said, Thou art my refuge and my portion in the land of the living.' God is a portion in present possession, and not a portion in reversion. The psalmist does not say, You may be my portion in another world, but 'Thou art my portion in the land of the living'; nor he does not say, You will be my portion in another world, but 'Thou art my portion in the land of the living.'

Look, as Elkanah gave Hannah a worthy portion in hand, 1 Sam. 1:5, so God gives himself to his saints as a worthy portion in hand. Many men wait, and wait long, for their earthly portions before they enjoy them; yea, their patience is often worn so threadbare in waiting, that they wish their parents in Abraham's bosom; aye, and sometimes in a worser place, that so they may inherit their honours, lordships, lands, treasures, *etc.* Look, as a bird in the hand is worth two, aye, ten, in the bush, so a portion in possession is worth two, aye, ten, in reversion. Now, God is a portion in present possession, and that speaks out the excellency of the saints' portion. As he in Plutarch said of the Scythians, that although they had no music nor vines among them, yet, as a better thing, they had gods, so I may say, though the saints have not this, nor that, nor the other earthly portion among them, yet, as a better thing, they have God for their present portion; and what can they desire more? But,

(2.) *Secondly*, As God is a present portion, so God is *an immense portion*, he is a vast large portion, he is the greatest portion of all portions: 1 Tim. 6:15, 'Which in his times he shall shew, who is the blessed and only Potentate, the King of kings, and Lord of lords.' These words are a stately and lofty description of the greatness of God. The apostle heaps up many words together, to show that in greatness God excels all: Isa. 40:15-17, 'Behold, the nations are as a drop of a bucket, and are counted as the small dust of the balance: behold, he taketh up the isles as a very little thing. And Lebanon is not sufficient to burn, nor the beasts thereof sufficient for a burnt offering. All nations before him are as nothing; and they are counted to him less than nothing, and vanity.' Not only one nation, but many nations; yea, not only many nations, but all nations, in comparison of God, are but as the drop of a bucket; and what is lesser than a drop? and as the small dust of a balance; and what is of lighter weight and lesser worth than the small dust or powder of the balance that hangs on the scale, and yet never alters the weight? yea, they are nothing, they are less than nothing. And though Lebanon was a very great spacious forest, and had abundance of beasts in it, yet God was a God of that infinite greatness, that though all the beasts harbouring in that stately forest should be slain, and all the wood growing on it cut down to burn them with it, all would not make up a sacrifice any way answerable or proportionable to his greatness with whom they had to do.

And so in Psa. 147:5, 'Great is our Lord, and of great power: his understanding is infinite,' or as the Hebrew has it, 'of his understanding there is no number.' Such is his greatness, that he knows not only all kinds and sorts of things, but even all particulars, though they exceed all number: Psa. 145:3, 'Great is the Lord, and greatly to be praised; and his greatness is unsearchable,' or as the Hebrew has it, 'of his greatness there is no search.' God is infinitely above all names, all notions, all conceptions, all expressions, and all parallels: Psa. 150:2, 'Praise him for his mighty acts: praise him according to his excellent greatness,' or greatness of greatness, or abundance of greatness, or according to the multitude of his greatness, as the Hebrew and Greek carries it; and so in Deut. 10:17, 'For the Lord your God is God of gods, and Lord of lords, a great God, a mighty, and a terrible, which regardeth not persons, nor taketh reward.'[1] God is the original cause of all greatness. All that greatness that is in any created beings, whether they are angels or men, is from God; all their greatness is but a beam of his sun, a drop out of his sea, a mite out of his treasury. God is a God of that infinite greatness, that he fills heaven and earth with his presence; he is everywhere, and yet circumscribed to no place; he is in all things, and without all things, and above all things, and this speaks out his immensity, Psa. 139.

Job had a very large portion, before God made a breach upon him: 'He had seven thousand sheep, and three thousand camels, and five hundred yoke of oxen, and five hundred she asses, and a very great household,' Job 1:3; but at last God gives him twice as much as he had at first, 'for he had fourteen thousand sheep, and six thousand camels, and a thousand yoke of oxen, and a thousand she asses,' Job 42:12. Cattle are only instanced in, because the wealth of that country consisted especially in cattle; but yet, doubtless, Job had a great many other good things, as goods, lands, possessions, and stately habitations; but what is all this to a saint's portion? Certainly, had not Job had God for his portion, he had been but a rich fool, a golden beast,

[1] In Daniel, God is called *El Elim*, the mighty of mighties.

notwithstanding all the great things that God had heaped upon him.

And so Ahasuerus had a very large portion, 'he reigned from India unto Ethiopia, over a hundred and seven and twenty provinces,' Esther 1:1, 2; but what were all his provinces but as so many handfuls of dust, in comparison of the saints' portion? The whole Turkish empire, says Luther, is but a crust that God throws to a dog. Had a man all the world for his portion, it would be but a poor pittance.

Nebuchadnezzar had a very great portion: Dan. 5:18, 19, 'O thou king, the most high God gave thy father Nebuchadnezzar a kingdom, and majesty, and glory, and honour. And for the majesty that he gave him, all people, nations, and languages trembled and feared before him: whom he would he slew; and whom he would he kept alive; and whom he would he set up; and whom he would he put down.' And so in Jer. 27:5-8, 'I have made the earth, the man, and the beast that are upon the ground, by my great power and by my outstretched arm, and I have given it unto whom it seemed meet unto me. And now have I given all these lands into the hand of Nebuchadnezzar, king of Babylon, my servant; and the beasts of the field have I given him also to serve him. And all nations shall serve him, and his son, and his son's son, until the very time of his land come: and then many nations and great kings shall serve themselves of him. And it shall come to pass, that the nation and kingdom which will not serve the same Nebuchadnezzar, the king of Babylon, and that will not put their neck under the yoke of the king of Babylon, that nation will I punish, saith the Lord, with the sword, and with the famine, and with the pestilence, until

I have consumed them by his hand.'[1] The portion that here God gives to Nebuchadnezzar is a wonderful large portion; and yet all these nations that God gave to him were but as so many molehills, or as so many birds' nests, compared with a saint's portion. All nations are but as a drop of a bucket, that may in a moment be wiped off with a finger, in comparison of God, nay, they are all nothing; but that word is too high, for they are less than nothing. Had a man as many worlds at his command as there be men on earth, or angels in heaven, yet they would be but as so many drops, or as so many atoms to a saint's portion.

When Alcibiades was proudly boasting of his lands that lay together, Socrates wittily rebukes his pride by bringing him a map of the world, and wishing him to show him where his lands did lie; his lands would hardly amount to more than the prick of a pin. England, Scotland, and Ireland are but three little spots to the vast continents that be in other parts of the world; and what then is your palace, your lordships, your manors, your farm, your house, your cottage, but a little *minum*, but a prick of a pin to God, who is so great, so vast a portion! Oh, sirs! had you the understanding of all the angels in heaven, and the tongues of all the men on earth, yet you would not be able to conceive, express, or set forth the greatness and largeness of a saint's portion. Can you tell the stars of heaven, or number the sands of the sea, or stop the sun in his course, or raise the dead, or make a new world? Then, and not till then, will you be able to declare what a great, what an immense portion God is. If 'eye hath not seen, nor ear heard, neither hath it entered 'the heart of man to conceive, the great things

[1] See also Jeremiah 28:14.

that God hath laid up in the gospel' (for so 1 Cor. 2:9 is to be understood), oh how much less, then, are they able to declare the great things that God has laid up for his people in another world! But,

(3.) *Thirdly*, As God is an immense portion, a large portion, so God is *an all-sufficient portion*: Gen. 17:1, 'And when Abram was ninety years old and nine, the Lord appeared to Abram, and said unto him, I am the Almighty God: walk before me, and be thou perfect.' 'I am God Almighty,' or as some carry the words, 'I am God all-sufficient, or self-sufficient.'[1] God has self-sufficiency and all-sufficiency in himself. Some derive the word *Shaddai*, that is here rendered almighty or all-sufficient, from *Shad*, a *dug*,[2] because God feeds his children with sufficiency of all good things, as the tender mother does the sucking child: Gen. 15:1, 'After these things the word of the Lord came unto Abram in a vision, saying, Fear not, Abram: I am thy shield, and thy exceeding great reward'; I will be your buckler to defend you from all kinds of mischief and miseries, and I will be your exceeding great reward to supply you with all necessary and desirable mercies; and what can a saint desire more? Psa. 84:11, 'For the Lord God is a sun and shield; the Lord will give grace and glory: and no good thing will he withhold from them that walk uprightly.' The sun, which among all inanimate creatures is the most excellent, notes all manner of excellency, provision, and prosperity; and the shield, which among all artificial creatures is the chiefest,

---

[1] *In quo nihil desiderari possit boni* [In whom no further good could be desired].—Zanchius, de nat. Dei, lib. iv. cap. i. qu. 1.

[2] [That is, a woman's breast.]

notes all manner of protection whatsoever. Under the name of grace, all spiritual good is wrapped up; and under the name of glory, all eternal good is wrapped up; and under the last clause, 'no good thing will he withhold,' is wrapped up all temporal good: all put together speaks out God to be an all-sufficient portion. Before the world was made, before angels or men had a being, God was as blessed and as glorious in himself as now he is.

God is such an all-sufficient and such an excellent being, that nothing can be added to him to make him more excellent. Man in his best estate is so great a piece of vanity, Psa. 39:5, that he stands in need of a thousand thousand things; he needs the air to breathe in, the earth to bear him, and fire to warm him, and clothes to cover him, and a house to shelter him, and food to nourish him, and a bed to ease him, and friends to comfort him, *etc.* But this is the excellency of God, that he has all excellencies in himself, and stands in need of nothing. Were there as many worlds as there are men in the world, and were all those worlds full of blessed saints, yea, were there as many heavens as there are stars in heaven, and were all those heavens full of glorious angels, yet all these saints and angels together could not add the least to God; for what can drops taken out of the sea add to the sea? what can finite creatures add to an infinite being? Though all the men in the world should praise the sun, and say, The sun is a glorious creature, yet all this would add nothing to the light and glory of the sun; so, though all the saints and angels shall be blessing, and praising, and admiring, and worshipping God to all eternity, yet they shall never be able to add anything to God, who is blessed for ever.

O Christians! God is an all-sufficient portion: his power is all-sufficient to protect you; his wisdom is all-sufficient to direct you; his mercy is all-sufficient to pardon you; his goodness is all-sufficient to provide for you; his word is all-sufficient to support you and strengthen you; and his grace is all-sufficient to adorn you and enrich you; and his Spirit is all-sufficient to lead you and comfort you; and what can you desire more?

O sirs! God has within himself all the good of angels, of men, and universal nature; he has all glory, all dignity, all riches, all treasures, all pleasures, all delights, all comforts, all contents, all joys, all beatitudes in himself. All the scattered excellencies and perfections that be in the creatures are eminently, transcendently, and perfectly in him. Look, as the worth and value of many pieces of silver are contracted in one piece of gold, so all the whole volume of perfections which is spread through heaven and earth are epitomised in God, according to that old saying, *Omne bonum in summo bono*, all good is in the chiefest good.[1] God is one infinite perfection in himself, which is eminently and virtually all perfections of the creatures. All the good, the excellency, the beauty and glory, that is in all created beings, are but parts of that whole that is in God; and all the good that is in them is borrowed and derived from God, who is the first cause, and the universal cause, of all that good that is in angels or men. God is a sufficient portion to secure your souls, and to supply all your wants, and to satisfy all your desires, and to answer all your expectations, and to suppress all your

---

[1] God is *omnia super omnia* [the everything above everything else]; and many of the very heathens counted God *optimum maximum*, the best and the greatest.

enemies, and, after all, to bring you to glory; and what can you desire more?

But now all earthly portions are insufficient portions; they can neither prevent afflictions, nor support the soul under afflictions, nor mitigate afflictions, nor yet deliver a man from afflictions; they can neither arm the soul against temptations, nor comfort the soul under temptations, nor lead the soul out of temptations.[1] All the creatures in the world are but as so many cyphers without God; when God frowns, all the creatures in the world are not sufficient to cheer the soul; when God withdraws, all the creatures in the world are not sufficient to sustain the soul; when God clouds his face, all the creatures in the world are not sufficient to make it day with the soul, *etc*. There is not enough in the whole creation to content, quiet, or satisfy one immortal soul. He that has most of the world would have more, and he that has least of the world has enough, if his soul can but groundedly say, 'The Lord is my portion.' But,

(4.) *Fourthly*, As the Lord is an all-sufficient portion, so the Lord is *a most absolute, needful, and necessary portion*. The want of an earthly portion may trouble me, but the want of God for my portion will damn me. It is not absolutely necessary that I should have a portion in gold, or silver, or jewels, or goods, or lands; but it is absolutely necessary that I should have God for my portion. I may have union and communion with God, though, with the apostles, I have neither gold nor silver in my purse, Acts 3:6; I may be holy

---

[1] A golden crown cannot cure the headache, nor a purple robe cannot fray away a burning fever, nor a bed of gold cannot give ease to a distempered body, nor the velvet slipper cannot take away the pain of the gout.

and happy, though, with Lazarus, Luke 16:20, 21, I have never a rag to hang on my back, nor never a dry crust to put into my belly; I may to heaven at last, and I may be glorious in another world, though, with Job, I should be stripped of all my worldly glory, and set upon a dunghill in this world, Job 1, *etc.*; but I can never be happy here, nor blessed hereafter, except God be my portion. Though I could truly say that all the world were mine, yet if I could not truly say that the Lord is my portion, I should be but miserable under all my worldly enjoyments. To have God for my portion is absolutely necessary, for without it I am for ever and ever undone, Eph. 2:12. In this verse you have several *withouts*, and it is very observable that they that were without God in the world, they were without Christ, without the church, without the covenant, without the promise, and without hope in the world; and therefore, such persons must necessarily be in a most sad and deplorable condition, *etc.*

[1.] First, In relation to the soul, and in relation to salvation, God is the most absolute necessary portion. If God be not my portion, my soul can never enjoy communion with him in this world; if God be not my portion, my soul can never be saved by him in the other world. But,

[2.] Secondly, When sinners are under terrors and horrors of conscience, when their consciences are awakened and convinced of the vileness of their natures, of the unspeakable evil that is in sin, yea, in the least sin, and of their lost, undone, and miserable estate out of Christ, Oh then! what would they not give to have God for their portion?[1] Oh, then they would give all the gold and silver

---

[1] *Una guttula malae conscientiae totum mare mundani gaudii absorbet* [One little stain of an evil conscience sucks up the whole sea of worldly joy].—Luther.

they have in the world to have God for their portion; oh, then they would give, Mic. 6:6, 7, 'thousands of rams, and ten thousands of rivers of oil'; yea, they would give their first-born, they would give the very fruit of their bodies, that they might have God to be the portion of their souls; oh, then they would say, as Mephibosheth said to the king, 'Let Ziba take all, forasmuch as my lord the king is come again in peace unto his own house,' 2 Sam. 19:29, 30. Under distress of conscience, poor sinners will cry out, Oh! let who will take all our honours, and all our manors, and all our treasures, and all our stores, and all our lands, and all our lordships, and all our bags, so we may have God for our portion. Oh! let us but have God for our portion, and we care not a straw who takes all. Now, what does this speak out, but that, of all portions, God is the most absolute necessary portion? But,

[3.] Thirdly, On a dying bed, an awakened sinner sets the highest price, value, and esteem on such as have God for their portion. Now he esteems a saint in rags that has God for his portion above a wicked emperor in his royal robes, who has only the world for his portion. What though wicked men, when they are in the height of their worldly prosperity, felicity, and glory, do slight the saints, and revile and scorn the saints, and contemn[1] and undervalue the saints, Lam. 2:14, 15; Zeph. 2:8-10, *etc.*; yet, when death knocks at their doors, and when their consciences are startled, and when hell fire flashes in their faces, and when the worm within begins to gnaw, oh now, if all the world were a lump of gold, and in their hands to dispose of, they would give it all, so they might have that honour and happiness

[1] [That is, treat or regard with contempt; to despise.]

to change conditions with those who have God for their portion: Num, 23:10, 'Let me die the death of the righteous, and let my last end be like his.' Though men who have their portion in this life do not love to live the life of the righteous, yet, when they come to die, they are often desirous that they might die the death of the righteous. And this many hundred ministers and Christians can witness from their own experience.

Lazarus having God for his portion, when he died he went to heaven without a rag on his back, or a penny in his purse; whereas Dives, who had not God for his portion when he died, went tumbling down to hell in all his riches, bravery, and glory.[1] Oh! it is infinitely better to go to heaven

---

[1] See Wisdom [Ecclesiasticus] 5:1-8. All these verses are worth their weight in gold.

['1. Do not rely on your wealth; do not say: "I have the power."

Do not walk after your heart or your eyes, by walking after the desire of your soul.

'2. Do not rely on your soul and strength in following the desires of your heart.

'3. Do not say: "Who can prevail against me?" for Jehovah will exact the punishment.

'4. Do not say: "I have sinned, yet what has befallen me?" for Jehovah bides his time. Do not say: "Jehovah is merciful, and all my sins he will blot out."

'5. Do not be overconfident of forgiveness, adding sin upon sin.

'6. Do not say: "Great is his mercy; he will forgive my many sins." For mercy and anger alike are with him; upon the wicked alights his wrath.

'7. Do not delay your conversion to Jehovah, do not put it off from day to day; for suddenly his wrath flames forth; at the time of vengeance, you will be destroyed.

'8. Do not rely upon deceitful wealth, for it will be no help on the day of wrath.']

a beggar than to go to hell an emperor; and this the sinner understands when his conscience comes to be enlightened upon a dying bed, and therefore he cries out, Oh send for such a minister, and send for such and such a Christian, and let them pray with me, and counsel me, and, if it be possible, give out some drops of comfort to me. Oh that I had never derided nor reviled them! Oh that I had never opposed and persecuted them! Oh that I had lived at such a rate of holiness and exactness as they have done! Oh that I had walked with God as they have walked! Oh that I had laid out my time, my strength, my treasure, my parts, my all for God, as they have done! Oh that my estate was as good, as safe, and as happy as theirs is! Oh that I could as truly say that the Lord is my portion, as they can say that the Lord is their portion! And what does all this speak out, but that high esteem and value that they set upon those that have God for their portion? So that upon this threefold account, we may safely conclude that God is a most absolute, needful, and necessary portion. But,

(5.) *Fifthly*, As the Lord is a most absolute, needful, and necessary portion, so the Lord is *a pure and unmixed portion*. God is an unmixed good, he has nothing in him but goodness; he is an ocean of sweetness, without one drop of bitterness; he is a perfect beauty, without the least spot or shadow of deformity, Deut. 32:4; Hab. 1:13. All other portions are a bitter sweet; but God is a rose without prickles; he is a good, in which there is not the least evil: 1 John 1:5, 'God is light, and in him is no darkness at all.' There are no mixtures in God. God is a most clear, bright, shining light, yea, he is all light, and in him is no darkness at all.

God is all light and all love, all sweetness and all goodness, all kindness and all graciousness, and there is no uncomeliness, no unloveliness, no bitterness, nor no darkness at all in God. The moon when it shines brightest has her dark spots and specks; but God is a light that shines most gloriously without the least spot or speck; God is a most pure, clear, splendid light. It is very observable, that the apostle, to illustrate the perfect purity of God, adds a negative to his affirmative, 'in him is no darkness at all'; that is, God is so pure, that not the least spot, the smallest speck of vanity or folly, can cleave to him. God is a pure, a most pure act, without the least potentiality, defectibility, or mutability, and therefore in the highest sense he 'is light, and in him is no darkness at all.' By this metaphorical description of God the apostle would not have us think that the nature of God is changed into the nature of light; but by this similitude the apostle would represent something of the purity and excellency of God to us. The sun is light, the moon is light, and the stars are light; but it would be blasphemy for us to imagine that the essence of God is the same with this of the creatures; but this, sirs! you must remember, that there are many excellent properties of light, for which God is often in the Scripture resembled to light. As,

[1.] First, *Light is pure, and so is God*: Hab. 1:13, 'Thou art of purer eyes than to behold evil, and canst not look on iniquity.' There are four things that God cannot do:

(1.) He cannot lie.

(2.) He cannot die.

(3.) He cannot deny himself, nor

(4.) He cannot look with a favourable eye upon iniquity.

He is a God of that infinite purity, that he cannot look upon iniquity but with a hateful eye, an angry eye, a revengeful eye, and with a vindictive eye.

[2.] Secondly, *All things are conspicuous to the light, and so they are to God*:[1] Heb. 4:13, 'Neither is there any creature that is not manifest in his sight: but all things are naked and open unto the eyes of him with whom we have to do.' The Greek word τετραχηλισμένα [*tetrachēlismena*], is a metaphor, say some, that is taken from the priests under the law, who when they killed the beasts for sacrifice, all things that were within the beasts were laid naked and bare before the priest, that so he might see what was sound and what was corrupted. Others say, the apostle alludes to the anatomising of such creatures, in which men are very cautious and curious to find out every little vein or muscle, though they lie never so close. Others say, that it is a metaphor taken from those that lie with their faces upwards, that all passengers[2] may see who they are. All agree in this, that all men's insides and outsides are anatomised, dissected, quartered, and laid naked to the eye of God: Job 34:21, 22, 'For his eyes are upon the ways of man, and he seeth all his goings. There is no darkness, nor shadow of death, where the workers of iniquity may hide themselves.' 'If you cannot hide yourself from the sun, which is God's minister of light, how impossible will it be to hide yourself from him whose eyes are ten thousand times brighter than the sun,' says Ambrose. But,

[3.] Thirdly, *Without light nothing can be seen; so without the beams of heavenly light no heavenly things can be seen.*

---

[1] Psa. 41:12; 1 Sam. 2:1, 3; Psa. 16:8; 119:168. God is *totus oculus*, all eye. Athenodorus, a heathen, could say, that God was everywhere, and beheld all that was done. [This Athenodorus was surnamed Cananites.—G.]

[2] [That is, wayfarers, travellers, passers-by.]

A man cannot see God, but in that light that comes down from above; a man cannot see Christ without he be first enlightened by Christ; a man cannot see heaven, but in that light that comes from heaven, James 1:17; 1 Cor. 2:10, 12, 14-16. Were it not for the sun, it would be perpetual night in the world, notwithstanding all the torches that could be lighted, yea, notwithstanding all the light of the moon and stars; so it would be perpetual night with poor souls, notwithstanding all the torchlight of natural parts, and creature comforts, and notwithstanding all the starlight of civil honesty and common gifts, and notwithstanding all the moonlight of temporary faith and formal profession, did not the Sun of righteousness arise and shine upon them. But,

[4.] Fourthly, *There is nothing more pleasant than the light*: Eccles. 11:7, 'Truly the light is sweet, and it is a very pleasant thing to behold the sun.' A philosopher being asked whether it were not a pleasant thing to behold the sun? answered, that that was a blind man's question, because life without light is but a lifeless life. Now, as there is nothing more pleasant and delightful to the eye than light, so there is nothing more pleasant and delightful to the soul than God. The poor northern nations, in Strabo, that want the light of the sun for some months together, when the term of his return approaches, they climb up into the highest mountains to spy it; and he that spies it first was accounted the best and most beloved of God, they chose him king almost, as the Tyrians did Strato. Now the return of the sun is not more pleasant and delightful to those poor northern nations, than God is pleasant and delightful to all gracious souls. But,

[5.] Fifthly, *The light shines and scatters its rays over all the world, over east, west, north, and south, and so does the presence and goodness of God*, Psa. 139. But,

[6.] Sixthly, *The light is a creature of a most resplendent beauty, lustre, and glory; it dazzles the eyes of the beholders; and, so God is a God of that transcendent beauty, majesty, and glory, that the very eyes of the angels are dazzled, as not being able to behold the brightness of his glory*: Isa. 6:2. 'God dwells in that light which no man can approach unto,' 1 Tim. 6:16. But,

[7.] Seventhly, and lastly, *The light of all bodies is the most incompound light; it will never mix with darkness; no more will God*: 2 Cor. 6:14, 'What communion hath light with darkness?' The nature of God is void of all composition. Light expels darkness, it never mixes nor mingles with it. By what has been said, you see that God is a pure and an unmixed light, and that in him there is no darkness at all.

But now all worldly portions are mixed with many troubles, sorrows, cares, fears, hazards, dangers, vexations, oppositions, crosses, losses, and oftentimes with many gripes of conscience too. All earthly portions are mixed portions; the goodness of all creatures is a mixed goodness; our wine is mixed with water, our silver with tin, our gold with dross, our wheat with chaff, and our honey with gall, *etc*. Every bee has his sting, and every rose has his prickles; and this mixture speaks out all earthly portions to be 'vanity and vexation of spirit,' Eccles. 1:14.[1] That great prince Xerxes was accustomed to say, You look upon my crown

---

[1] All earthly riches are true gardens of Adonis, where we can gather nothing but trivial flowers, surrounded with many briars and thorns.

and my purple robes, but did you know how they were lined with thorns, you would not stoop to take them up. And who is there in this our English Israel that cannot with both hands subscribe to this? The emblem of King Henry VII, in all his buildings, in the windows, was still a crown in a bush of thorns; wherefore, or with what historical allusion he did so, is uncertain; but surely it was to imply thus much, that great places are not free from great cares, that no man knows the weight of a sceptre but he that sways it. This made Saul to hide himself amongst the stuff, when he should have been made king. Many a sleepless night, many a restless day, many a sad temptation, and many a busy shift,[1] will their ambition cost them, that affect such places of eminency. Besides, high places are commonly very slippery; he that stands in them may suddenly fall, and wound his conscience, or easily fall and break his neck. But,

(6.) *Sixthly*, As God is a pure and unmixed portion, so he is *a glorious, a happy, and a blessed portion*, Psa. 16:5, 6. He is so in himself, and he makes them so too who enjoy him for their portion: Psa. 33:12, 'Blessed is the nation whose God is the Lord; and the people whom he has chosen for his own inheritance.' All the happiness and blessedness of the people of God stands in this, that God is their God, and that he is their portion, and that they are his inheritance. The Hebrew word *ashrei*, that is here rendered *blessed*, is, Oh the blessedness! or Oh the heaped up happiness of those whose God is the Lord! The happiness of such is so great and so glorious, as cannot be conceived, as cannot be uttered. The words are a joyful acclamation for their felicity that have

[1] 'Expedient.'—G.

God for their portion: Psa. 144:15, 'Happy is that people, that is in such a case: yea, happy is that people, whose God is the Lord.' David having prayed for many temporal blessings in the behalf of the people, from verses 12-15, at last concludes, 'Blessed are the people that are in such a case'; but presently he checks and corrects himself, and eats, as it were, his own words, but rather, 'happy is that people whose God is the Lord.' The Syriac renders it question-wise, 'Is not the people [happy] that is in such a case?' The answer is, '*No*,' except they have God to boot, Psa. 146:5. Nothing can make that man truly miserable that has God for his portion, nor nothing can make that man truly happy that wants God for his portion. God is the author of all true happiness; he is the donor of all true happiness; he is the maintainer of all true happiness, and he is the centre of all true happiness and blessedness; and, therefore, he that has him for his God, for his portion, is the only happy man in the world.[1]

But now all earthly portions cannot make a man truly happy and blessed. A crown, a kingdom cannot; for Saul and other princes have found it so. Honours cannot; for Haman and others have found it so. A high and noble birth cannot; for Absalom, Amnon, and others have found it so. Riches cannot; for the rich fool in the Gospel, and many thousand others, have found it so. Large dominions and great commands cannot; for Ahasuerus, Nebuchadnezzar, Belshazzar, and others, have found it so. Policy cannot; for Ahithophel and other great counsellors have found it

---

[1] If a man should make a critical inquiry after true happiness, from the highest angel in heaven to the lowest worm on earth, the joint voice of all the creatures would be, that happiness is not in them.

so. Glorious apparel and delicate fare cannot; for Dives and others have found it so. Applause and credit among the people cannot; for Herod and others have found it so. Learning and great gifts cannot; for the scribes and Pharisees, and many others, have found it so. No earthly thing, nor earthly creature, can give happiness nor blessedness to man. *Non dat quod non habet*, nothing can give what it has not. If the conduit has no water, it can give no water; if the sun has no light, it can give no light; if the physician has no remedy, he can give no remedy, *etc.*

But now it is a very true observation, though it be a very sad observation, *viz., That every wicked man's portion is cursed unto him.*

Do but compare the scriptures in the margin together,[1] and then let conscience judge. All a wicked man's relations are cursed to him, and all a wicked man's contentments and enjoyments are cursed to him, and all his mercies within doors are cursed to him, *etc.* What though a man should match with one that has many thousand bags of gold for her portion, yet if the plague should be in every bag, would you count him happy in this match? Surely no. Verily this is the case of every man that has not God for his portion. But,

(7.) *Seventhly*, As God is a glorious portion, so he is *a peculiar portion*, he is a portion peculiar to his people, Psa. 142:5, 6; Jer. 10:16. This is evident in the text, and in all the scriptures cited to prove the point, Psa. 16:5; and so in Psa. 67:6, 'Then shall the earth yield her increase, and God, even our own God, shall bless us': and so Psa. 68:20, 'He that is our God is the God of salvation,' or 'God of salvations,' as it is

[1] Deut. 28:17-20; Job 20:22-29; 24:18; Prov. 3:33; Mal. 2:2, *etc.*

in the Hebrew. God is a God of all manner of salvations; he has all sorts and ways of salvations; he is not only powerful, but also skilful, to save his people from ten thousand deaths and dangers. Faith is an appropriating grace, it is much in appropriating of God to itself: 'My Lord and my God,' and my Redeemer and my Saviour and my portion;' Psa. 73:26, 'My flesh and my heart faileth: but God is the strength of my heart, and my portion for ever.' In Gideon's camp every soldier had his own pitcher, Judg. 7:16; amongst Solomon's men of valour, every man wore his own sword, 1 Chron. 26:30; and the five wise virgins had every one oil in her own lamp, Matt. 25:4. Luther was accustomed to say, that there lay a great deal of divinity couched up in pronouns, as in *meum*, *tuum*, *suum*, mine, yours, his: and so faith's appropriating of God to the soul, as its own portion, is all in all.

God is a portion peculiar to the saints; he is the hidden manna, the new name, the white stone, the bread to eat that others know not of. There is never a hardened Pharaoh in the world that can truly say, 'The Lord is my portion'; nor there is never a murdering Saul in the world that can truly say, 'The Lord is my portion'; nor there is never a painted bloody Jezebel in the world that can truly say, 'The Lord is my portion'; nor there is never a cunning Ahithophel in the world that can truly say, 'The Lord is my portion'; nor there is never a proud Haman in the world that can truly say, 'The Lord is my portion'; nor there is never a tyranni- cal Nebuchadnezzar in the world that can truly say, 'The Lord is my portion'; nor there is never a crafty Herod in the world that can truly say, 'The Lord is my portion nor there is never a rich Dives in the world that can truly say, 'The

¹ John 20:28; Job 19:25; Luke 1:47.

Lord is my portion'; nor there is never a treacherous Judas in the world that can truly say, 'The Lord is my portion'; nor there is never a hypocritical Simon Magus in the world that can truly say, 'The Lord is my portion'; nor there is never an apostatizing Demas in the world that can truly say, 'The Lord is my portion'; nor there is never a persecuting scribe or Pharisee in the world that can truly say, 'The Lord is my portion.' It is only the saint that can truly say, 'The Lord is his portion,' for God is peculiarly his, he is only his.

But now all earthly portions are common portions; they are all common to good and bad, to the righteous and to the wicked, to the clean and to the unclean, to him that sacrifices and to him that sacrifices not, to him that swears and to him that fears an oath, Eccles. 9:1-3. Was Abraham rich? so was Dives too; was David a king? so was Saul too; was Daniel a great favourite at court? so was Haman too, *etc.* And indeed usually the basest and the worst of men have the largest share in earthly portions; which made Luther say, that the whole Turkish empire was but a crust that God cast to a dog. Abraham gave unto his sons of the concubines gifts, and sent them away, but unto Isaac he gave all that he had, Gen. 25:5, 6.

So all earthly portions, which are giftless gifts, God gives them to the worst and vilest of men; Daniel 4:17, 'This matter is by decree of the watchers, and the demand by the word of the holy ones: to the intent that the living may know, that the most High ruleth in the kingdom of men, and giveth it to whomsoever he will, and setteth up over it the basest of men'; and so in Daniel 11:21, 'And in his estate shall stand up a vile person, to whom they shall not give the honour of the kingdom: but he shall come in peaceably, and obtain the kingdom by flatteries.' Interpreters generally agree, that by this vile person in the text is meant Antiochus Epiphanes, that was so great and mighty a prince, that when the Samaritans did write to him, they wrote, *Antiocho magno deo*, to Antiochus the great god. And indeed his very name speaks him out to be some great and glorious person, for *Antiochus Epiphanes* is Antiochus the illustrious, the famous; and yet you see that the Holy Spirit, speaking of him, calls him a vile person. Ah! how vile in the eyes of God are the greatest men in the world who have not God for their portion! Augustus in his solemn feasts gave trifles to some, but gold to others. God gives the trifling portions of this world to the vilest and worst of men, but his gold, his Christ, himself, he gives only to his saints: Gal. 2:20, 'And the life which I now live in the flesh I live by the faith of the Son of God, who loved me, and gave himself for me.' Haws,[1] that are for hogs, grow upon every hedge; but roses, that are for men, they only grow in pleasant gardens; you know how to apply it. Though many have counterfeit jewels, yet there are but a few that have the true diamond; though many have their earthly portions, yet there are but a few that have God for their portion. But,

(8.) *Eighthly,* As God is a peculiar portion, so he is a *universal portion.* He is a portion that includes all other portions. God has himself the good, the sweet, the profit, the pleasure, the delight, the comfort, *etc.,* of all portions.[2] There is no good in wife, child, father, friend, husband,

---

[1] Fruit of the hawthorn.—G.

[2] Rom. 8:32, God is the *bonum in quo omnia bona* [the good in which all other goods are embraced].

health, wealth, wit, wisdom, learning, honour, *etc.*, but is all found in God: Rev. 21:7, 'He that overcometh shall inherit all things; and I will be his God, and he shall be my son'; or as the Greek hath it, ὁ νιχῶν (*ho nichōn*), he that is overcoming, though he has not yet overcome, yet if he be striving for the conquest, and will rather die than he will give up the bucklers, 'he shall inherit all things'; that is, he shall inherit God in all and all in God:[1] Gen. 33:9, 'And Esau said, I have enough, my brother; keep that thou hast unto thyself'; as the Hebrew has it, *Li Rab*, 'I have much, my brother.' And indeed it was very much that an Esau should say he had much; it is more than many of the Esaus of these times will say. But Jacob speaks at a far higher rate in verse 11: 'Take, I pray thee, my blessing that is brought to thee; because God hath dealt graciously with me, and because I have enough'; or rather, as the Hebrew hath it, *Li chol*, I have all. Esau had much, but Jacob had all, because he had all in God, and God in all. *Habet omnia qui habet habentem omnia*, he has all that has the haver of all: 2 Cor. 6:10, 'As having nothing, and yet possessing all things.' There is in God an immense fulness, an ocean of goodness, and an overplus of all that graciousness, sweetness, and kindness that is to be found in all other things or creatures.

As Noah had a copy of every kind of creature in that famous library of the ark, out of which all were reprinted to the world, so he that has God for his portion has the original copy of all blessings, out of which all may easily be renewed. All the goodlinesses and all the glories of all the creatures are eminently and perfectly to be enjoyed in God.

[1] *Qui habet hoc unum, habet unum universale* [Whoever has this one thing, has the one thing of universal significance].

God is a universal excellency. All the particular excellencies that are scattered up and down among angels, men, and all other creatures, are virtually and transcendently in him, he has them all in his own being, Eph. 1:3.[1] All creatures in heaven and earth have but their particular excellencies; but God has in himself the very quintessence of all excellencies. The creatures have but drops of that sea, that ocean, that is in God, they have but their parts of that power, wisdom, goodness, righteousness, holiness, faithfulness, loveliness, desirableness, sweetness, graciousness, beauty, and glory that is in God. One has this part, and another has that; one has this particular excellency, and another has that; but the whole of all these parts and excellencies is to be found only in God. There is none but that God, that is a universal good, that can truly say, All power, all wisdom, all strength, all knowledge, all goodness, all sweetness, all beauty, all glory, all excellency, *etc.*, dwells in me. He that can truly say this, is a god, and he that cannot is no god. There is no angel in heaven, nor saint on earth, that has the whole of any one of those excellencies that are in God; nay, all the angels in heaven, and all the saints on earth, have not among them the whole of any one of those glorious excellencies and perfections that be in God. All the excellencies that are scattered up and down in the creatures, are united into one excellency in God; but there is not one excellency in God that is fully scattered up and down among all the creatures. There is a glorious union of all excellencies in God, and only in God.

[1] When Paulinus Nolanus, a great man, had his city taken away from him by the barbarians, he prayed thus: Lord, let me not be troubled at the loss of my gold, silver, honour, *etc.*, for you are all, and much more than all these to me.

Now this God, that is such a universal good, and that has all excellencies dwelling in himself, he says to the believer, as the king of Israel said to the king of Assyria, 'I am thine, and all that I have,' 1 Kings 20:4. Our propriety reaches to all that God is, and to all that God has, Jer. 32:38, 42. God is not parted, nor divided, nor distributed among his people, as earthly portions are divided among children in the family; so as one believer has one part of God, and another believer has another part of God, and a third another part of God; oh no, but every believer has whole God wholly, he has all of God for his portion. God is not a believer's portion in a limited sense, nor in a comparative sense, but in an absolute sense. God himself is theirs, he is wholly theirs, he is only theirs, he is always theirs. As Christ looks upon the Father, and says, 'All thine is mine, and mine is thine,' 1 Cor. 3:23; John 17:10, that may a saint say, looking upon God as his portion. He may truly say, O Lord, you are mine, and all that you have; and I am yours, and all that I have. A saint may look upon God and say, O Lord, not only your gifts but your graces are mine, to adorn me and enrich me; and not only your mercies and your good things are mine to comfort me, and encourage me, but also you yourself are mine; and this is my joy and crown of rejoicing. To be able to say that God is mine, is more than if I were able to say that ten thousand worlds, yea, and as many heavens, are mine; for it is God alone that is the sparkling diamond in the ring of glory. Heaven would be but a low thing without God, says Augustine; and Bernard had rather enjoy Christ in a chimney-corner, than to be in heaven without him; and Luther had rather be in hell with Christ, than in heaven without him. It is God alone that makes heaven to be heaven.

Now God is so every particular believer's portion, as that he is every believer's portion: 1 Cor. 1:1, 2 'Paul, called to be an apostle of Jesus Christ, through the will of God, and Sosthenes our brother, unto the church of God which is at Corinth, to them that are sanctified in Christ Jesus, called to be saints, with all that in every place call upon the name of Jesus Christ our Lord, both theirs and ours.' As the sun is every man's sun to see by, to walk by, to work by; and as the sea is every man's sea to trade by, *etc.*; so God is every believer's portion. He is a poor saint's portion as well as a rich saint's portion; he is the despised believer's portion, as well as the exalted believer's portion; he is the weak believer's portion, as well as the strong believer's portion; he was as much his portion who miscalled his faith, and who in the behalf of his son cried out with tears, 'Lord, I believe, help my unbelief,' Mark 9:24, as he was Abraham's portion, who, in the strength of his faith, offered up his only son, Gen. 22; he was as much Job's portion sitting on a dunghill, as he was David's portion sitting on a royal throne; he was as much Lazarus' portion, that had never a penny in his purse, as he was Solomon's portion, who made gold and silver as plenteous in Jerusalem as the stones of the street, 2 Chron. 1:15. God is not my portion alone, but he is every saint's portion in heaven, and he is every saint's portion on earth. The father is every child's portion, and though they may wrangle and quarrel, and fall out one with another, yet he is all their portions; and so it is here; and oh what a spring of joy and comfort should this be to all the saints. Riches are not every believer's portion, but God is every believer's portion; honour and preferment in the world is not every believer's portion, but God is every believer's portion;

liberty and freedom is not every believer's portion, but God is every believer's portion; credit and applause in the world is not every believer's portion, but God is every believer's portion; prosperity and success is not every believer's portion, but God is every believer's portion, *etc.*

God is a universal portion, all things receive their being, essence, and existence from him, for the fulness of all things is in him, really and eminently. The heathen philosophers of old called God τό πᾶν (*to pan*), *i.e.* all or everything, and in that oracle 'great Pan is dead,' of which Plutarch makes mention. Christ is called the greater Pan, because, say some, he is the Lord of all, and contains all things in himself: Exod. 33:19, 'I will make all my goodness pass before thee,' to wit, because in God are all good things, God is all things, God is everything. The cream, the good, the sweet, the beauty, and the glory of every creature, and of every thing, centres in God. But,

(9.) *Ninthly*, As God is an universal portion, so God is *a safe portion, a secure portion*. He is a portion that none can rob or wrong you of; he is a portion that none can touch or take from you: he is a portion that none can cheat or spoil you of. God is such a portion, that no friend, no foe, no man, no enemy, no devil can ever rob a Christian of.[1] O Christians, God is so yours in Christ, and so yours by covenant, and so yours by promise, and so yours by purchase, and so yours by conquest, and so yours by donation, and so yours by marriage union and communion, and so yours by the earnest of the Spirit, and so yours by the feelings and

---

[1] These things I have formerly handled more largely, and, therefore, a touch here must suffice, *etc.*

witnessings of the Spirit, that no power or policy on earth can ever finger your portion, or cheat, or rob you of your portion: Psa. 48:14, 'For this God is our God for ever and ever, and he will be our guide even unto death.' He is not only our God for the present, nor he will not be only our God for a short time longer; oh no, but he will be our God for ever and ever. If God be once your portion, he will be for ever your portion. It must be a power that must overmatch the power of God, and a strength that must be above the strength of God, that must rob or spoil a Christian of his portion; but who is there that is stronger than God? Is the clay stronger than the potter, or the stubble than the flame, or weakness than strength? yea, is not the very weakness of God stronger than man? and who then shall ever be able to take away a Christian's portion from him? Rom. 9; 1 Cor. 1:25; 10:22.

But now a man may be easily deprived of his earthly portion. How many have been deprived of their earthly portions by storms at sea, and others by force and violence, and others by fraud and deceit, and others by hideous lying and hellish swearing? Many have lost their earthly portions by treachery, knavery, perjury, subtlety, robbery, *etc.* Some play away their earthly portions, and others with Esau fool away their earthly portions, and not a few, with the prodigal, sin away their earthly portions. Ahab's fingers itched to be fingering of Naboth's vineyard. 1 Kings 21:1-4. A man can no sooner come to enjoy an earthly portion, but other men's fingers itch to be fingering of his portion, as daily experience does sufficiently evidence. But God is a portion that the fire cannot burn, nor the floods cannot drown, nor the thief cannot steal, nor the enemy cannot sequester, nor the soldier cannot plunder a Christian of. A man may take away my gold from me, but he cannot take away my God from me. The Chaldeans and the Sabeans could take away Job's estate from him, but they could not take away Job's God from him, Job 1. And the Amalekites burnt Ziklag, and robbed David of his substance, and of his wives, but they could not rob him of his God, 1 Sam. 30. And those persecutors in Hebrews 10 and 11 plundered the saints of their goods, but they could not plunder them of their God. Till weakness can make a breach upon strength, impotency upon omnipotency, the pitcher upon the potter, and the crawling worm upon the Lord of hosts, a saint's portion is safe and secure.

It is true, sickness and disease may take away my health and my strength from me, and death may take away my friends and my relations from me, and enemies may take away my estate, my liberty, my life from me; but none of all these can take away my God from me. I have read of the men of Tyrus, how that they chained and nailed their god Apollo to a post, that so they might be sure of him, supposing that all their safety lay in the enjoyment of him. Certainly God is so chained, and so linked, and so nailed to his people by his everlasting love, and by his everlasting covenant, and by the blood of his Son, and by his oath, and by that law of relation that is between him and them, that no created power shall ever be able to deprive them of him. But,

(10.) *Tenthly*, As God is a safe portion, a secure portion, so he is a *suitable portion*, Psa. 4:6, 7. No object is so suitable and adequate to the heart as he is. He is a portion that punctually, exactly, and directly suits the condition of the soul, that suits the desires of the soul, the necessities of the soul, the wants of the soul, the longings of the soul, and the prayers of the soul. The soul can crave nothing, nor wish for nothing, but what is to be found in this portion. Here is light to enlighten the soul, and wisdom to counsel the soul, and power to support the soul, and goodness to supply the soul, and mercy to pardon the soul, and beauty to delight the soul, and glory to ravish the soul, and fullness to fill the soul, *etc.* Health is not more suitable to the sick man, nor wealth to the poor man, nor bread to the hungry man, nor drink to the thirsty man, nor clothes to the naked man, nor balm to the wounded man, nor ease to the tormented man, nor health to the diseased man, nor a pardon to the condemned man, nor a guide to the blind man, *etc.* than this portion is suitable to all the necessities of man; and this speaks out the excellency of this portion above all other portions.

Now there is no earthly portion that can suit an immortal soul; he is a fool upon record that said, 'Soul, thou hast goods laid up for many years; take ease, eat, drink, and be merry,' Luke 12:18-20. If the man, says Ambrose upon the words, had the soul of a swine, what could he have said more? for those things were more suitable to swine than they were to an immortal soul. Man's soul is a spiritual and immortal substance, it is capable of union and communion with God; it is capable of a choice enjoyment of God here, and of an eternal fruition of God hereafter. A great shoe will not fit a little foot, nor a great sail a little ship, nor a great ring a little finger; no more will any earthly portion suit an immortal soul. The soul is the breath of God, the beauty of man, the wonder of angels, and the envy of devils. It is of an angelical nature; it is a heavenly spark, a celestial plant, and of a divine offspring. So that nothing can suit the soul below God, nor nothing can satisfy the soul without God. The soul is so high and so noble a piece, that all the riches of the east and west Indies, nor rocks of diamonds, nor mountains of gold, can fill it, or satisfy it, or suit it.

When a man is in prison, and condemned to die, if one should come to him, and tell him, that there is such a friend or such a relation that has left him a very fair estate, a brave[1] seat, *etc.*, yet all this would not please him, nor joy him, because it does not suit his present condition; oh, but now let a man bring him his pardon, sealed under his prince's hand, oh how will this delight him and joy him! And so tell a man that is ready to starve, that such and such loves him, and that such and such intends well towards him, *etc.*, yet all this does not take him, it does not satisfy him, and all because it does not suit him; oh, but now, but bring him food to eat, and this will joy him and delight him, and all because it suits him. That is the highest good, that is the most suitable good to the soul, and such a good is God; that is the most excellent portion, that is the most suitable portion to the soul, and such a portion is God. But,

(11.) *Eleventhly*, As God is a suitable portion, so he is *an incomprehensible portion*. No created understanding can comprehend what a portion God is, Psa. 147:5; Job 26:14. It is true God is not incomprehensible, in regard of his own understanding, for he perfectly understands himself, else he could not be God; but God is incomprehensible in regard of us, and the angels, who are no ways able to comprehend

[1] [That is, excellent, splendid.]

infiniteness: 1 Kings 8:27, 'But will God indeed dwell on the earth? behold, the heaven and heaven of heavens, cannot contain thee; how much less this house that I have builded?'[1] God is an infinite being, and therefore he cannot be contained in any place, nor comprehended by any created being. Such multiplied phrases and Hebraisms as are here, as heaven, and the heaven of heavens, very emphatically set out the immensity and incomprehensibleness of God: Job 37:23, 'Touching the Almighty, we cannot find him out.' We are as well able to comprehend the sea in a cockle shell, as we are able to comprehend God.

God is above all name, all notion, and all comprehension. God is so incomprehensible, that you shall as soon tell the stars of heaven, and number the sand of the sea, and stop the sun in his course, and raise the dead, and make a world, as you shall be able to comprehend the infiniteness of God's essence: Psa. 145:3, 'His greatness is unsearchable.' The most perfect knowledge that we can have of God is, that we cannot perfectly know him, because we know him to be infinitely and incomprehensibly perfect: Rom. 11:33, 'Oh the depth both of the wisdom and knowledge of God! how unsearchable are his judgments, and his ways past finding out!' When men and angels search farthest into God's perfection, they then most of all discover their own imperfection; for it is utterly impossible for angels or men, by their most accurate disquisition, to find out the Almighty to perfection, 1 Tim. 6:16, 'who only hath immortality,

---

[1] Aristotle, that great secretary of nature, being not able to comprehend the reason of the sea's ebbing and flowing, cast himself into it; oh, how much less able was he to comprehend God, blessed for ever!

dwelling in the light which no man can approach unto, whom no man hath seen, nor can see.' Here is a denial both of the fact and the possibility. It is a good observation of Chrysostom on the words, *Diligentiae Pauli attende, non dicit lucem incomprehensibilem, etc.* Observe the diligence of Paul, he does not say a light incomprehensible, but a light inaccessible, which is much more; for that which, being sought and searched for, cannot be comprehended, we say is incomprehensible; but that which suffers not by any means the labour of searching after, and which no one can come near, that is inaccessible. There is infinitely more in God than the tongues of men or angels can express.[1] There is much in God beyond the apprehension and comprehension of all created beings. The sum of all that philosophers and schoolmen have attained to concerning this great principle, amounts to no more than this, *viz.*, that men and angels can never comprehend that perfection which dwells in God; for the perfection of God is infinite, and therefore incomprehensible. God, says Dionysius, is a super-substantial substance, an understanding not to be understood, a word never to be spoken.

When one was asked what God was, he answered, that he must be God himself, before he could know God fully.

When the tyrant Hiero asked the poet Simonides what God was, he craved a day to study an answer; but the more he sought into the nature of God, the more difficult he found it to express; the next day, after being questioned, he asked two days, and the third time he craved four, and so

---

[1] If one man had all the reason, gifts, graces, and excellencies that are in angels and men, yet would he never be able to comprehend an incomprehensible God.

went on, doubling the number; and being asked why he did so, he answered, that the more he studied the nature of God, the less he was able to define what God was. He being so incomprehensible in his nature, the more this poor heathen inquired, the more he admired, and the less he understood.

It was a notable observation of Chrysostom, who being very busy and studious in searching into the nature of God, says, I am like a man digging in a deep spring; I stand here, and the water rises upon me; and I stand there, and still the water rises upon me. Indeed, this is a knowledge that passes knowledge, Eph. 3:19.

The Turks build their mosques or churches without any roof, because they hold as we do, that God is incomprehensible. God is a circle whose centre is everywhere, and whose circumference is nowhere, all which speaks out his infiniteness and incomprehensibleness.

But now all earthly portions are easily apprehended and comprehended. A portion in money, or plate, or goods, or lands, or jewels, is easily cast up, and so many hundreds or thousands a year are quickly told. There are few, except it be children or fools, but can readily give an account of all earthly portions. The child's portion, and the wife's portion, and the servant's portion, and the soldier's portion, and the poor man's portion, and the rich man's portion, are talked on all the city over, and all the town over, and all the country over; but God is such an incomprehensible portion, that there is not a man in town, city, or country that is able to comprehend him, Prov. 3:15. But,

(12.) *Twelfthly*, As God is an incomprehensible portion, so God is *an inexhaustible portion*; a portion that can never be spent, that can never be exhausted; a fountain that still overflows; a rich mine that has no bottom; a spring that can never be drawn dry, but continues always full, without augmentation or diminution: John 4:14, 'But whosoever drinketh of the water that I shall give him shall never thirst; but the water that I shall give him shall be a well of water springing up into everlasting life.' If grace in the soul be such a perpetual flowing fountain, that it shall never be exhausted till grace be swallowed up in glory, then certainly the God of grace is much more an inexhaustible fountain that can never be drawn dry. Angels, saints, and sinners have lived upon this portion almost this six thousand years, and it is not in the least diminished, Col. 1:16, 17. God has his city-house, and his country-house, where millions have been kept at his table, and lived upon his purse, his charge, even days without number, and yet God is not one penny the poorer for all this. This portion is like the meal in the barrel, and the oil in the cruse,[1] which never failed: 1 Kings 17:14-16, 'For thus saith the Lord God of Israel, The barrel of meal shall not waste, neither shall the cruse of oil fail, until the day that the Lord sendeth rain upon the earth. And the barrel of meal wasted not, neither did the cruse of oil fail, according to the word of the Lord, which he spake by Elijah.' God is such a portion as cannot be wasted nor diminished; he is such a portion as can never fail. Should all Christians now live to the age of the patriarchs, who lived many hundred years, and should they all live freely, and keep open house every day in the year, yet at the end, not a dram, not a penny, no not a farthing of this portion will be expended or diminished.

[1] [That is, an earthenware pot or jar.]

Though men have never so great a stock, yet if they still spend upon it they will certainly consume it; oh, but God is such a stock as can never be spent, as can never be consumed. If a sparrow should but fetch a drop of water out of the sea once a day, yea, once in a thousand years, yet in time it would be exhausted; oh but God is such a sea, such an ocean, that if every angel in heaven, and every saint and sinner on earth, should drink whole rivers at a draught, yet not one drop could be diminished. If a child should take but a cockle-shell of water out of the sea every day, the sea would be really the less, though not visibly the less, and in time it would be exhausted, and drawn dry; but let all created beings be every day drawing from God, yet they shall never lessen him, they shall never draw him dry. The mother's breasts are often drawn dry, but the more you draw at the breasts of God, the more milk of grace and comfort will flow in upon you: Isa. 66:10, 11, 'Rejoice ye with Jerusalem, and be ye glad with her, all ye that love her: rejoice for thy joy with her, all ye that mourn for her: that ye may suck, and be satisfied with the breasts of her consolation; that you may milk out, and be delighted with the abundance of her glory.' God keeps open house for all comers and goers, for all created creatures both in heaven and earth; and though they are perpetually sucking at his breasts, yet the more they draw, the more the heavenly milk of divine joy, content, and satisfaction flows in abundantly upon them, Psa. 104:24.

All creatures, both high and low, rich and poor, honourable and base, noble and ignoble, bond and free, Jews and Gentiles, are all maintained upon God's own cost and charge; they are all fed at his table, and maintained by what comes out of his treasury, his purse; and yet God is not a pin the poorer for all this. It would break and beggar all the princes on earth, to keep but one day the least part of that innumerable company that God feeds, and clothes, and cherishes, and maintains every day upon the account of his own revenue, which is never the poorer for all the vast expenses that he is daily at. There is still in God a fulness of abundance, and a fulness of redundance, notwithstanding the vast sums that he has, and does daily expend. It were blasphemy to think that God should be a penny the poorer by all that he has laid out for the maintenance of those millions of angels and men, that have had their dependence upon him, from their first creation to this very day. Look, as the sun has never the less light for filling the stars with light, and as the fountain has never the less water for filling the lesser vessels with water that are about it; so though God fills all the vessels, both of grace and glory, with his own fulness, yet he is never the less full himself; there is still in God *plenitudo fontis*, the fulness of a fountain. Look, as the overflowing fountain pours out water abundantly, and yet after all it remains full; so though the Lord be such an overflowing fountain as that he fills all, yet still he retains all fulness in himself.

I have read of a Spanish ambassador, that, coming to see the treasury of Saint Mark in Venice, that is so much cried up in the world, he fell groping at the bottom of the chests and trunks, to see whether they had any bottom; and being asked the reason why he did so, answered in this among other things, My master's treasure differs from yours, and excels yours, in that his has no bottom as yours have, alluding to the mines in Mexico, Peru, and other parts of the

[45]

western India.[1] All men's mints, bags, purses, and coffers may be quickly exhausted and drawn dry, but God is such an inexhaustible portion, that he can never be drawn dry; all God's treasures are bottomless, and all his mints are bottomless, and all his bags are bottomless. Millions of thousands in heaven and earth feed every day upon him, and yet he feels it not; he is still giving, and yet his purse is never empty; he is still filling all the court of heaven, and all the creatures on earth, and yet he is a fountain that still overflows. There be them that say, that it is most certainly true of the oil at Rheims, that though it be continually spent in the inauguration of their kings of France, yet it never wastes; but whatever truth is in this story, of this I am most sure, that though all the creatures in both worlds live and spend continually on Christ's stock, yet it never wastes.

But now all earthly portions are frequently exhausted and drawn dry. The prodigal quickly spent his patrimony upon his harlots, Luke 15; and how many drunkards, and gluttons, and wantons, and gamesters, and roysters,[2] *etc.*, daily bring a noble to ninepence! Prov. 23:20, 21. 'Hast thou entered into the treasures of the snow?' says God to Job 38:22, *etc.* Now, says Gregory, the treasures of the snow are worldly riches, which men rake together, even as children do snow, which the next shower washes away, and leaves nothing in the room of it but dirt. And ah! how many merchants, and shopkeepers, and others in these breaking times, have found all their riches and earthly portions to

---

[1] [That is, the West Indies. In the seventeenth century the term was used by European nations to describe their acquired territories in the continent of America.]

[2] [That is, those engaged in noisy merrymaking; revellers.]

melt away as snow before the sun! how many of late have been very rich one week, and stripped of all the next, and set with Job upon the dunghill! All earthly portions are like water in a cistern, that may easily and quickly be drawn dry; but God is an inexhaustible portion, that can never be drawn dry; and this discovers the excellency of this portion above all other portions. But,

(13.) *Thirteenthly*, As God is an inexhaustible portion, so God is *a soul-satisfying portion*, Psa. 17:15. He is a portion that gives the soul full satisfaction and content: Psa. 16:5, 6, 'The Lord is the portion of mine inheritance and of my cup: thou maintainest my lot. The lines are fallen unto me in pleasant places; yea, I have a goodly heritage.' It was well with him as his heart could wish. And so in Psa. 73:25, 'Whom have I in heaven but thee? and there is none upon earth that I desire besides thee'; or as some render it, 'I would I were in heaven with you'; or as others read the words, 'I have sought none in heaven or earth besides you'; or as others, 'I desire none in heaven or earth besides you,' or 'I affect none in heaven, nor none on earth like you; I love none in heaven, nor none on earth, in comparison of you; I esteem you instead of all other treasure, and above all other treasures that are in heaven, or that are on earth.' The holy prophet had spiritual and sweet communion with Christ to comfort and strengthen him; he had a guard of glorious angels to protect him and secure him, and he had assurance of heaven in his bosom to joy and rejoice him; and yet it was none of these, nay, it was not all these together, that could satisfy him, it was only an infinite good, an infinite God, that could satisfy him. He very well knew that the substantials of all true happiness and blessedness lay in God, and his enjoyment of God, It was not his high dignities nor honours that could satisfy him; it was not the strength, riches, security, prosperity, and outward glory of his kingdom that could satisfy him; it was not his delightful music, nor his noble attendance, nor his well furnished tables, nor his great victories, nor his stately palaces, nor his pleasant gardens, nor his beautiful wife, nor his lovely children, that could satisfy him; all these without God could never satisfy him; but God without all these was enough to quiet him, and satisfy him: John 14:8, 'Philip said unto him, Lord, shew us the Father, and it sufficeth us.'

A sight of God will satisfy a gracious soul more than all worldly contentments and enjoyments, yea, one sight of God will satisfy a saint more than all the glory of heaven will do. God is the glory of heaven. Heaven alone is not sufficient to content a gracious soul, but God alone is sufficient to content and satisfy a gracious soul. God only is that satisfying good, that is able to fill, quiet, content, and satisfy an immortal soul. Certainly, if there be enough in God to satisfy the spirits of just men made perfect, whose capacities are far greater than ours, Heb. 12:23-25; and if there be enough in God to satisfy the angels, whose capacities are far above theirs; if there be enough in God to satisfy Jesus Christ, whose capacity is unconceivable and inexpressible; yea, if there be enough in God to satisfy himself, then certainly there must needs be in God enough to satisfy the souls of his people. If all fulness, and all goodness and infiniteness will satisfy the soul, then God will. There is nothing beyond God imaginable, nor nothing beyond God desirable, nor nothing beyond God delectable; and therefore the soul that enjoys him, cannot but be satisfied with him.

God is a portion beyond all imagination, all expectation, all apprehension, and all comparison; and therefore he that has him cannot but sit down and say, I have enough, Gen. 33:11; Psa. 63:5, 6, 'My soul shall be satisfied as with[1] marrow and fatness; and my mouth shall praise thee with joyful lips: when I remember thee upon my bed, and meditate on thee in the night watches.' Marrow and fatness cannot so satisfy the appetite, as God can satisfy a gracious soul; yea, one smile from God, one glance of his countenance, one good word from heaven, one report of love and grace, will infinitely more satisfy an immortal soul, than all the fat, and all the marrow, and all the dainties and delicates of this world can satisfy the appetite of any mortal man. 'My soul shall be satisfied with fatness and fatness'; so the Hebrew has it; that is, my soul shall be topful of comfort, it shall be filled up to the brim with pleasure and delight, in the remembrance and enjoyment of God upon my bed, or upon my beds, in the plural, as the Hebrew has it.

David had many a hard bed and many a hard lodging, whilst he was in his wilderness condition. It oftentimes so fell out that he had nothing but the bare ground for his bed, and the stones for his pillows, and the hedges for his curtains, and the heavens for his canopy; yet in this condition God was sweeter than marrow and fatness to him; though his bed was never so hard, yet in God he had full satisfaction and content: Jer. 31:14, 'My people shall be satisfied with goodness, saith the Lord'; and 'my God shall

---

[1] *Cheleb vade shen*, fat and fat; so the Hebrew has it; and hereby is meant satiety of pleasures, *etc.*

supply all your need according to his riches in glory, by Christ Jesus,' Phil. 4:19, saith Paul, that great apostle of the Gentiles. The Greek word πληρώσει (*plērōsei*) signifies to *fill up*, even as he did the widow's vessels, 2 Kings 4:4, till they did overflow. God will fill up all, he will make up all, he will supply all the wants and necessities of his people. That water that can fill the sea, can much more fill a cup: and that sun which can fill the world with light, can much more fill my house with light. So that God that fills heaven and earth with his glory, can much more fill my soul with his glory. To show what a satisfying portion God is, he is set forth by all those things that may satisfy the heart of man, as by bread, water, wine, milk, honours, riches, raiment,[1] houses, lands, friends, father, mother, sister, brother, health, wealth, light, life, *etc*. And if these things will not satisfy, what will? It is enough, says old Jacob, that Joseph is alive, Gen. 45:28; so says a gracious soul, It is enough that God is my portion. A pardon cannot more satisfy a condemned man, nor bread a hungry man, nor drink a thirsty man, nor clothes a naked man, nor health a sick man, *etc*., than God satisfies a gracious man. But,

Now worldly portions can never satisfy the souls of men, Eccles. 5:10: 'He that loveth silver shall never be satisfied with silver; nor he that loveth abundance with increase. This is also vanity.'[2] All the world cannot fill the soul, nor all the creatures in the world cannot stock the soul with complete satisfaction. As nothing can be the perfection of

[1] [That is, clothing.]

[2] Some read the words thus: He that loves silver shall not be satisfied with silver, and he that loves it in the multitude of it shall not have fruit.

the soul but he that made it, so nothing can be the satisfaction of the soul but he that made it. If a man be hungry, silver cannot feed him; if naked, it cannot clothe him; if cold, it cannot warm him; if sick, it cannot recover him; if wounded, it cannot heal him; if weak, it cannot strengthen him; if fallen, it cannot raise him; if wandering, it cannot reduce him; oh how much less able is it then to satisfy him! He that, out of love to silver, seeks after silver, shall love still to seek it, but shall never be satisfied with it. A man shall as soon satisfy the grave, and satisfy hell, and satisfy the stomach with wind, as he shall be able to satisfy his soul with any earthly portion. All earthly portions are dissatisfying portions, they but vex and fret, gall and grieve, tear and torment, the souls of men. The world is a circle, and the heart of man is a triangle, and no triangle can fill a circle.[1]

Some good or other will be always wanting to that man that has only outward good to live upon. Absalom's beauty could not satisfy him, nor Haman's honour could not satisfy him, nor Ahab's kingdom could not satisfy him, nor Balaam's gold could not satisfy him, nor Ahithophel's policy could not satisfy him, nor the scribes and Pharisees' learning could not satisfy them, nor Dives' riches could not satisfy him, nor Alexander's conquests could not satisfy him; for when, as he thought, he had conquered one world, he sits down and wishes for another world to conquer; and Cyrus the Persian king was wont to say, did men but know the cares which he sustained under his imperial crown, he thought no man would stoop to take it up. Gilimex, king of the Vandals, when he was led in triumph by Belisarius,

[1] If the whole world were changed into a globe of gold, it could not fill one heart, it could not satisfy one immortal soul.

cried out, 'Vanity of vanity, all is vanity.' Charles V, emperor of Germany, whom of all men the world judged most happy, cried out with detestation to all his honours, riches, pleasures, trophies, *Abite hinc, abite longe*, Get you hence, let me hear no more of you. And it has been long since said of our King Henry II,

> He whom, alive, the world could scarce suffice,
> When dead, in eight-foot earth contented lies.

By all these instances, it is most evident that no earthly portions can satisfy the souls of men. Can a man fill up his chest with air? or can he fill up the huge ocean with a drop of water? or can a few drops of beer quench the thirst of a man in a burning fever? or can the smell of meat, or the reeking fume of a ladle, or dreaming of a banquet, satisfy a hungry stomach? No! no more can any earthly portions fill or satisfy the heart of man. If emptiness can fill the soul, if vanity can satisfy the soul, or if vexation can give content to the soul, then may earthly portions satisfy the soul, but not till then. When a man can gather grapes of thorns, and figs of thistles, and turn day into night, and winter into summer, then shall he find satisfaction in the creatures; but not before. All earthly portions are weighed in the balance of the sanctuary, and they are found to be lighter than the dust of the balance; and this will rather inflame the thirst than quench it.

A man that has only the world for his portion, is like Noah's dove out of the ark, that was in continual motion, but could find no resting place; but a man that has God for his portion is like the dove, returning and resting in the ark, The soul can never be at rest, till it comes to rest and centre in God.[1] God himself is the soul's only home, no good but

[1] A reminiscence of Augustine's memorable saying, '*Fecisti nos*

the chiefest good can suffice an immortal soul. Look, as God never rested till he had made man, so man can never rest till he comes to enjoy God; the soul of man is of a very vast capacity, and nothing can fill it to the brim but he that is fulness itself. It is the breast, and not the baby[1] nor the rattle, that will satisfy the hungry child; and it is God, and not this or that creature, that can satisfy the soul of man. But,

(14.) *Fourteenthly*, As God is a soul-satisfying portion, so God is *a permanent portion, an indefinite portion, a never-failing portion, a lasting, yea, an everlasting portion*: Psa. 73:26, 'My flesh and my heart faileth: but God is the strength,' or the rock, 'of my heart, and my portion for ever.' God is a fountain which the hottest summer dries not, a bottomless treasure that can never be expended. God ever was, and ever will be. He cannot borrow his being from anything, who gives being and well-being to all things. God is Alpha and Omega, the first and the last, he is yesterday and today, and the same for ever, Rev. 1:8. God is the Almighty, which is, and which was, and which is to come. All the differences of time are united by some to connote the eternity of God, in Exod. 3:14, 'And God said unto Moses, I AM THAT I AM: and he said, Thus shalt thou say unto the children of Israel, I AM hath sent me unto you.'[2] Some translate this text, according to the full scope of the

---

ad te, Domine, et inquietum est cor nostrum donec requiescat in te,' ['You have made us for yourself, O Lord, and our heart is restless until it rests in you.'] Conf. i. 1.—G.

   [1] 'Doll.'—G,

   [2] *Omnia tempora conjuncta de Deo dicta eternitatem connotant* [All temporal expressions used of God alike denote eternity].

future amongst the Hebrews, 'I am that I am, that I was, and that I will be'; for the future amongst the Hebrews points at all differences of time, past, present, and to come; but others, observing the strict and proper signification of the future, translate it thus, 'I will be that I will be.' This name of God imports two of God's incommunicable attributes,

First, His eternity, when he says, 'I will be.'

Secondly, His immutability, when he says, 'That I will be.' The Rabbins, upon this text, express themselves after this manner: 'The blessed God said unto Moses, Say unto them, I that have been, and I the same now, and I the same for time to come,' *etc.*; but others, more agreeable to the Chaldee paraphrase, express themselves thus: 'I, he that is, and was, and hereafter will be, has sent me unto you.'[1] But it is observable, that the angel of the waters unites all differences of time in that great and glorious acknowledgment, Rev. 16:5, 'Thou art righteous, O Lord, which art, and wast, and shalt be, because thou hast judged thus.' God is a God of that infinite excellency and glory, that it is utterly impossible for him to be better, or other than he is. If God should in the least be alterable or mutable, he would presently cease to be God. God is a God of that transcendent excellency, that there can be nothing added to him, nor nothing subtracted from him. If you add anything to him, you deny him to be God; and if you take anything from him, you destroy his being, James 1:17; Psa. 90:2, 'From everlasting to everlasting,

---

[1] See Ainsworth and D. Rivetus on the place. The Hebrew words in this Exod. 3 and their several significations well agree with the name Jehovah, which implies, that God here sending Moses, is eternal in his being, faithful in his promises, and almighty in the performance thereof.

thou art God.' 'And Mary hath chosen the better part, which shall never be taken from her,' Luke 10:42.

God is eternal, as neither being capable of a beginning nor ending; and therefore the Egyptians used to signify God by a circle, and the Persians thought that they honoured God most, when, going up to the top of the highest tower, they called him the circle of heaven. Now you know a circle has no end. And it was a custom among the Turks to go up every morning to a high tower, and to cry out, 'God always was, and always will be,' and so salute their Muhammad. Some things have a beginning, but no ending, as angels and the souls of men; and some things have no beginning, and yet have an end, as the decrees of God in their final accomplishment; and some things have both a beginning and an ending, as all sublunary things; but God has neither beginning nor ending. All creatures have a lasting, angels have an outlasting, but God has an everlasting being: 1 Tim. 1:17, 'Now unto the King eternal, immortal, invisible, the only wise God, be honour and glory for ever and ever. Amen.' God is without beginning and end, first and last, past and to come: Psa. 102:25-27, 'Of old hast thou laid the foundation of the earth: and the heavens are the works of thy hands. They shall perish, but thou shalt endure: yea, all of them shall wax old like a garment; as a vesture shalt thou change them, and they shall be changed: but thou art the same, and thy years shall have no end.' Were there no other scripture to prove the eternity and immutability of God, this were enough.[1] Whatever changes may pass upon the heavens and the earth, yet God will always remain unchangeable

[1] He that made heaven and earth must needs be before them, and therefore eternal; but this God did, *ergo*.

and unalterable. By what has been said, it is most evident that God is an everlasting portion, that he is a never-failing portion.

But now all earthly portions are very uncertain; now they are, and anon they are not: Prov. 23:5, 'Wilt thou set thine eyes upon that which is not? for riches certainly make themselves wings; they fly away as an eagle towards heaven.' Though the foolish world call riches substance, yet they have no solid subsistence. All earthly portions are as transitory as a shadow, a ship, a bubble, a bird, a dream, an arrow, a post[1] that passes swiftly away. Riches were never true to any that have trusted in them. In this text, riches are said not to be, because they do not continue to be; they will not abide by a man, they will not long continue with a man, and therefore they are as if they were not.[2] All earthly things are vain and transitory, they are rather shows and shadows than real things themselves: 1 Cor. 7:31, 'For the fashion of this world passeth away.' The Greek word σχῆμα (*schēma*) signifies a mathematical figure, which is a mere notion, and nothing in substance. All the glory of this world is rather a matter of fashion than of substance, it is a body without a soul, it is a golden shell without a kernel, it is a show without a substance. There is no firmness, there is no solidness, there is no consistency, there is no constancy in any of the creatures. All the pomp, and state, and glory of the world is but a mere piece of pageantry, a mask, a comedy, a fantasy: Acts 25:23, 'And on the morrow, when Agrippa was

---

[1] [That is, a courier who travels swiftly with his message.]

[2] Crassus was so rich that he maintained an army with his own revenues; yet he, his great army, with his son and heir, fell together, and so his great estate fell to others.

come, and Bernice, with great pomp.' The original words, μετὰ πολλῆς φαντασίας, (*meta pollēs phantasias*) signifies *great fantasy*, or *vain show*. The greatest glory and pomp of this world, in the eye of God, in the account of God, is but as a fantasy or a shadow. It was a custom in Rome, that when the emperor went by upon some great day in all his imperial pomp, there was an officer appointed to burn flax before him, and to cry out, *Sic transit gloria mundi*, so the glory of this world passes away;¹ and this was purposely done to put him in mind that all his honour, pomp, glory, and grandeur should soon pass and vanish away, as the flax did that he saw burnt before his eyes. That great conqueror of the world, Alexander, caused a sword in the compass of a wheel, to be painted upon a table, to show that what he had gotten by the sword was subject to be turned about by the wheel of fortune; and many great conquerors, besides him, have found it so, and many now alive have seen it so.

Look, as the rainbow shows itself in all its dainty colours, and then vanishes away; so does all worldly honours, riches, and preferments show themselves and then vanish away; and how many in our days have found it so! When one was commending the riches and wealth of merchants; I do not love that wealth, said a heathen, which hangs upon ropes, for if they break, the ship and all her wealth miscarries. Certainly within these few months the miscarrying of several ships has caused several merchants sadly to miscarry. A storm at sea, a spark of fire, an unfaithful servant, a false oath, or a treacherous friend, may quickly bring a man to sit with Job upon a dunghill.

¹ Cf. Sibbes's *Works*, vol. iv. Notes *d* p. 58, and *k* p. 305, vol. vii. pp. 603, 604.—G.

Look, as the bird flies from tree to tree, and as the beggar goes from door to door, and as the pilgrim travels from place to place, and as the physician walks from patient to patient; so all the riches, honours, and glory of this world either fly from man to man, or else walk from man to man. Who knows not, that many times one is made honourable by another's disgrace? another is made full by another man's emptiness? and a third is made rich by another's poverty? How soon is the courtier's glory eclipsed, if the prince but frowns upon him! and how soon the prince becomes a peasant, if God but frowns upon him? Now one is exalted, and anon he is debased; now one is full, and anon he is hungry; now one is clothed gloriously, and anon he is clothed with rags; now one is at liberty, and anon he is under restraint; now a man has many friends, and anon he has never a friend. There is nothing but vanity and uncertainty in all earthly portions. But,

(15.) *Fifteenthly*, and lastly, As God is a permanent and never failing portion, so God is *an incomparable portion*; and this follows clearly and roundly upon what has been said; for,

(1.) If God be a present portion, a portion in hand, a portion in possession; and,

(2.) If God be an immense portion, if he be the vastest, the largest, and the greatest portion; and,

(3.) If God be an all-sufficient portion; and,

(4.) If God be the most absolute, needful, and necessary portion; and,

(5.) If God be a pure and unmixed portion; and,

(6.) If God be a glorious, a happy, and a blessed portion; and,

(7.) If God be a peculiar portion; and,

(8.) If God be a universal portion; and,

(9.) If God be a safe portion, a secure portion, a portion that none can rob or wrong us of; and,

(10.) If God be a suitable portion; and,

(11.) If God be an incomprehensible portion; and,

(12.) If God be an inexhaustible portion, a portion that can never be spent, that can never be exhausted or drawn dry; and,

(13.) If God be a soul-satisfying portion; and,

(14.) If God be a permanent and an everlasting portion: then it must very necessarily follow, that God is an incomparable portion. But such a portion God is, as I have proved at large; and, therefore, beyond all dispute, God must needs be an incomparable portion: Prov. 3:13-15, 'Happy is the man that findeth wisdom' (that is, the Lord Jesus Christ), 'and the man that getteth understanding. For the merchandise of it is better than the merchandise of silver, and the gain thereof than fine gold. She is more precious than rubies: and all the things thou canst desire are not to be compared to her.' All the gold of Ophir, and all the silver of the Indies, which are but the guts and garbage of the earth, are nothing, yea, less than nothing, compared with God. God is a portion more precious than all those things which are esteemed most precious. A man may desire, what not? he may desire that all the mountains in the world may be turned into mountains of gold for his use; he may desire that all the rocks in the world may be turned into the richest pearls for his use; he may desire that all the treasure that is buried in the sea may he brought into his treasuries; he may desire that all the crowns and sceptres of all the princes and emperors of the world, may he piled up at his gate, as they were once said to be at Alexander's; yet all these things are not comparable to a saint's portion, yea, they are not to be named in that day, in which the excellency of a saint's portion is set forth. Horace writes of a precious stone that was more worth than twenty thousand shekels, and Pliny valued the two precious pearls of Cleopatra at twelve hundred thousand shekels. But what were these, and what were all other precious stones in the world, but dung and dross, in comparison of a saint's portion? (Phil. 3:7, 9).

I have read a story of a man, whom Chrysostom did feign to be in prison.[1] Oh, says he, if I had but liberty, I would desire no more! He had it. Oh then, if I had but for necessity, I would desire no more! He had it. Oh then, had I for a little variety, I would desire no more! He had it. Oh then, had I any office, were it the meanest, I would desire no more! He had it. Oh then, had I but a magistracy, though over one town only, I would desire no more! He had it. Oh then, were I a prince, I would desire no more! He had it. Oh then, were I but a king, I would desire no more! He had it. Oh then, were I but an emperor, I would desire no more! He had it. Oh then, were I but emperor of the whole world, I would then desire no more! He had it; and yet then he sits down with Alexander, and weeps that there are no more worlds for him to possess. Now did any man enjoy what he is said to desire, it would be but a very mean portion compared with God.

We may truly say of all the honours, riches, greatness, grandeur, and glory of this world, compared with God, as Gideon sometimes said of the vintage of Abiezer,

[1] [That is, imagine or pretend to be in prison.]

'The gleanings of Ephraim are better than the vintage of Abiezer' (Judg. 8:2); so the very gleanings, yea, the smallest gatherings of God, are far better, and more excellent and transcendent, they are more satisfying, more delighting, more ravishing, more quieting, and more contenting than all earthly portions are or can be. What comparison is there between a drop of a bucket and the vast ocean? between a weak drop, which recollecting all its force, yet has not strength enough to fall, and the mighty waters? Or what comparison is there between the dust of the balance and the whole earth? Why, you will say, there is no comparison between these things; and I will say, there is less between all finite portions, and such an infinite portion as God is. For this is most certain, that there must needs be always an infinite distance between what is finite and what is infinite; and such a portion God is. By all that has been said, it is most evident that God is an incomparable portion.

But now all earthly portions are comparable portions. You may easily and safely compare one earthly portion with another, one prince's revenues may be comparable to another's, and one great man's lordships may be comparable to another's, and one merchant's estate may be comparable to another's, and one gentleman's lands may be comparable to another's, and one wife's portion may be comparable to another's, and one child's portion may be comparable to another's, but God is an incomparable portion. There is no comparison to be made between God and other portions. And thus I have in these fifteen particulars fully discovered the excellency of the saints' portion above all other portions.

And, therefore, I shall now come to the second thing, and that is, to show you,

Part II.
The Grounds of Title unto God as a Portion

II. *Upon what grounds their title unto God as their portion is founded and bottomed; and they are these that follow*:

(1.) *First, The free favour and love of God, the good will and pleasure of God*, is the true ground and bottom of God's bestowing of himself as a portion upon his people, Deut. 7:6-8; Ezek. 16:1-15. There was no loveliness nor comeliness in them that should move him to bestow himself upon them. They had neither portion nor proportion, and therefore there was no cause in them why God should bestow himself as a portion upon them. God, for the glory of his own free grace and love, has bestowed himself as a portion upon those who have deserved to have their portion amongst devils and damned spirits, in those torments that are endless, ceaseless, and remediless. The Ethnics[1] feign, that their gods and goddesses loved some certain trees, for some lovely good that was in them; for Jupiter loved the oak for durance, and Neptune the cedar for stature, and Apollo the laurel for greenness, and Venus the poplar for whiteness, and Pallas the vine for fruitfulness; but what should move the God of gods to love us, who were so unworthy, so filthy,

[1] That is, the heathens, applied to all nations, non-Jewish and non-Christian.—G.

so empty, so beggarly, that were trees indeed, but such as Jude mentions, 'corrupt, fruitless, twice dead, and plucked up by the roots'? Jude 12. The question may be resolved in three words, *Amat quia amat*, he loves us because he loves us. The root of all divine love to us lies only in the bosom of God. But,

(2.) *Secondly*, Their title to God as their portion is founded upon *God's free and voluntary donation of himself to them in the covenant of grace*, Ezek. 11:19; Heb. 8:10-13. In the covenant of grace, God has freely bestowed himself upon his people: Jer. 32:38, 40, 'And they shall be my people, and I will be their God: and I will make an everlasting covenant with them, that I will not turn away from them, to do them good; but I will put my fear in their hearts, that they shall not depart from me.' The covenant of grace is the great charter, it is the *Magna Charta* of all a saint's spiritual privileges and immunities. Now in this great charter, the Lord has proclaimed himself to be his people's God: Jer. 10:16, 'The portion of Jacob is the former of all things; the Lord of hosts is his name.' He that is the former of all things, even the Lord of hosts, is the portion of Jacob; and he is Jacob's portion, by virtue of that covenant of grace, which is a free, a full, a rich, and an everlasting covenant: a covenant that he will never break, nor alter, nor falsify; a covenant that he has sworn to make good, as you may see by comparing the scriptures in the margin together.[1] That covenant of grace, by which God gives himself to be his people's God and portion, he is bound to make good by his oath; and, therefore, certainly whoever is forsworn, God will never

[1] Psa. 89:34, 35; Isa. 54:9, 10; Psa. 111:5; Psa. 105:9; Mic. 7:20; Heb. 6:13-19; Luke 1:73.

be forsworn. The Egyptians, though heathens, so hated perjury, that if any man did but swear 'By the life of the king,' and did not perform his oath, that man was to die, and no gold was to redeem his life, as Paulus Fagius observes in his comment on Genesis. To think that God will not make good that covenant that he has bound himself by oath to make good, is blasphemy, yea, it is to debase him below the very heathens. All laws, both divine and human, have left no such bond of assurance to tie and fasten one to another, as that of an oath or covenant; which, as they are to be taken in sincerity, so they are to be kept inviolably. Certainly, the covenant and oath of the great God, is not like a gipsy's knot, that is fast or loose at pleasure. Whoever breaks with him, yet he will be sure, faithfully and inviolably to keep his covenant and his oath with his. But,

(3.) *Thirdly*, Their title to God as their God and portion, is founded and bottomed upon *that marriage union that is between God and his people*, Jer. 3:13, 14. Hos. 2:19, 20, 23, 'And I will betroth thee unto me for ever; yea, I will betroth thee unto me in righteousness, and in judgment, and in lovingkindness, and in mercies: I will betroth thee unto me in faithfulness: and thou shalt know the Lord. And I will sow her unto me in the earth; and I will have mercy upon her that had not obtained mercy; and I will say to them that are not my people, Thou art my people; and they shall say, Thou art my God.' This threefold repetition, 'I will betroth thee,' 'I will betroth thee,' 'I will betroth thee,' notes three things,

[1.] First, *The certainty of their marriage union and communion with God.*

[2.] Secondly, *The excellency and dignity of their marriage union and communion with God.* And,

[3.] Thirdly, *The difficulty of believing their marriage union and communion with God.* There is nothing that Satan so much envies and opposes, as he does the soul's marriage union and communion with God; and therefore God fetches it over again and again and again, 'I will betroth thee unto me.' And so in Isa. 61:10, 'I will greatly rejoice in the Lord, my soul shall be joyful in my God; for he hath clothed me with the garments of salvation, he hath covered me with the robe of righteousness, as a bridegroom decketh himself with ornaments, and as a bride adorneth herself with her jewels.' And so, Isa. 62:5, 'For as a young man marrieth a virgin, so shall thy sons marry thee: and as a bridegroom rejoiceth over the bride, so shall thy God rejoice over thee.'[1] I have read of five sisters, of the same birth, pedigree, and race, whereof one was married to a knight, another to an earl, a third to a gentleman, a fourth to a mean man, and the fifth to a filthy beggar. Though they were all alike by birth and descent, yet their difference lay in their marriage. We are all alike by creation, by the fall, by nature, and by the first birth; it is only our marriage union and communion with God that differences us from others, and that exalts and lifts us up above others. Look, as the husband is the wife's by marriage union and communion, so God is the believer's God and portion, by virtue of that marriage union and communion that is between God and the believer. And let thus much suffice for the second thing.

---

[1] What was said by one of the Rabbins concerning Methuselah's wife, that she had nine husbands in one, is very applicable to the believer that has God for his husband.

Part III.
The Improvement of God as Your Portion

III. I shall come now to the third thing, and that is, *to make some improvement of this blessed and glorious truth to ourselves*; and, therefore,

Is it so, that God is the saint's portion, and that he is such an excellent, and such a transcendent portion above all other portions, as has been fully evidenced? Then,

(1.) *First*, Let not the saints that have God for their portion *fret and vex themselves, because of those earthly portions that God commonly bestows upon the worst of men.* There is a great aptness in the best of men to envy those earthly portions that God often bestows upon the worst of men. The lights of the sanctuary have burnt dim, stars of no small magnitude have twinkled, men of eminent parts, famous in their generations for religion and piety, have staggered in their judgments, to see the flourishing estate of the wicked.[1] It made Job to complain, Job 21:7-16;

---

[1] Diogenes, the Cynic philosopher, seeing Harpalus, a vicious person, still thriving in the world, he was bold to say, that wicked Harpalus' living long in prosperity, was an argument that God had cast off his care of the world, that he cared not which end went forward; and no wonder if this heathen stumbled at the prosperity of the wicked, when so many of the precious sons of Zion have stumbled at that stumbling-stone.

24:12, and Jeremiah to expostulate with God, Jer. 12:1, 2, and David even to faint and sink, Psa. 73. To see the prosperity of the ungodly, to see the wicked in wealth and the saints in want, the wicked in their robes and the saints in their rags, the wicked honoured and the saints despised, the wicked exalted and the saints debased, the wicked upon thrones and saints upon dunghills, is a sight that has sadly put the best of men sometimes to it. But this is a temper of spirit that no way becomes those that have God for their portion; and therefore the psalmist, in Psalm 37, cautions the saints against it no less than three several times, as you may see in verses 1, 7, 8. There is nothing that so ill becomes a saint that has God for his portion, as to be sick of the *frets*; and to prevent this mischief, this sickness, the precept is doubled, and redoubled, 'fret not, fret not, fret not.' Though they that have sore eyes are offended at bright clear lights, yet they that have God for their portion should never fret or fume, storm or rage, because some are greater than they, or richer than they, or higher than they, or more honourable than they, because all their prosperity is nothing but an unhappy happiness; it is nothing but a banquet, like Haman's, before execution; and what man is there, that is in his wits, that would envy a malefactor who meets with honourable entertainment as he is going along to execution? All a wicked man's delicate meats, his fine bits, and his murdering morsels, are sauced, and all his pleasant and delightful drinks are spiced, with the wrath and displeasure of an angry God; and why then should you fret and vex at their prosperity? What madness and folly would it be in a man that is heir to many thousands per annum, to envy a stage player that is clothed in the habit of a king, but yet not heir to one foot of land, no, nor worth one penny in all the world, and who at night must put off his royal apparel, and the next day put on his beggarly habit? Oh, sirs! it will be but a little, little while before the great God will disrobe the wicked of all their prosperity, felicity, and worldly glory, and clothe them with the rags of shame, scorn, and contempt for ever; and therefore, oh what folly and madness would it be for those that are heirs of God, and joint heirs with Christ of all the glory of heaven, to envy the prosperity of the wicked, Rom. 8:17.

The prosperity of the wicked lays them open to the worst and greatest sins.

[1.] First, *It lays them open to all uncleanness and filthiness*, Jer. 5:7, 8.

[2.] Secondly, *It lays them open to pride and contempt of God*, Psa. 73:3-13; Deut. 32:15.

[3.] Thirdly, *It lays them open to vex, oppress, tyrannize, persecute, insult, and triumph over the poor people of God*, as you may see in Pharaoh, Saul, Ahab, Jezebel, Haman, and the scribes and Pharisees.

[4.] Fourthly, *It lays them open to a neglect and slighting of the ways of God, and of the ordinances of God*, Job 21:5-16; Mal. 3:13-15; Jer. 22:21. When the protestants in France were in their prosperity, they slighted powerful preachings, and began to affect a vain frothy way of preaching and living, which ushered in the massacre upon them. Peter du Moulin hit it, when, speaking of the French protestants, he said, when the papists hurt us and persecute us for reading the scriptures, we burn with zeal to be reading of them; but now persecution is over, our Bibles are like old almanacs.

[5] Fifthly, *It lays them open to a stupidness, unmindfulness, and forgetfulness of the afflictions of the people of God*, Amos 6:1-8. Pharaoh's chief butler was no sooner set down in the seat of prosperity, but quite contrary to his promise, he easily forgets Joseph in misery.

[6.] Sixthly, *It lays them open to dreadful apostasy from the ways and worship of God*, Deut. 32:15-18. No sooner was Israel possessed of the good land that flowed with milk and honey, but they forsook the true worship of God, and fell to the worshipping of idols, for which at last the good land spewed them out as a generation cursed and abhorred by God.

[7.] Seventhly, *It lays them open to all carnal security*, as you may see in the old world: their prosperity cast them into a bed of security, and their security ushered in a flood of sin, and that flood of sin ushered in a flood of wrath, Matt. 24:37-39.

[8.] Eighthly, *It lays them open to idolatry, which is a God-provoking and a land-destroying sin*, Hos. 2:6-8; 4:6, 7, *etc.* Ah, sirs! who can seriously consider of the dreadful sins that the prosperity of the wicked lays them open to, and yet fret and vex at their prosperity?

Again, as their prosperity lays them open to the greatest sins, so their prosperity lays them open to *the greatest temptations*. Witness their tempting of themselves, and their own lusts, and witness their temptings of others to the worst of wickedness and villanies, and witness their frequent tempting and provoking of the great God to his own face, and witness their daily, yea, their hourly tempting of Satan to tempt their own souls. O sirs! as there is no condition that lays persons open to such great transgressions as prosperity does, so there is no condition that lays persons open to such horrid temptations as prosperity does; and why then should God's holy ones envy wicked men's prosperity, and worldly glory.

Again, *Their prosperity, and worldly felicity and glory, is all the portion, and all the heaven and happiness that ever they are like to have*: Psa. 17:14, 'From men of the world, which have their portion in this life.' Certainly, men whose hearts are worldly, whose minds are worldly, whose spirits are worldly, whose desires are worldly, whose hopes are worldly, and whose main ends are worldly, have only the world for their portion; and what a pitiful perishing portion is that! Men that choose the world as their portion, and that delight in the world as their portion, and that trust to the world as their portion, and that in straits run to the world as their portion, and that take content and satisfaction in the world as their portion; doubtless these have never known what it is to have God for their portion. That is a very heart-cutting and soul-killing word that you have in Matt. 6:2, 'Verily I say unto you, that they have their reward.' The scribes and Pharisees proposed to themselves, the eyes of men, the praise of men, and the applause of men, for a reward of their alms, *etc.*, and Christ tells them, that they have their reward; not God's reward, but theirs; that is, that reward that they had propounded to themselves, as the prime and ultimate end of their actions; and doubtless that word was a thunderbolt to Dives, 'Son, remember that thou in thy lifetime received thy good things, and likewise Lazarus his evil,' *etc.*, Luke 16:25. Wicked men have their best here, their worst is to come; they have their comforts here, their torments are to come; they have their joys here, their sorrows are to come; they have their heaven here, their hell is to come. Gregory being advanced to great preferment, professed that there was no scripture that struck so much terror and trembling into his heart, as that scripture did, 'Here you have your reward.' Had wicked men but their eyes in their heads, and a little understanding in their hearts, and life in their consciences, they would quickly conclude that it is hell on this side hell, for a man to have his portion in this world; and why then should you envy the prosperity of the wicked?

Again, *All their prosperity is cursed unto them*; as you may see by comparing the scriptures in the margin together.[1] All their comforts are cursed without doors, and all their comforts are cursed within doors; there are snares on all their tables, and poison in all their cups, and the plague in all their brave clothes. Dionysius the tyrant, to show Damocles, one of his flatterers, the felicity, or rather the infelicity, of a king, attired him as a king, and set him at the table, served as a king; and whilst he was in his imperial robes, he caused a naked sword, with the point downward, to be hung just over his head by a horse hair, which made Damocles to tremble, and to forbear both meat and mirth. Though the feast was a royal feast, and the attendance royal attendance, and the music royal music, yet Damocles, for his life, could not taste of any of those varieties that were before him, nor take any comfort or contentment in any other part of his royal entertainment, because of the sword, the sword, that hung but by a single hair over his head. O sirs! a sword, a sharp sword, a two-edged sword, a sword of displeasure, a sword of wrath, a sword of vengeance, hangs over the head of every wicked person when he is in his most

[1] Deut. 28:15-68; Lev. 26:14-39; Prov. 3:33; Mal. 2:2.

prosperous and flourishing condition; and had sinners but eyes to see this sword, it would be as the handwriting upon the wall; it would cause their thoughts to be troubled, and their countenances to be changed, and their joints to be loosed, and their knees to be dashed one against another; and why, then, should Christians fret and vex at the prosperity of the wicked?

Again, *When wicked men are at the highest, then are they nearest their fall*; as you may see in the 37th Psalm, and the 73rd Psalm, and in those great instances of Pharaoh, Adoni-bezek, Benhadad, Ahab, Sennacherib, Haman, Nebuchadnezzar, Belshazzar, and Herod, *etc.*[1] Look, as the ship is soonest cast away when she is top and top-gallant, so when wicked men are top and top-gallant, when they are at the height of all their pomp, bravery, and worldly glory, then God usually tumbles them down into the very gulf of misery. The great ones of the world have suddenly fallen from their highest honours and dignities, and have been sorely and sadly exercised with the greatest scorns and calamities. Let me give you this in a few remarkable instances.

Valerian, the Roman emperor, fell from being an emperor to be a footstool to Sapor, the king of Persia, as often as he took horse.

Valens the emperor, a furious Arian, being wounded in a fight with the Goths, in his flight he betook himself to a poor cottage, in which he was burnt by the Goths.

Aurelianus, the Roman emperor, brought Tetricus his opposite, and the noble queen Zenobia of Palmerina, in triumph to Rome in golden chains.

[1] Exod. 14; Judg. 1:6, 7; 1 Kings 20; 22; 2 Kings 19; Esther 6:4; Dan. 5.

Bajazet, a proud emperor of the Turks, being taken prisoner by Tamberlain,[1] a Tartarian emperor, he bound him in chains of gold, and used him for a footstool when he took horse; and when he ate meat, he made him gather crumbs under his table and eat them for his food.

Caesar, having bathed his sword in the blood of the senate and his own countrymen, is, after a while, miserably murdered in the senate by his own friends, Cassius and Brutus, to show that they are but the scourges and rods of the Almighty, which he will cast into the fire as soon as he has done with them.

The victorious emperor, Henry IV, who in sixty-two pitched battles for the most part became victorious, fell to that poverty and misery before he died, that he was forced to petition to be a prebend in the church of Spire to maintain him in his old age, which the bishop of that place denied him; whereupon he broke forth into that speech of Job, 'Have pity upon me, O my friends; for the hand of the Lord hath touched me,' Job 19:21. He died of grief and want.

And Procopius reports of king Guidimer, who was sometimes a potent king of the Vandals, that he was brought so low as to entreat his friend to send him a sponge, a loaf of bread, and a harp: a sponge to dry up his tears, a loaf of bread to maintain his life, and a harp to solace himself in his misery.

Dionysius, king of Sicily, was such a cruel tyrant that his people banished him. After his banishment he went to Corinth, where he lived a base and contemptible life. At last he became a schoolmaster, that so, when he could no longer tyrannize over men, he might over boys.

[1] Tamerlane.—G.

Great Pompey, that used to boast that he could raise all Italy in arms with a stamp of his foot, had not so much as room to be buried in.

And William the Conqueror's corpse lay three days unburied, his interment being hindered by one that claimed the ground to be his.

And Pythias pined to death for want of bread, who once was able to entertain and maintain Xerxes' mighty army.

And Philip de Comines reports of a Duke of Exeter, who though he had married Edward IV's sister, yet he saw him in the low countries begging barefoot.

And so Belisarius, a most famous general, and the only man living in his time for glorious victories, riches, and renown, yet in his old age he had his eyes put out by the empress Theodora; and being led at last in a string, he was forced to cry out, *Date panem Belisario, etc.*, Give a crust to old blind Belisarius, whom virtue advanced, but envy has brought into this great misery. By all these royal instances, you see the truth of that which once a royal slave hinted to Sesostris. The story runs thus:

Sesostris having taken many of his neighbour kings prisoners, he made them to draw his chariot by turns. Now, it so happened that one of these royal slaves, as he was drawing in the chariot, had his eye almost continually fixed on the wheels, which Sesostris observing, asked him why he looked so seriously upon the wheels. He answered, that the falling of that spoke lowest which was even now highest, put him in mind of the instability of fortune. Sesostris, duly weighing the parable, would never after be drawn by his royal slaves any more.

By what has been said, it is more evident that when

wicked men are highest they are nearest their fall; and that none fall so certainly and so suddenly, and under such dreadful calamities and miseries, as those that have been the most highly advanced in all worldly dignities and glories. And why, then, should any fret or vex at their outward prosperity or worldly felicity?

Again, *God will bring them to an account for all those talents of power, of honour, of riches, of trust, of time, of interest that God has given them in the world*; and the more they have employed the liberality and bounty of God against God or his glory, or interest, or people, the shorter shall be their felicity, and the more endless shall be their misery, Matt. 25:14-30. The greatest account and the greatest damnation commonly attends the great ones of the world. I have read of Philip III of Spain, whose life was free from gross evils, professing that he would rather lose all his kingdoms than offend God willingly; yet being in the agony of death, and considering more thoroughly of that account he was to give to God, fear struck him, and these words brake from him, 'Oh, would to God I had never reigned! Oh that those years I have spent in my kingdom, I had lived a private life in the wilderness! Oh that I had lived a solitary life with God, how much more confidently should I have gone to the throne of God! What does all my glory profit me now, but that I have so much the more torment in my death, and the greater account to give up to God!'

I have read of a soldier, who, being condemned to die for taking a bunch of grapes contrary to his general's command, as he was going along to execution, he went eating of his grapes, whereupon one of his fellow-soldiers rebuked him, saying, What! are you eating your grapes now you are going to execution? The poor fellow replied, Please, friend, do not envy me my grapes; for I shall pay a dear price for them, I shall lose my life for them; and so accordingly he did. So I say, Oh you that have God for your portion, do not envy, do not fret and vex, at the prosperity of the wicked; for what though they have more than their heart can wish, what though they live in pleasure and wallow in all carnal and sensual delights, *etc.*, yet they have a sad account to give up to God, and they shall pay dear at last for all their worldly enjoyments. For without sound repentance on their sides, and pardoning grace on God's, they shall not only lose their lives, but they shall also for ever lose their immortal souls; and therefore never fret at their prosperity.

O sirs, do you not remember that Lazarus did not fret nor fume because Dives had robes for his rags, and delicates for his scraps? *etc.* for he very well knew that though he was *sine domo*, yet not *sine Domino*.[1] He had a guard of glorious angels to transport his holy, precious, heaven-born soul into Abraham's bosom. He knew that it was better to beg on earth, than to beg in hell. O sirs, what is darkness to light, earth to heaven, chaff to wheat, tin to silver, dross to gold, or pebbles to pearls? No more are all earthly portions to that God who is the saints' portion; and, therefore, let not the saints, that have such a matchless portion, envy the prosperity and felicity of wicked men. It is the justice of envy to kill and torment the envious; and, therefore, shun it as you would poison in your meat, or a serpent in the way. A man were better to have a serpent tumbling up and down in his bowels, than to have envy gnawing in his soul. Envy is as pernicious a wickedness, as it is a foolish and

---

[1] [without a home, yet not without the Lord.]

a groundless wickedness. Envy is a scourge to scourge the soul; it is a serpent to sting the soul; it is a poison to swell the soul; it is a saw to saw the soul; it is a moth that corrupts the soul, and it is a canker that eats up the soul; and therefore fly from it, as you would fly from the most cruel and destroying adversary.

O sirs, to be angry, because God is bountiful to others; to frown, because God smiles upon others; to be bitter, because God is sweet in his dealings with others; and to sigh, because God multiplies favours and blessings upon others; what is this but to turn others' good into our own hurt, others' glory and mercy into our own punishment and torment? And if this be not to create a hell in our own hearts, I am much mistaken. I shall conclude this first inference with the counsel of the prophet in Psa. 49:16, 17, 'Be not thou afraid when one is made rich, when the glory of his house is increased; for when he dieth he shall carry nothing away: his glory shall not descend after him.' When the bodies of the wicked are rotting in their graves, and their souls are roaring in hell, none of their worldly greatness, pomp, state, glory, gallantry, riches, rents, or revenues, shall descend after them to administer one drop of comfort to them; and therefore never envy their outward prosperity or worldly glory, *etc*. But,

(2.) *Secondly*, If the saints have such an excellent, such a transcendent, and such a matchless portion, oh then, let them *be content with their present condition, let them sit down satisfied and contented, though they have but a handful of meal in their barrel, and a little oil in a cruse*, 1 Kings 17:12. O sirs, in having of God you have much, in having of God you have enough, in having of God you have all; and why then should you not sit down quiet with your present allowance? Certainly, if much will not satisfy you, if enough will not satisfy you, if all will not satisfy you, nothing will satisfy you: Heb. 13:5, 'Let your conversation be without covetousness (or love of silver, as the Greek word signifies); and be content with such things as you have (or as the Greek has it, ἀρχούμενοι τοῖς παρουσιν, [*archoumenoi tois parousin*] be content with present things): for he hath said, I will never leave thee, nor forsake thee.' There are five negatives in the Greek, 'I will not, not, not, not, not leave you nor forsake you'; fully to assure and fully to satisfy the people of God that he will never forsake them, and that he will everlastingly stick close to them. What does this unparalleled gemination,[1] 'I will never, never, never, never, never,' import but this, 'I will ever, ever, ever, yea and for ever and ever take care of you, and look after you, and be mindful of you.' Though they had changed their glory for contempt, Heb. 11:36-38, their fine raiment for sheepskins and goatskins, their silver for brass, their plenty for scarcity, their fullness for emptiness, their stately houses for holes and caves, and dens of the earth, yet they are to be contented and satisfied with present things, upon this very ground, that God will always cleave to them, and that he will never turn his back upon them. The Hebrews had been stripped and plundered of all their goods that were good for anything, and yet they must be contented, they must sit down satisfied, with their hands upon their mouths, though all were gone, Heb. 10:34.

---

[1] [Gemination literally means 'twinning' and comes from the same Latin root as 'Gemini.' Here it refers to duplication or repetition.]

Though men cannot bring their means to their minds, yet they must bring their minds to their means, and then they will sit down in silence, though they have but a rag on their backs, a penny in their purse, and a crust in their cupboards, *etc.* O sirs! a little will serve nature, less will serve grace, though nothing will serve men's lusts; and why then should not Christians be contented with a little?[1]

O friends! you have but a short journey to go, you have but a little way home, and a little will serve to bear your charges till you come to heaven, and therefore be contented with a little. To have more than will serve to bring a man to his journey's end is but a burden. One staff is helpful to a man in his journey, but a bundle is hurtful; and this, doubtless, Jacob well understood when he made that proposal in Gen. 28:20, 21, 'If God will give me bread to eat, and raiment to put on, then shall the Lord be my God.' Jacob does not say, If God will give me delicates and junkets[2] to eat, he shall be my God! Oh no! But if he will give me but bread to eat, though it be never so coarse, and never so black, and never so dry, he shall be my God. He does not say, If God will give me so many hundreds, or so many thousands a year, he shall be my God! Oh no! But if he will give me bread to eat, he shall be my God. Nor does he say, If God will give me so many hundred pounds in my purse, a comfortable habitation, and a thriving trade, he shall be my God! Oh no! But if he will give me bread to eat, he shall be my God. Nor does he say, If God will give me costly apparel, or rich and royal raiment to put on, he shall be my God! Oh no! But

---

[1] Nature is content with a little, as not to starve, not to thirst, says Galen.

[2] [A dish of sweetened and flavoured curds of milk.]

if God will give me raiment to put on, though it be never so mean and poor, he shall be my God. If Jacob may but have a little bread to feed him, and a few clothes to cover him, it is as much as he looks for. Look, as a wicked man in the fullness of his sufficiency is in straits, as Job speaks, Job 20:22, so a holy man, in the fullness of his straits, enjoys an all-sufficiency in God, as you may see in Jacob.

O Christians! though you have but little, yet you have the highest, and the noblest title that can be to that little that you do enjoy; for you hold all *in capite,*[1] as the apostle shows in that large charter of a Christian, 1 Cor. 3:21-23, which the wicked do not. Now, a hundred a year upon a good title is a better estate than a thousand a year upon a cracked, crazy title. Saints have the best title under heaven for all they enjoy, be it little or be it much. But all the titles that sinners have to their earthly enjoyments are but crazy titles, yea, in comparison of the saints' titles, they are no titles.

Again, That little that a saint has, he has it from *the special love and favour of God*; he has it from a reconciled God, Prov. 15:17. Now, a little from special love is better than a great deal from a general providence. A penny from a reconciled God is better than a pound from a bountiful God; a shilling from God as a father is a better estate than a hundred from God as a creator. The kiss that a king gave to one in the story, was a greater gift than the golden cup that he gave to another; a little, with the kisses of God's mouth, is better than all the gold of Ophir, Song of Sol. 1:2. A drop of mercy from special love is better than a sea of mercy from common bounty. Look, as one draught of clear, sweet spring water is more pleasing, satisfying, and delightful to

[1] [in the head, *i.e.* in Christ.]

the palate than a sea of brackish salt water, so one draught out of the fountain of special grace is more pleasing, satisfying, and delightful to a gracious soul than a whole sea of mercy from a spring of common grace: and therefore do not wonder when you see a Christian sit down contented with a little.

Again, The little that a Christian has *shall be certainly blessed and sanctified to him*, 1 Tim. 4:3-5; Titus 1:15; Jer. 32:41, *etc.* Though your mercies, O Christian, are never so few, and never so mean, yet they shall assuredly be blessed to you. The Lord has not only promised that he will bless your blessings to you, but he has also sworn by himself that in blessing he will bless you; and how dare you then, O Christian, think that the great and faithful God will be guilty of a lie, or that which is worse, of perjury? Gen. 22:16, 17. Now, a little blessed is better than a great deal cursed; a little blessed is better than a world enjoyed; a pound blessed is better than a thousand cursed; a black crust blessed is better than a feast cursed; the gleanings blessed are better than the whole harvest cursed; a drop of mercy blessed is better than a sea of mercy cursed; Lazarus' crumbs blessed was better than Dives' delicates cursed; Jacob's little blessed to him was better than Esau's great estate that was cursed to him. It is always better to have scraps with a blessing than to have manna and quails with a curse; a thin table with a blessing is always better than a full table with a snare, Psa. 78:18, 32; a threadbare coat with a blessing is better than a purple robe cursed; a hole, a cave, a den, a barn, a chimney-corner, with a blessing, is better than stately palaces with a curse; a woollen cap blessed is better than a golden crown cursed; and it may be that emperor understood as much, that said of his crown, when he looked on it with tears, If you knew the cares that are under this crown, you would never stoop to take it up.[1] And, therefore, why should not a Christian be contented with a little, seeing his little shall be blessed to him? Isaac tills the ground, and sows his seed, and God blesses him with a hundred fold, Gen. 26:12; and Cain tills the ground, and sows his seed, but the earth is cursed to him, and commanded not to yield to him his strength, Gen. 4:12. Oh, therefore, never let a Christian murmur because he has but a little, but rather let him continue to bless the God that has blessed his little, and that does bless his little, and that will bless his little to him.

Again, That little estate that a righteous man has *is most commonly a more lasting, a more abiding, a more permanent, and a more enduring estate than the great and large estates of the wicked are*, Prov. 15:16; 16:8. Psa. 37:16, 'A little that a righteous man hath, is better than the riches of many wicked.' One old piece of gold is worth more than a thousand new counters, and one box of pearls is worth more than many loads of pebbles, and one hundred pounds a year for ever is better than many hundreds in hand. It is very observable the psalmist does not simply say, *the estate*, but *the rich estate*; the riches not of one, or a few, but of *many* wicked, are not comparable to that little that a righteous man has. The Hebrew word המון, *Hamon*, that is here rendered *riches*, signifies also a multitude, or an abundance, or store of riches.[2] A little that a righteous man has is better than the multitude of riches, or the abundance of riches, or the store of riches that many wicked men have; and he

---

[1] Cyrus.—G.

[2] From this word *Hamon* comes the word *Mammon*, Luke 16:9.

gives you the reason of this in the 17th verse: 'For the arms of the wicked shall be broken: but he upholdeth (or under-props) the righteous.' By 'the arms of the wicked,' you are to understand their strength, their valour, their power, their wit, their wealth, their abundance, which is all the arms they have to support and bear up themselves in the world with. Now, these arms shall be broken, and when they are broken, then, even then, will God uphold the righteous, that is, God will be a continual overflowing fountain of good to his righteous ones, so that they shall never want, though all the springs of the wicked are dried up round about them.

O Sirs! there are so many moths, and so many dangers, and so many crosses, and so many losses, and so many curses that daily attend the great estates of wicked men, that they are very rarely long-lived. Ah! how many in this great city are there that have built their nests on high, and that have thought that they had laid up riches for many years, and that have said in their hearts, that their lands, and stocks, and trades, and houses, and pompous estates should abide for ever, who are now broken in pieces like a potter's vessel.

Ah! how often does the pride, the oppression, the lying, the cheating, the over-reaching, the swearing, the cursing, the whoring, the covetousness, the drunkenness, and the wantonness of the wicked, cut the throat of all their mercies! These are the wickednesses that as a fire burns up all their outward enjoyments, and that turns their earthly paradise into a real hell. It is the wickedness of the wicked that causes their prosperity to wither, and that provokes God to turn their plenty into scarcity, their glory into contempt, and their honour into shame. It is very observable, that in the holy Scriptures the prosperous estates of the wicked are frequently compared to things of an abrupt existence,[1] to a shadow which soon passes away; to chaff, which a puff, a blast of wind easily disperses and scatters; to grass, which quickly withers before the sun; to tops of corn, which in an instant are cut off; to the unripe grape, which on a sudden drops down; yea, to a dream in the night; and what is a dream, but a quick fancy, and a momentary vanity? All the riches that the wicked gain, either by their trades, or by their friends, or by their great places, or by their high offices, or by their subtle contrivances, or by their sinful compliances; and all the honour they gain in the court, or in the camp, or in the school, is but light and inconstant; it is but like the crackling of thorns under a pot. They are fading vanities, that commonly die before those that enjoy them are laid in the dust.

Oh, therefore, let all Christians be contented with their little, seeing that their little shall outlast the large estates of wicked and ungodly men. A man that has God for his portion can truly say that which no wicked man in the world can say, *viz.*, 'Surely goodness and mercy shall follow me all the days of my life: and I will dwell in the house of the Lord for ever,' Psa. 23:6. The psalmist does not say that goodness and mercy should follow him a day, or a few days, or many days, but that goodness and mercy should follow him all the days of his life. The Hebrew word *radaph*, that is here rendered *to follow*, signifies *to persecute*; says the psalmist, 'Goodness and mercy shall follow me, as the persecutor follows him he persecutes'; that is, it shall follow me frequently, it shall follow me constantly, it shall follow

---

[1] Job 14:2; 21:17, 18; Isa. 29:5; 2 Kings 19:26; Job 24:24; 15:33; 20:8.

me swiftly, it shall follow me earnestly, it shall follow me unweariedly. The word signifies a studious, anxious, careful, diligent following; it is a metaphor that is taken from beasts and birds of prey, that follow and fly after their prey with the greatest eagerness, closeness, and unweariedness imaginable. Why thus should mercy and loving-kindness follow David all the days of his life; and if in a temptation, he should prove so weak and so foolish as to run from goodness and mercy, yet goodness and mercy should follow him, like as the sun going down follows the passenger that goes eastward with his warm beams.

O, but now the mercies of the wicked are short-lived. Though the wicked flourish and spread themselves like a green bay tree one day, yet they are cut down the next, and there is neither root nor branch to be found, tale nor tidings to be heard of them; for in a moment, they, with all their greatness, state, pomp, and glory, are utterly vanished and banished out of the world, Psa. 37:35-37. And so, Psa. 34:10, 'The young lions do lack and suffer hunger: but they that seek the Lord shall not want any good thing.' Young lions are lusty, strong, fierce, and active to seek their prey, and have it they will if it be to be had: and yet for all that they shall lack and suffer hunger. By *young lions*, the learned understand,

[1.] *First*, All wicked rulers; men that are in the highest places and authority, as the lion is the king of beasts, Prov. 28:15; Ezek. 32:2.

[2.] *Secondly*, By lions they understand all cruel oppressors, that are still oppressing and grinding of the faces of the poor: Prov. 30:30, '*rich cormorants*,' as the Septuagint renders it, 'who live on the spoil of the poor, and are never satisfied.'

[3.] *Thirdly*, By lions, they understand the tyrants and the mighty Nimrods of the world, which are sometimes called lions, Jer. 2:15; 1 Chron. 11:22; Nahum 2:13.

[4.] And *lastly*, By lions, they understand all the crafty and subtle politicians of the earth: Ezek. 38:13, 'The lion lurks very craftily and secretly for his prey.' The sum of all is this, That wicked men that are in the highest authority, and that great oppressors, cruel tyrants, and crafty politicians shall be impoverished, and brought to penury, beggary, and misery. And this we have often seen verified before our eyes.

O Christian! what though you have but a little of this world, yet the God of all mercies, and all the mercies of God, the God of all comforts, and all the comforts of God, are yours; and what would you have more? In God is fullness, all fullness, infinite fullness; and if this, with a little of the world, will not satisfy you, I know not what will. If a God for your portion will not content you, all the world will never content you. Shall Diogenes, a heathen, be more content with his tub to shelter him, and with his dish to drink in, than Alexander was with all his conquests?[1] And shall not a Christian sit down contented and satisfied in the enjoyment of God for his portion, though he has but a tub to shelter him, bread to feed him, and a dish of water to refresh him? I shall conclude this head with a weighty saying of Cato's, *Si quid est quo utar utor, si non scio quis sum; mihi vitio vertunt, quia multis egeo, et ego illis, quia nequeunt egere*. I have neither house, nor plate, nor garments of any price in my hands; what I have I can use; if not, I can want it: some blame me because I want many things, and I blame them

---

[1] The immortal 'tub,' belonging to the Metroum or temple of the mother of the gods.—G.

because they cannot want. Oh let not nature do more than grace! Oh let not this heathen put Christians to a blush! But,

(3.) *Thirdly*, If God be the saint's portion, *the sinners are much mistaken, that judge the saints to be the most unhappy men in the world.* There are no men under heaven in such a blessed and happy estate as the saints are, Balaam himself being judge, Num. 23:5-11. A man that has God for his portion, is honourable even in rags, Psa. 16:3. He has some beams, some rays, of the majesty and glory of God stamped upon his soul, and shining upon his face, and glittering in his life; and he that is so blind as not to behold this, is worse than Balaam the witch. Though the blind Jews could see no form, nor comeliness, nor beauty in Christ that they should desire him, Isa. 53:2; yet the wise men that came from the east could see his divinity sparkling in the midst of the straw; they could see a heavenly majesty and glory upon him when he lay among the beasts, when he lay in a manger, Luke 2:7. Witness their tedious journey to find him, and witness their worshipping of him, and witness those rich and royal presents that they brought to him, Matt. 2:11. So though the blind sots[1] of the world can see no loveliness nor comeliness, no beauty nor glory, in the saints, or upon the saints, that should render them amiable and desirable in their eyes, yet God, and Christ, and angels, and those that are wise in heart and wise to salvation, can see a great deal of divine beauty, majesty, and glory upon all those that have God for their portion.

There is no happiness to that of having God for a man's portion: Psa. 144:15, 'Happy is that people, that is in such

---

[1] [That is, foolish persons.]

a case' (but give me that word again), 'yea, happy is that people, whose God is the Lord.' He that has not God for his portion can never be happy, and he that enjoys God for his portion can never be miserable. Augustine, speaking of one who, passing by a stately house which had fair lands about it, and asking another whom he met to whom that house and lands belonged, he answered, to such an one. Oh, says he, that is a happy man indeed. No, says the other, not so happy as you think; for it is no such happiness to have that house and land, but he is happy indeed that has the Lord for his God, for that is a privilege that exceeds all things whatsoever. For, says he, he that has honour and riches may go to hell for all them, but he that has God to be his God, is sure to be everlastingly happy. According as a man's portion is, so is he. Now, if God be a man's portion, who is the spring, the fountain, the top of all excellency and glory, then certainly that man must needs be an excellent man that has God for his portion; and upon this score it is that the righteous man is more excellent than his neighbour.[1] Let the righteous man's neighbour be never so great, and never so rich, and never so mighty, and never so noble, yet if he has not God for his portion, the righteous man is more excellent than he. And the reason is evident, because he has that God for his portion that is most eminent and excellent.

O sirs! if God be most excellent, if God be alone excellent, then they must needs be most excellent that have God for their portion. It is very observable that, according to the excellency of God, the excellency of the saints is in some

---

[1] Prov. 12:26. A man that hath God for his portion, doth as much excel and outshine such as have only Mammon for their portion, as the sun excels and outshines the stars.

proportion hinted at in Scripture; as in Deut. 33:26, 29, 'There is none like unto the God of Jeshurun'; and presently it follows, 'Happy art thou, O Israel: who is like unto thee!' or, Oh your happinesses, O Israel! Oh the multiplied happiness, the heaped-up happiness, that attends Israel! The saints that have God for their portion are the world's paragons; they are worthies 'of whom this world is not worthy'; they are such great, such noble, such worthy worthies, that this world is not worthy to think on them, to look on them, to wait on them, or to enjoy their company. One saint that has God for his portion, is worth more than all the millions of sinners in the world that have not God for their portion. God delights to reflect his glory upon his saints; for as there are none like to God, so there are none like to the people of God. Look, as God is a nonsuch,[1] so his people are a nonsuch; and so in 2 Sam. 7:22, 23 'Wherefore thou art great, O Lord God: for there is none like thee, neither is there any God besides thee, according to all that we have heard with our ears. And what one nation in the earth is like thy people?' Look, as the excellency of God rises, so in a proportion the excellency of the saints rises; and look, as there are no gods in all the world that are so excellent as God is, so there are no people in all the world that are so excellent as the people of God are. Every one that has God for his portion resembles the child of a king, as Zebah and Zalmunna said to Gideon of his brethren, Judg. 8:18. If you look upon their divine and heavenly origin, you shall find that they are born of the blood-royal, and that they are his sons who is the King of kings, and Lord of lords; yea, all the saints that have God for their portion are kings: Rev.

[1] [That is, without equal.]

1:6, 'And hath made us kings and priests unto God and his Father.'[1] They have the power, sovereignty, and authority of kings, they are privileged as kings, they are guarded as kings, they are adorned as kings, they are entertained as kings, they feed as kings, they feed high, they live upon God and Christ, and all the glory of heaven; and they are clothed as kings, they are clothed with Christ's righteousness, and with the garments of joy and gladness. Kings have great alliance, and so have the saints that have God for their portion. Kings have a very great influence, and so have they that have God for their portion. A man in rags that has God for his portion is a more honourable person than the greatest monarch on earth that has only the world for his portion.

I have read of Alexander the Great, and of Pompey the Great, and of Charles the Great, and of Abner the Great, and of Herod the Great; but what were all these great men but grasshoppers to the saints that have God for their portion? Men that have had God for their portion have been very famous, illustrious, and glorious, when they have been friendless, and houseless, and penniless; yea, when they have been under the swords, and saws, and harrows of persecution.[2] When Maximian, the tyrant, had plucked out one of Paphnutius the Confessor's eyes, that good emperor Constantine saw such a lustre, beauty, and glory upon Paphnutius, that he fell upon him and kissed him; and he kissed that very hole most in which one of the Confessor's eyes had been, as being most ravished and delighted with that hole. His name that has God for his portion shall live,

---

[1] Rev. 17:14; 5:10; Dan. 7:27; 1 Cor. 3:22, 23; Psa. 34:14; Heb. 1:14; Psa. 45:13; 1 Cor. 1:30.

[2] As you may see in the 10th and 11th chapters of Hebrews.

when the name of the wicked shall rot (Prov. 10:7; Psa. 112:9). His name shall be written in golden characters upon marble, when the name of the wicked shall be written in the dust.

The blind besotted world are sadly out, who are ready to set the crown of honour and happiness upon any heads, rather than upon theirs that have God for their portion. Look, as Samuel, beholding the beauty and stature of Eliab, would surely have him anointed, and the crown set upon his head, when the crown was designed for David at the sheepfold, 1 Sam. 16:6, 12, so vain men are very apt to set the crown of happiness upon their heads who have the greatest share in this world, when the crown of happiness and blessedness is only to be set on their heads that have God for their portion. What the Queen of Sheba said of Solomon's servants, 'Happy are thy men, happy are these thy servants, which stand continually before thee, and that hear thy wisdom' (1 Kings 10:8), is here very applicable to the saints: 'Happy, happy, yea, thrice happy are those precious sons and daughters of Sion that have God for their portion.' A man that has God for his portion shall live happily and die happily, and after death he shall remain happy to all eternity; and therefore we may well cry out, 'Oh, the happiness and blessedness of that man that has God for his portion!' But,

(4.) *Fourthly*, If the saints have such an excellent, such a matchless, portion, oh, then, let them never *set their hearts and affections upon any earthly portions*, Prov. 23:5. It is true, O Christian, you may lay your hand upon an earthly portion, but you must never set your heart upon an earthly portion: Psa. 62:10, 'If riches increase, set not your heart upon them.' The Hebrews put the heart for the thoughts, affections, love, desire, joy, hope, confidence, *etc.* If riches increase, oh, set not your thoughts upon them; if riches increase, oh, set not your affections upon them; if riches increase, oh, set not your love upon them, set not your desires upon them, set not your joy and delight upon them, nor never place your hope or confidence in them. Oh! what a shame and dishonour would it be to see men of great estates to rake in dunghills, and to sweep channels, and to carry tankards of water, and to cry trifles[1] up and down the streets! And is it not a greater shame, a greater dishonour, to see those that have the great God for their portion, to set their hearts and affections upon a little white and yellow clay?

It was a generous speech of that heathen, Themistocles, who, seeing something glister[2] like a pearl in the dark, scorned to stoop for it himself, but bid another stoop, saying, You stoop, for you art not Themistocles. Oh! it is below a generous Christian, a gracious Christian, a noble Christian, that has God for his portion, to stoop to the things of this world. A true-bred Christian will set his feet upon those very things that the men of the world set their hearts: Rev. 12:1, 'And there appeared a great wonder in heaven, a woman clothed with the sun, and the moon under her feet, and upon her head a crown of twelve stars.' The church is compared to a woman for her weakness, for her lovingness, for her comeliness, and for her fruitfulness; and being clothed with the Sun of righteousness, she has the moon, that is, the world, under her feet. The church

---

[1] [That is, things of little value, substance, or importance.]

[2] [That is, sparkle, glitter.]

treads under her feet all temporary and transitory things, which are as changeable as the moon. She treads upon all worldly and carnal enjoyments and contentments, as things below her, as things not worthy of her. What vanity is it for a great man to set his heart on birds' nests, and paper kites that boys make fly in the air? And as great, yea, a greater vanity it is for the saints that have God for their portion, to set their hearts upon the poor little low things of this world. It is not for you to be fishing for gudgeons, but for towns, forts, and castles, said Cleopatra to Mark Antony. So say I, it is not for you that have God for your portion, to be fishing for the honours, riches, and preferments of the world; but for more grace, more holiness, more communion with God, more power against corruptions, more strength to withstand temptations, more abilities to bear afflictions, more sense of divine love, and more assurance of interest in Christ, and in all that glory and happiness that comes by Christ.

When Alexander heard of the riches of India, he regarded not the kingdom of Macedonia, but gave away his gold; and when he was asked, what he kept for himself? he answered, *Spem majorem et meliorum*, the hope of better and greater things. O sirs! when you look upon those riches of grace, those riches of glory, those riches of justification, those riches of sanctification, and those riches of consolation that are in that God that is your portion, how should you disregard, how should you despise, how should you scorn the great things, and the carefree things of the world! It was a notable speech of Erasmus, if his wit were not too quick for his conscience. I desire, said he, neither wealth nor honour, no more than a feeble horse does a heavy cloak-bag. O

Christians! you have many thousand excellencies in God to set your affections upon, and you have many thousand excellencies in Christ to set your affections upon, and you have many thousand excellencies in the Spirit to set your affections upon, and you have many thousand excellencies in the covenant to set your affections upon, and you have many thousand excellencies in the gospel to set your affections upon, and you have many thousand excellencies in the ordinances to set your affections upon, and you have many thousand excellencies in promises to set your affections upon, and you have many thousand excellencies in prophecies to set your affections upon, and you have many thousand excellencies in rare providences to set your affections upon, and you have many thousand excellencies in the saints to set your affections upon; and therefore, for shame, set not your affections upon things below, set not your hearts upon things that perish, Col. 3:1. A man can never come to set his heart upon any earthly portion, but that God will either embitter it, or lessen it, or cloud it, or wholly strip him of it; and therefore sit loose, I say again, sit loose in your affections to all worldly enjoyments. But,

(5.) *Fifthly*, If the saints have such a glorious, such an incomparable portion; then let them *be cheerful and comfortable under all worldly crosses, losses, and troubles*, Acts 5:17-42; Rom. 5:2-4. With what a Roman spirit do many vain men of great estates bear up under great losses and crosses; and shall not grace do more than nature? Shall not the Spirit of God do more than a Roman spirit? O sirs, how can you look upon God as your portion, and not bear up bravely under any worldly loss? Heb. 10:34, 'For ye had compassion of me in my bonds, and took joyfully the spoiling of your goods, knowing in yourselves that ye have in heaven a better, and an enduring substance.' They had God for their portion, and the joy of the Lord was their strength, and therefore they could rejoice in whatever damage came upon them by the hand of violence. And so David could comfort himself in his God, and encourage himself in his God, when Ziklag was burned, his wives and children carried captive, and the people in a readiness to stone him, 1 Sam. 30:6. Now all was gone, he looks up to God as his portion, and so he bears up bravely and cheerfully in the midst of all extremity of misery.[1]

And so Habakkuk was a man of the same noble temper, as you may see in Hab. 3:17, 18: 'Although the fig-tree shall not blossom, neither shall fruit be in the vines, the labour of the olive shall fail, and the fields shall yield no meat, the flock shall be cut off from the fold, and there shall be no herd in the stalls; yet I will rejoice in the Lord, I will joy in the God of my salvation.' 'Although the fig tree shall not blossom, yet I will rejoice in the Lord.' Aye, but that is nothing, to rejoice in the Lord as long as there is fruit in the vines; aye, but says he, 'Though there be no fruit in the vines, yet I will rejoice in the Lord.' Aye, but that is nothing, to rejoice in the Lord so long as the labour of the olive does not fail; aye, but says he, 'Though the labour of the olive shall fail, yet I will rejoice in the Lord.' Aye, but that is nothing, to rejoice in the Lord so long as the fields do yield their meat; aye, but says he, 'Though the fields shall yield no meat, yet I will rejoice in the Lord.' Aye, but that is nothing, to

---

[1] Better is that hell on earth which makes way for heaven, than that heaven on earth which makes way for hell.

rejoice in the Lord, so long as the flock is not cut off from the fold; aye, but says he, 'Though the flock shall be cut off from the fold, yet I will rejoice in the Lord.' Aye, but that is nothing, to rejoice in the Lord, so long as there be herds in the stalls; aye, but says he, 'Though there be no herd in the stalls, yet will I rejoice in the Lord, and joy in the God of my salvation.' Habakkuk could rejoice in the Lord, and joy in that God that was his portion, not only when all delightful comforts and contentments should fail, but also when all necessary comforts and contentments should fail. Habakkuk was a man of raised spirit, he knew that he had that God for his portion that did contain in himself all comforts and contentments, and that could easily make up the want of any comfort or contentment, and that would certainly lie himself in the room of every comfort and contentment, that either his children should need or desire; and in the power of this faith he rejoices and triumphs in a day of thick darkness and gloominess: 1 Sam. 1:5, 18, 'But unto Hannah he gave a worthy portion; for he loved Hannah, and her countenance was no more sad.' O my brethren, it no way becomes those that have God for their portion to walk up and down the world with clouded countenances, with saddened countenances, or with dejected countenances, and therefore, under all your crosses and losses, wipe your eyes, and walk up and down with pleasant countenances, with cheerful countenances, and with smiling countenances, and this will be an honour to God, and an honour to religion, and an honour to profession, and an honour to that saintship that is too much slighted and scorned in the world.

Indeed, when wicked men are exercised with crosses and losses, it is no wonder to see them take on like madmen, and see them take on bitterly, like Micah, when he cried out, 'They have taken away my gods, and what have I more? and what is this that ye say unto me, What aileth thee?' Wicked men's bags and goods are their gods; they are their portion, they are their all; and when these are gone, all is gone with them; when these are taken away, all is taken away with them; and therefore it is no wonder to hear them cry out, 'Undone, undone!' and to see them sit down and weep, as if they were resolved to drown themselves in their own tears. But you that have God for your portion, you have such a portion that shall never be taken from you. As Christ told Mary, 'Thou hast chosen the better part that shall never be taken from thee,' Luke 10:42; and therefore it highly concerns you to bear up bravely, as well when you have but little, as when you have much; and as well when you have nothing, as when you have everything. You shall be sure to enjoy all in God, and God in all; and what would you have more? Seneca once told a courtier that had lost his son, that he had no cause to mourn either for that or anything else, because Caesar was his friend! O then, what little cause have the saints to mourn for this or that loss, considering that God is their friend; yea, which is more, that God is their portion.

I have read of a company of poor Christians, who, being banished to some remote parts, and one standing by, seeing them pass along, said, that it was a very sad condition that those poor people were in, to be thus hurried from the society of men, and to be made companions with the beasts of the field; True, said another, it were a sad condition indeed, if they were carried to a place where they could not find their God; but let them be of good cheer, for God goes along with them, and will follow them with the comforts of his grace wherever they go. Would it not make a man either sigh or laugh to see a man lament and take on bitterly for the loss of his shoestrings, when his purse is safe; or for the loss of a little lumber, when all his goods are safe; or for the burning of a pigsty, when his dwelling house is safe; or for the loss of his scabbard, when his life is safe? And why, then, should a Christian lament and take on for the loss of this or that, so long as his God is safe, and his portion is safe? But,

(6.) *Sixthly*, If the saints have such an excellent and such a transcendent portion, as has been discovered, then *away with all sinful shifts, ways, courses, and compliances to gain an earthly portion*. Was it not horrid, yea, hellish baseness in Ahab, who had a whole kingdom at his devotion, to possess himself of poor Naboth's vineyard, by false swearing, hypocrisy, treachery, cruelty, and blood? 1 Kings 21. But, certainly, it is a far greater baseness and wickedness in those that have God for their portion, or at least pretend to have God for their portion, to be sharking,[1] and shifting, and complying with the lusts of men, and with the abominations of the times; and all to hold what they have, or else to raise themselves, and greaten[2] themselves, and enrich themselves, by others' ruin. These men might do well to make Jer. 17:11 their daily companion: 'As the partridge sitteth on eggs, and hatcheth them not; so he that getteth riches, and not by right, shall leave them in the midst of his days, and at his end shall be a fool.' The crafty fox in

---

[1] 'Swindling'—G.
[2] [That is, make themselves great.]

the fable hugged himself to think how he had cozened[1] the crow of his breakfast; but when he had eaten it, and found himself poisoned with it, he wished that he had never meddled with it.

O sirs! there is a day coming, in which men shall wish that they had never laboured to sin themselves into honours, riches, preferments, high offices, and high places, when God shall let some scalding drops of his wrath to fall upon their spirits, who have sold all Christ's and Christians' concernments, and their own consciences, to gain riches and high offices! How will they curse the day in which they were born, and be ready, by the knife or the halter, to put an end to their most wretched days! Oh what a sad and lamentable thing would it be to see men worth many thousands a year purloining from others! But it is a far more sad and lamentable thing to see men who pretend to have God for their portion, to act all this, and more than this, and all to lay up an earthly portion for themselves and others.

How many be there in these days who pretend very high towards God, and yet 'sell the righteous for silver, and the poor for a pair of shoes,' Amos 2:6; yea, that pollute the name of God, the worship of God; and that slay the souls of men for handfuls of barley, and pieces of bread; and that will say anything, or swear anything, or bow, or crouch to anything, for a piece of silver and a morsel of bread, or to be put into one of the priest's offices, Ezek. 13:19; 1 Sam. 2:36. O Christian, you have all honours and riches and preferments in that God that is your portion; and why then should you go about to sin yourself into the enjoyment of those things which you have already in your God? Have you forgotten

---

[1] [That is, tricked or deceived.]

that Solomon got more hurt by his wealth, than ever he got good by his wisdom? and that David was best in a wilderness, and that our stomachs are usually worse in summer, and that the moon is furthest from the sun when it is fullest of light; and that all that a man gets by breaking with God and his conscience, he may put in his eye; and that the coal that the eagle carried from the sacrifice to her nest, set all on fire. Have you forgotten what is said of Abraham in Gen. 13:2, *viz.*, 'That he was very rich in cattle, in silver, and in gold?' The Hebrew word *cabbedh*, that is here rendered *rich*, signifies *heavy*, to show that riches are a very heavy burden, and often a hindrance in the way to heaven. Oh! how vain, how uncertain, how vexing, and how dividing are the great things of the world! How unfit do they make many men to live, and how unwilling do they make many men to die! Oh what is gold in the purse, when there is guilt upon the conscience! What are full bags, when sin and wrath are at the bottom of them! O sirs! you have an infinite fullness in that God that is your portion, and that fills all in all; and why then should you break the hedge to gain the world? But,

(7.) *Seventhly*, If the saints have such an excellent, glorious, and incomparable portion (1 Cor. 1:31), oh then let them *glory in their portion, let them rejoice and delight themselves in their portion*. Man is a creature very apt and prone to glory in earthly portions, when he should be glorying in the Lord: Jer. 9:23, 24, 'Thus saith the Lord, Let not the wise man glory in his wisdom, neither let the mighty man glory in his might, let not the rich man glory in his riches: but let him that glorieth glory in this, that he understandeth and

knoweth me, that I am the Lord which exercise lovingkindness, judgment, and righteousness, in the earth, for in these
things I delight, saith the Lord'; Isa. 41:16, 'Thou shalt rejoice
in the Lord, and shalt glory in the Holy One of Israel'; and
Isa. 45:25, 'In the Lord shall all the seed of Israel be justified,
and shall glory.' Oh how should the saints, that have God
for their portion, make their boast of their God, and rejoice
in their God, and glory in their God! Shall the men of the
world glory in an earthly portion, and shall not a saint glory
in his heavenly portion? Shall they glory in a portion that
they have only in hope, and shall not a Christian glory in
that portion that he has already in hand? Shall they glory
in a portion that they have only in reversion, and shall not
a saint glory in that portion that he has in present possession? Shall they glory in their hundreds and thousands a
year, and shall not a Christian glory in that God that fills
heaven and earth with his glory? In all the scriptures there
is no one duty more pressed than this, of rejoicing in God;
and indeed, if you consider God as a saint's portion, there
is everything in God that may encourage the soul to rejoice
in him, and there is nothing in God that may in the least
discourage the soul from rejoicing and glorying in him.[1]

O Christians, the 'joy of the Lord is your strength' (Neh.
8:10); it is your doing strength, and your bearing strength,
and your suffering strength, and your prevailing strength;
it is your strength to work for God, and it is your strength
to wait on God, and it is your strength to exalt and lift up
God, and it is your strength to walk with God; it is your
strength to live, and your strength to die, and therefore be

---

[1] Compare these scriptures together: Phil. 3:1; 4:4; Ezek. 10:17;
Joel 2:23; Psa. 33:1; 79:12, 13; 149:1, 2.

sure to keep up your joy in God. It is one of the saddest sights in all the world to see a man that has God for his portion, with Cain to walk up and down this world with a dejected countenance. It was holy joy and cheerfulness that made the faces of several martyrs to shine as if they had been the faces of angels. One observes of Crispina, that she was cheerful when she was apprehended, and joyful when she was led to the judge, and merry when she was sent to prison, and so she was when bound, and when lifted up in a cage, and when examined, and when condemned.

O Christians! how can you number up the several souls that you deject, the foul mouths that you open, and the bad reports that you bring upon the Lord and his ways by your sad, dejected, and uncomfortable walking! It is very observable that the Lord takes it so very unkindly at his people's hands when they go sighing, lamenting, and mourning up and down, when they should be rejoicing and delighting of themselves in him and his goodness, that he threatens to pursue them to the death with all manner of calamities and miseries upon that very score: Deut. 28:47, 48, 'Because thou servedst not the Lord thy God with joyfulness, and with gladness of heart, for the abundance of all things; therefore shalt thou serve thine enemies which the Lord shall send against thee, in hunger, and in thirst, and in nakedness, and in want of all things: and he shall put a yoke of iron upon thy neck until he have destroyed thee.' But,

(8.) *Eighthly*, If the saints have such a great, such a large, and such an all-sufficient portion as has been shown they have, *then certainly they shall never want anything that is good for them*. David tells you that his cup runs over, Psa.

23:5, 6. The words are an allusion to the Hebrew feasts. David's table was richly and nobly spread, both in sight and spite of all his enemies. In one God is every good; and what can he want that enjoys that God? God is a bundle of all goodness and sweetness. And look, as God is the best God, so he is the greatest and the fullest good. He can as easily fill the most capacious souls up to the very brim with all inward and outward excellencies and mercies, as Christ did once fill those waterpots of Galilee up to the very brim with wine, John 2:1-11. If God has enough in himself for himself, then certainly he has enough in himself for us; that water that can fill the sea can much more easily fill my cup or my pot: 'My people shall be satisfied with goodness, saith the Lord,' Jer. 31:14; 'And I will make an everlasting covenant with them, that I will not turn away from them, to do them good. Yea, I will rejoice over them to do them good, and I will plant them in this land assuredly with my whole heart and with my whole soul,' Jer. 32:40, 41; 'My God shall supply all your need,' Phil. 4:19, or, 'My God shall (πληρωσει, *plērō-sei*) fill up all your need,' as he did the widow's vessels in 2 Kings 4:3-6. Godliness has the promise both of this life and that which is to come, 1 Tim. 4:8.

He that has God for his portion shall have all other things cast into his store, as paper and packthread is cast into the bargain, or as a handful of corn is cast into the corn you buy, or as hucksters cast in an overcast among the fruit you buy, or as an inch of measure is given into an ell of cloth,[1] Matt. 6:25, 31-33. O sirs, how can that man be

[1] [The 'ell' was an ancient measure of length mostly used for measuring cloth. It came from the Latin for arm 'ulnia' and was assumed to be the average length of a person's arm.]

poor, how can that man want, that has the Lord of heaven and earth for his portion? Surely he cannot want light that enjoys the sun, nor he cannot want bread that has all sorts of grain in his barns, nor he cannot want water that has the fountain at his door; no more can he want anything that has God for his portion, who is everything, and who will be everything to every gracious soul. O sirs! the thought, the tongue, the desire, the wish, the conception, all fall short of God, and of that great goodness that he has laid up for them that fear him, Psa. 31:19; and why then should they be afraid of wants? Psa. 104:10-31. How does that pretty bird the robin-redbreast cheerfully sit and sing in the chamber window, and yet does not know where he shall make the next meal, and at night must take up his lodging in a bush. Oh what a shame is it that men that have God for their portion should act below this little bird.

I have read of famous Mr Dod, who is doubtless now high in heaven,[1] who intended to marry, was much troubled with fears and cares how he should live in that condition, his incomes being so small that they would but maintain him in a single condition; and looking out at a window, and seeing a hen scraping for food for her numerous brood about her, thought thus with himself: This hen did but live before it had these chickens, and now she lives with all her little ones; upon which he added this thought also, I see the fowls of the air neither sow nor reap, nor gather into barns, and yet my heavenly Father feeds them, Matt. 6:26; and thus he overcame his fears of wanting.[2] O Christians! you have such a Father for your portion, as will as soon cease to

[1] Died 1645, aged 96.—G.
[2] See Life of Dod in Benjamin Brook's 'Puritans,' vol. iii. *seq.*—G.

be, as he will cease to supply you with all things necessary for your good. It was a good saying of one, I would desire neither more nor less than enough; for I may as well die of a surfeit as of hunger, and he is rich enough that lacks not bread, and high enough in dignity that is not forced to serve. Plutarch's reasoning is good, τα τῶν φιλῶν παντα κοινα (*ta tōn philōn panta koina*), friends have all things in common; but God is our friend, *ergo* we cannot want; a rare speech from a heathen. Rather than Israel should want, did not God feed them with manna in the wilderness? and rather than Elijah and the widow should not have their wants supplied, did not God work a miracle, by causing the handful of meal in the barrel, and the little oil in the cruse, to last and hold out till he supplied them in another way? Rather than Elijah shall want, God will feed him with a raven, and by that miraculous operation save him from a perishing condition.

O sirs! all the attributes of God are so engaged for you that you cannot want, and all the promises of God are so engaged to you that you cannot want, and all the affections of God are so set upon you that you cannot want; and why then should you fear wants? O sirs! has God given you his Son, his Spirit, his grace, his glory, yea, himself, and will he deny you lesser things,[1] Rom. 8:32. Has he given you those things that are more worth than ten thousand worlds, and will he not give you bread to eat, and raiment to put on? Has he given you those spiritual riches that infinitely exceed and excel all the riches, rubies, and pearls in the

[1] Gregory the Great was wont to say, that he was a poor man, whose soul was void of grace, not he whose coffers were empty of money.

world; and will he deny you a little money in your purses to bear your charges till you come to heaven? Has he given you a crown, and will he deny you a crust? Has he given you his royal robes, and will he deny you a few rags? Has he given you a royal palace, and will he deny you a poor cottage to shelter you from the stormy winter and from the scorching summer? yea, does he feed his enemies, and clothe his enemies, and protect his enemies, and provide for his enemies, which are the generation of his wrath and curse, and will he not do as much for you, 'O ye of little faith'? Will he do so much for them that hate him, and will he not do as much for you that love him? Doubtless he will. Will he feed the ravens, and provide for the ox and the ass, and clothe the grass of the field; and will he suffer you, who are his love, his joy, his delight, to starve at his feet, for want of necessaries? Surely no.

But suppose you were under many real wants, yet certainly this very consideration, that the Lord is your portion, should quiet your hearts, and bear up your spirits bravely under them all. Jerome tells us of one Didymus, a godly preacher, who was blind; Alexander, a godly man, coming to see him, asked him, whether he was not sorely troubled and afflicted for want of his sight. Oh yes, said Didymus, it is a very great affliction and grief to me. Whereupon Alexander chided him, saying, Has God given you the excellency of an angel, of an apostle, and are you troubled for that which rats and mice, and brute beasts enjoy? O sirs! if God has given you himself for a portion, then certainly it is a sinful thing, a shameful thing, an unworthy thing for you to be so troubled, afflicted, and grieved, because you want this and that worldly contentment and enjoyment, which God bestows upon such whose wickedness has debased them below the ox and the ass, I mean, men of beastly spirits, and beastly principles, and beastly practices, Isa. 1:2, 3. Look, as Benjamin's mess[1] was five times greater than his brethren's (Gen. 43:34); so those that have God for their portion have five thousand times a greater portion than the wicked of the world, whose portion only lies in perishing trifles, and in tried vanities; and therefore there is no just reason, no Scripture reason, why they should be afraid of wants. But,

(9.) *Ninthly*, If the saints have such a great, such a large, such an all-sufficient, such an infinite, and such an incomparable portion, as has been made evident they have, oh then *away with all inordinate cares for the things of this life.* Oh say to all vexing, wasting, distracting, and disturbing cares, as Ephraim once said to his idols, 'Get you hence, for what have I any more to do with you?' Hos. 14:8. Christ's counsel should lie warm upon every man's heart that has God for his portion, 'Take no thought, saying, What shall we eat? or, What shall we drink? or, Wherewithal shall we be clothed?' Matt. 6:31, and so should the apostle's, 'Cast all your care on him; for he careth for you,' 1 Pet. 5:7, and so should the psalmist's also, 'Cast thy burden (or as the Greek well turns it, thy care) upon the Lord, and he shall sustain thee: he shall never suffer the righteous to be moved,' Psa. 55:22. Some write, that lions sleep with their eyes open and shining; but the Lion of the tribe of Judah, the Lord Jesus Christ, who is the keeper of Israel, never slumbers nor sleeps; his eyes are always open upon the upright; he still

[1] [That is, portion of food.]

stands sentinel for his people's good, and therefore why should inordinate cares eat up the hearts of Christians? O Christians! of all burdens the burden of carking[1] cares will sit the heaviest upon your spirits. There is no burden that will bow you and break you like this. Inordinate cares vex the heart, they divide the heart, they scratch and tear the heart, they pierce and wound the heart through and through with many sorrows, 1 Tim. 6:10. Inordinate cares will either crowd out duties, as in Martha, Luke 10:40, or else they will crowd into duties and spoil duties, as in Luke 8:14, 'the cares of the world choke the word.' Look, as Pharaoh's ill-favoured lean cattle ate up the fat, Gen. 41:4, so all inordinate ill-favoured cares will eat up all those fat and noble cares for God, for his glory, for heaven, for holiness, for grace, for glory, for power against corruptions, for strength to resist temptations, and for support and comfort under afflictions, etc., with which the soul should be filled and delighted. Oh that you would for ever remember these few things, to prevent all inordinate, distrustful, and distracting cares.

[1.] First, *That they are a dishonour and a reproach to the all-sufficiency of God*; as if he were not able to supply all your wants, and to answer all your desires, and to succour you in all your distresses, and to deliver you out of all your calamities and miseries.

[2.] Secondly, *Inordinate cares are a dishonour and a reproach to the omnisciency of God.*[2] As if your wants were not as well known to him as his own works, and as if he had not a fixed eye upon all the straits and trials that lie upon

---

[1] [That is, cares that cause distress or worry.]

[2] Psa. 139:11; 40:5; Job 31:4; 2 Chron. 16:9.

you, and as if he did not know every burden that makes you to groan, and did not behold every affliction that makes you to sigh, and did not observe every tear that drops from your eyes; whereas his eye is still upon you: Deut. 11:11, 12, 'But the land, whither ye go to possess it, is a land of hills and valleys, and drinketh water of the rain of heaven: a land which the Lord thy God careth for: the eyes of the Lord thy God are always upon it, from the beginning of the year, unto the end of the year.' And do you think that he will not have as great a care, and as tender a regard of you who are his jewels, his treasure, his joy, yea, who are the delight of his soul, and the price of his Son's blood?

[3.] Thirdly, *Inordinate cares are a dishonour and a reproach to the authority of God.* As if the earth were not the Lord's and the fullness thereof, and as if all creatures were not at his command and at his disposal, when he is the great proprietary, and all is his by primitive right, and all the creatures are at his service, and are ready at a word of command to serve where he pleases, and when he pleases, and as he pleases, and whom he pleases (Psa. 24:1; 50:10).

[4.] Fourthly, *Inordinate cares are a dishonour and a reproach to the mercy, bounty, and liberality of God.* They proclaim God to be a hard master, and not to be of so free, so noble, and so generous a spirit, as Scripture and the experiences of many thousands speaks him to be. I have read of a duke of Milan, that marrying his daughter to a son of England, he made a dinner of thirty courses, and at every course he gave so many gifts to every guest at the table, as there were dishes in the course. Here was a rich and royal entertainment, here was noble bounty indeed; but this bounty is not to be named in the day in which the bounty and liberality of God to his people is spoken of. Princes' treasures have been often exhausted and drawn dry, but the treasures of God's bounty and liberality were never, nor never shall be, exhausted or drawn dry.[1] O sirs! you are as well able to tell the stars of heaven, and to number the sands of the sea, as you are able to number up the mercies and favours of God that attends his people in one day, yea, that attends them in one hour of the day, or in one minute of an hour; such is his liberality and bounty towards them. God is always best, when he is most in the exercise of his bounty and liberality towards his people. His favours and mercies seldom come single. There is a series, a concatenation[2] of them, and every former draws on a future; yea, such is the bounty and liberality of God, that he never takes away one mercy, but he has another ready to lay in the room of it; as Joshua began to shine before Moses' candle was put out; and before Joshua went to bed, Othniel the son of Kenaz was raised up to judge. Eli was not gathered to his fathers, before Samuel appeared hopeful; nor Sarah was not taken away till Rebekah was ready to come in her stead. The Jews have a saying, that never an illustrious man dies, but there is another born as bright on the same day.

[5.] Fifthly, *Inordinate cares are a reproach and a dishonour to the fidelity of God.* As if he were not the faithful witness, the faithful God, that has bound himself by promise, by covenant, and by oath, to take care of his people, and to provide for his people, and to look after the

---

[1] Mercy and bounty is as essential to God, as light is to the sun, or as heat is to the fire.

[2] [That is, a series of interconnected things.]

welfare of his people.[1] God is that ocean and fountain from where all that faithfulness that is in angels and men issues and flows, and his faithfulness is the rule and measure of all that faithfulness that is in all created beings, and his faithfulness is unchangeable and perfect. Though the angels fell from their faithfulness, and Adam fell from his, yet it is impossible that God should ever fall from his. God's faithfulness is a foundation-faithfulness; it is that foundation upon which all our faith, hope, prayers, praises, and obedience stands; and therefore, whoever is unfaithful, God will be sure to show himself a faithful God, in making good all that he has spoken concerning them that fear him. I had rather, said Plutarch, that men should say there was never any such person in the world as Plutarch, rather than say that Plutarch is unfaithful. Men were better to say that there is no God, than to say that God is an unfaithful God; and yet this is the constant language of inordinate cares.

O sirs! God's goodness inclines him to make good promises, precious promises; and his faithfulness engages him to make those promises good, 2 Pet. 1:4. If the word be once gone out of his mouth, heaven and earth shall sooner pass away, than one jot of that word shall fail, Matt. 5:18. Men say and unsay what they have said; they often eat their words as soon as they have spoke them; but so will not God. This faithfulness of God Joshua stoutly asserts to the height; he throws down the gauntlet, and, as it were, challenges all Israel to show but that one thing that God had failed them in of all the good things that he had promised, Josh. 23:14, 15. If God in very faithfulness afflicts his people to make

---

[1] Rev. 1:5; 3:14; Isa. 49:7; 1 Cor. 1:9; 10:13; 2 Thess. 3:3; Heb. 10:23; Rev. 19:11; Heb. 6:13-19.

good his threatenings, oh, how much more in faithfulness will he preserve and provide for his people, to make good his promises! Psa. 119:75. God has never broken his word nor cracked his credit by deceiving, or by compounding for one penny less in the pound than what he has promised to make good. God stands upon nothing more than his faithfulness, and glories in nothing more than his faithfulness; and yet all inordinate cares leaves a blot upon his faithfulness. But,

[6.] Sixthly and lastly, *Inordinate cares are a reproach to the pity and compassion of God*, Matt. 6:32. They speak out God to be a God of no pity, of no bowels,[1] of no tenderness; whereas God is all pities, all bowels, all compassions, all tendernesses: Psa. 103:13, 'Like as a father pitieth his children, so the Lord pitieth them that fear him.' There is an ocean of love and pity in a father's heart to his children, Gen. 33:13, 14; and there is much more in God's to his. Hence he is called the Father by way of eminency; and indeed, originally and properly, there is no Father to him, there is no Father like him, there is no Father besides him; and he is called the Father of all mercies, because all the mercies, all the pities, all the bowels, all the compassions that are in all the fathers on earth, are but a drop of his ocean, a spark of his flame, a mite out of his treasury.[2] That father that sees his child in want, and pities him not, and pitying, if able, relieves him not, forfeits the very name of father, and may better write himself monster than man. I have read of a young man who,

---

[1] [Or, all heart.]

[2] Eph. 3:15. God is *pater miserationum; tam pius nemo, tam pater nemo*, [Father of mercies; none so devoted, none so fatherlike], says Bernard.

being at sea in a mighty storm, was very merry when all the passengers were at their wits' end for fear; and when he was asked the reason of his mirth, he answered, that the pilot of the ship was his father, and he knew that such was his father's pity and compassion, that he would have a care of him. O sirs! whatever storms the people of God may be in, yet such is his pity and compassion towards them, that he will be sure to have a care of them. The Lord is all that to his people, and will be all that to his people, yea, and infinitely more than that which *Isis Mammosa* was to the Egyptians, a god full of dugs;[1] and whilst he has a breast, there is no reason why his children should fear the want of milk. That golden promise, Heb. 13:5, were there no more, has enough in it to steel and arm the soul against all inordinate cares. The Greek has five negatives, and may thus be rendered: 'I will not, not leave thee, neither will I not, not forsake thee.'[2] Five times, as one well observes, is this precious promise renewed, that we may suck and be satisfied with the breasts of its consolations, that we may milk out and be delighted with the abundance of its glory. O sirs! shall the word, the promise, the protest of a king, arm us and cheer us up against all inordinate cares, and shall not the word, the promise, the protest of the King of kings, so often repeated, much more arm us against all base, distrustful, and distracting cares? O Christians! the remembrance of this blessed truth, that God is your portion, should make you sing care away, as that famous martyr said, 'My soul is turned to her rest; I have taken a sweet nap in Christ's lap; and therefore I will now

[1] [That is, breasts.]

[2] οὐ μή οὐ δε οὐ μή (*ou mē ou de ou mē*), never, in no wise, in no case; whatever I do, I will not do this, whatever shift I make.

sing away care, and will be careless, according to my name.'[1] If the sense of God's being a man's portion will not burn up all those inordinate cares that commonly fills his head, and that disturbs, and distracts, and racks his heart, I profess I cannot tell what will. It was a strange speech of Socrates, a heathen: Since God is so careful for you, says he, what need you be careful for anything yourselves? But,

(10.) *Tenthly*, If God be the saints' portion, *then all is theirs.* As he said, *Christus meus et omnia*, Christ is mine, and all is mine; so may a Christian say, *Deus meus et omnia mea*, God is mine, and all is mine.[2] If God be your portion, then heaven and earth are yours; then all the good and all the glory of both worlds are yours; then all the upper and the nether springs are yours: 1 Cor. 3:21, 'All things are yours'; verse 22, 'whether Paul, or Apollos, or Cephas, or the world, or life, or death, or things present, or things to come; all are yours.' The scope of the apostle is not to show that such as are saints, and have God for their portion, have a civil and common interest in all men's earthly possessions; but it is to show that all things are prepared, ordered, and ordained by God to serve the interest of his people, to work for the good of his people, and to help on the happiness and blessedness of his people. All the gifts, and all the graces, and all the experiences, and all the excellencies, and all the mercies of the ministers of the gospel, whether they are ordinary or extraordinary, are all for the information, edification, confirmation, consolation, and

---

[1] John Carless in a letter to Mr Philops—Acts and Mon. fol. 1743. [Foxe by Townsend, vol. viii. p. 172, and *sub nomine.*—G.]

[2] Cf. Sibbes's Works, vol. ii., note *u*, p. 195.—G.

salvation of the church; and all the good and all the sweet of the creatures are to be let out for the good of the people of God, and for the comfort of the people of God, and for the encouragement of the people of God; all changes, all conditions, all occurrences, shall be sure 'to work together for their good,' Rom. 8:28, that have God for their portion. Whatever the present posture of things are, or whatever the future state of things shall be, yet they shall all issue in their good, in their profit, in their advantage, that have God for their portion.

Look, as the wife communicates in her husband's honour and wealth, and as the branches partake of the fatness and sweetness of the root, and as the members derive sense and motion from the head; so the saints communicate in all that good which in God is communicable to them. God is communicative, as the fig tree, the vine, and the olive is. O sirs! if God be your portion, then every promise in the book of God is yours, and every attribute in the book of God is yours, and every privilege in the book of God is yours, and every comfort in the book of God is yours, and every blessing in the book of God is yours, and every treasury in the book of God is yours, and every mercy in the book of God is yours, and every ordinance in the book of God is yours, and every sweet in the book of God is yours; if God be yours, all is yours. When Alexander asked King Porus, who was then his prisoner, how he would be used? he answered in one word, Βασιλικῶς [Basilikos] like a king; Alexander again replying, Do you desire nothing else? No, says he, all things are in Βασιλικῶς, in this one word, *like a king*; so all things are in this one word, 'The Lord is my portion.' He that has God for his portion, has all things, because God is all things; he is a good that contains all good in himself. All the good that is to be found in honours, in riches, in pleasures, in preferments, in husband, in wife, in children, in friends, is to be found only and eminently in God. You have all in that great God that is the saints' great all, Col. 3:11. But,

(11) *Eleventhly*, If God be the saint's portion, and such a portion as I have at large discovered him to be, then certainly *God is no injurious portion, no mischievous portion, no hurtful portion, no prejudicial portion*. Surely there can be no danger, no hazard, no hurt in having God for a man's portion. Oh! but often earthly portions do a great deal of hurt, a great deal of mischief; they ruin men's bodies, they blast and blot men's names, and they lay men open to such sins, and snares, and temptations, that for ever undoes their immortal souls. Oh what a trappan¹ are worldly portions to most men! yea, what fuel are they to corruption! and how often do they lay persons open to destruction! Eccles. 5:13, 'There is a sore evil which I have seen under the sun, namely, riches kept for the owners thereof to their hurt.' Though riches in themselves are God's blessings, yet through the corruptions that are in men's hearts, they prove weapons of wickedness and engines to evil. 'There is a sore evil,' the Septuagint reads it, *infirmitas pessima*, a sore disease; Pagnin and Arias Montanus reads it *mala infirmitas*, an evil disease; others read it *languor pessimus*, a sore weakness. The Hebrew word, *cholah*, signifies such a sore evil as sticks close and is not easily removed; they are kept a thousand thousand ways for their hurt. Latimer, in a sermon before

¹ 'Trepan' = snare.—G.

king Edward VI, tells a story of a rich man, that when he lay upon his sick bed, some told him that came to visit him, that by all they were able to discern he was a dead man; he was no man for this world. As soon as ever he heard these words, says Latimer, What, must I die? said the sick man: send for a physician; wounds, sides, heart, must I die, and leave these riches behind me? wounds, sides, heart, must I die, and leave these things behind me? and nothing else could be got from him but wounds, heart, sides, must I die, and leave these riches behind me? Do you think, sirs, that riches were not kept for this man's hurt? Without a peradventure[1] in this man's heart was written 'the god of this present world.'

And the same father Latimer elsewhere says, that if he had an enemy to whom it was lawful to wish evil, he would chiefly wish him great store of riches, for then he should never enjoy any quiet. As I have read of one Pheraulas, a poor man, on whom king Cyrus bestowed so much that he knew not what to do with his riches; being wearied out with care in keeping of them, he desired to live quietly, though poor, as he had done before, than to possess all those riches with discontent; therefore he gave away all his wealth, desiring only to enjoy so much as might relieve his necessities, and give him a quiet possession of himself.

Queen Mary said, when she was dying, that if they should open her when she was dead, they should find Calice[2] lying at the bottom of her heart, implying that the loss of it broke her heart.

---

[1] [That is, without a doubt.]
[2] 'Calais.'—G.

The historian observes that the riches of Cyprus invited the Romans to hazard many dangerous fights for the conquering of it.

When the Indians had taken some of the Spaniards, who made gold their god, they filled their mouths with it, and so choked them; they melted their gold, and poured it down their throats, resolving that they should have their fill of gold, who preferred gold before the lives and souls of men. How many millions of bodies and souls have the Spaniards destroyed, to possess themselves of the riches of the West Indies! But let me a little further show you how hurtful, how dangerous and pernicious earthly riches, earthly portions, are oftentimes to their owners; and this I shall do by a brief induction of these particulars.

[1.] First, *Riches encourage and advantage persons to make the strongest and the stoutest opposition against anything that is good*.[1] Rich persons usually are the greatest opposers both of religion and of religious persons: James 2:6, 7, 'But ye have despised the poor. Do not rich men oppress you, and draw you before the judgment seats? Do not they blaspheme that worthy name by which ye are called?' And this you may see also in the rich citizens of Jerusalem, and in King Herod; and the very same spirit you may run and read in the scribes and Pharisees, who were the rich and the great men of the times, and the very same opposing spirit lives and works strongly in the hearts of many great ones this day. But,

[2.] Secondly, *Earthly portions estrange the heart from God*; as you see in the prodigal, Luke 15, and in those wealthy monsters that say to God, 'Depart from us; for we

---

[1] Not only the history of the ten persecutions, but also all other histories do very strongly evince this.

desire not the knowledge of thy ways. What is the Almighty, that we should serve him? and what profit should we have, if we pray unto him?' Job 21:13-15. But,

[3.] Thirdly, A*s earthly portions estrange the soul from God; so they often swell the soul, and puff up the soul*, Psa. 10:1-7, *etc*. Salvian counts pride the rich man's inheritance. Men's minds ebb and flow with their means, their blood commonly rises with their outward good. Pride, says Bernard, is the rich man's cousin, it blows him up like a bladder with a quill, it makes him grow secure, and so prepares him for sudden ruin: so that he may well sing his part with those sad souls, 'What hath pride profited us? or what profit hath the pomp of riches brought us? All those things are passed away like as a shadow, and as a post that passeth by,' Wisdom 5:8, 9.[1] But,

[4.] Fourthly, *Earthly riches commonly cast men into a deep sleep of security*.[2] Thus they served David in Psa. 30:6, 7, and thus they served the fool in the Gospel, Luke 12:16-22, and thus they served the old world; and so they did Sodom and Gomorrah afterwards, and so they did the two kings of Midian, Zebah and Zalmunna, and their hosts, Judg. 8:11, 12, and so did the people of Laish, in Judg. 18:6-28; and so the peace, plenty, and prosperity of the Bohemians cast them into so great a security, that they began to grow very loose and base in their lives, and very cold and careless in the things of God, and in all the concerns of their soul's; insomuch that many of their most pious and prudent men did presage, that certainly some horrible storm would suddenly arise, and that some dreadful tempest without

---

[1] [Wisdom of Sirach, or Ecclesiasticus in the Apocrypha.]
[2] Amos 1:12-14; ponder the words.

all peradventure would beat upon them; and accordingly it came to pass. Alexander slew him whom he found asleep on the watch; and God finding the Bohemians in a deep sleep of sin and security, he brought the devouring sword upon them. Mercury could not kill Argus, till he had cast him into a sleep, and with an enchanted rod closed his eyes. No more can the devil or the world hurt any man, till by dandling him on the knee of prosperity, they come to lull him asleep in the bed of security. But,

[5.] Fifthly, *Earthly riches frequently divert the souls of men from embracing and closing with the golden seasons and opportunities of grace.* Riches are the thorns that choke the word, and that make men barren and unfruitful under the word, Matt. 13:22. Rich Felix had no leisure to hear poor Paul, though the hearing of a sermon might have saved his soul, and made him happy in both worlds, Acts 24:24-27; and the rich fool in the Gospel was so taken up in pulling down his barns, and in building of them greater, and in bestowing of his fruits and his goods, that he had no time to prevent the ruin of his soul, Luke 12:15-22; and Dives was so taken up with his riches, pomp, state, and with his royal apparel, royal attendance, and royal fare, that he never minded heaven, nor never dreaded hell, till he did awake with everlasting flames about his ears, Luke 16:19-31. Sicily is so full of sweet flowers, that dogs cannot hunt there: and so what do all the sweet profits, pleasures, and preferments of this world, but make men lose the scent of grace, the scent of glory, the scent of holiness, and the scent of happiness.[1] It is true, rich men will have their eating times,

---

[1] Some say, where gold grows, no plant will prosper; certainly, where riches bear the bell [*i.e.* take the lead], no good, no grace, will thrive or prosper.

and their drinking times, and their trading times, and their sporting times, and their sleeping times, and that which is worse, their sinning times, *etc.* But ah, how rare is it to see rich men covet after hearing times and praying times, and reading times, and meditating times, and mourning times, and repenting times, and reforming times. Rich men will have time for everything, but to honour God, exalt Christ, obey the Spirit, love the saints, attend ordinances, and save their own immortal souls. Oh the time, the thoughts, the strength, the spirits that rich men spend and consume upon their riches, whilst their precious souls lie bleeding to death, and an eternity of misery is posting upon them. But,

[6.] Sixthly, *Earthly riches commonly load the soul with a multitude of cares, fears, griefs, and vexations, which mightily disturb the soul, distract the soul, yea, often rack, torture, and torment the soul.* What if such a friend should be unfaithful to his trust? what if such a ship should miscarry? what if such a one should break, that owes me so much? what if my title to such a lordship should not prove good? what if flaws be found in my evidences for such and such lands? what if fire should consume my habitation? what if thieves should rob me of my treasure? *etc.*, and what do all these *whats* tend to, but to break a man's heart in a thousand pieces? But,

[7.] Seventhly, *Earthly riches are many times fuel for the greatest and the grossest sins*; as pride, oppression, revenge, cruelty, tyranny, gluttony, drunkenness, wantonness, and all manner of uncleanness and filthiness. Riches are a bawd[1] to those very sins that require the largest stock to maintain them. Vices are more costly than virtues. Virtue observes a

[1] [That is, a woman in charge of a brothel.]

mean, but vice knows none; vice is all for extremes; witness the prodigious wickedness of these times.[1] But,

[8.] Eighthly, *Earthly riches are many times reserved as witnesses against the rich in the great day of their account.* James 5:1-3, 'Go to now, ye rich men, weep and howl for the miseries that shall come upon you. Your riches are corrupted, and your garments motheaten. Your gold and silver is cankered; and the rust of them shall be a witness against you, and shall eat your flesh as it were fire. Ye have heaped treasure together for the last days.' The rust of the rich man's cankered gold and his motheaten apparel shall be brought in as dreadful witnesses against him in the great day. The poet feigned Pluto to be the god of riches and of hell too, as if they were inseparable. By all these particulars you see how hurtful, how prejudicial earthly portions often prove to their owners.

Oh, but now God is a portion that will never hurt a man, that will never harm a man, that will never in the least prejudice a man. Among all 'the spirits of just men made perfect' (Heb. 12:22, 23), there is not one to be found that will give in his witness against this sweet and blessed truth that I have asserted; and among all the saints on earth you shall not find one, but will with both hands readily subscribe to this glorious maxim, *viz.*, That God is such a portion, that has never hurt them, that has never harmed them, yea, that he is such a portion that has done them good all their days, and one upon whom they have lived, and by whom they have been maintained ever since they 'hung upon the breasts' (Psa. 22:9). Holy Polycarp hit

[1] Compare these scriptures together, Psa. 73:1-13; Deut. 32:15-17; Jer. 5:7, 8; Hos. 13:6; James 5:1-7.

it, when he said, 'This sixty-eight years have I served the Lord, and he never did me any hurt; and shall I now forsake him?'[1] Surely not. But now earthly riches, for the most part, do a world of mischief and hurt to their owners. Oh the souls that earthly riches have pierced through and through with many sorrows! Oh the minds that earthly riches have blinded! Oh the hearts that earthly riches have hardened! Oh the consciences that earthly riches have benumbed! Oh the wills that earthly riches have perverted! Oh the affections that earthly riches have disordered! Oh the lives that earthly riches have corrupted! And oh the souls that earthly riches have destroyed! But,

[9.] Ninthly and lastly, *Earthly riches, for the most part, make men unwilling to die.* Oh how terrible is the king of terrors to the rich and the great ones of the world! (1 Sam. 28:20; Dan. 5:1-7). And so Henry Beaufort, that rich and wretched cardinal, in the reign of Henry VI, perceiving death at hand, spoke thus: Why should I die, being so rich? If the whole realm would save my life, I am able either by policy to get it, or by riches to buy it; fie,[2] said he, will not death be hired? will money do nothing?[3] It is reported that Queen Elizabeth could not endure so much as to hear death named; and Sigismund the emperor, and Louis XI, king of France, straitly charged all their servants, that when they saw them sick, they should never dare to name that bitter word death in their ears. Vitellius, an emperor of Rome – a notorious glutton, as you may easily judge, by his having at

[1] Martyred.—G.

[2] [An exclamation used to express disgust or outrage.]

[3] A great man wrote thus a little before his death, *Spes et fortuna valete* ['Fortune and hope, adieu'].

one supper two thousand fishes, and seven thousand birds – when he could not fly death, he made himself drunk that he might not be sensible of the pangs of death.[1] It was a very prudent and Christian speech of Charles V to the duke of Venice, who when he had showed him the glory of his princely palace and earthly paradise, instead of admiring it, or him for it, he only returned him this grave and serious memento, *Haec sunt quae faciunt invitos mori*, these are the things which make us unwilling to die, *etc*. And by daily experience we find that of all men wealthy men are most unwilling to die.

Oh, but now God is such a portion as fits and disposes the soul to die, yea, as makes the soul look and long for death, and that makes death more desirable than life itself. A man that has God for his portion, that has God in his arms, may well sing it out with old Simeon, 'Lord, let thy servant depart in peace, according to thy word: for mine eyes have seen thy salvation' (Luke 2:25, 29, 30); and with Paul, 'I desire to be dissolved, and to be with Christ' (Phil. 1:23); and with the church, 'Make haste, my beloved, and be thou like a roe, or to a young hart upon the mountains of spices' (Song of Sol. 8:14); and, 'Come, Lord Jesus, come quickly' (Rev. 22:20). Did Christ die for me that I might live with him? I will not therefore desire to live long from him. All men go willingly to see him whom they love, and shall I be unwilling to die that I may see him whom my soul loves? Surely no. Augustine longed to die that he might see that head that was once crowned with thorns. The dying words of my young Lord Harrington were these: 'O my God, when

---

[1] Erasmus hit it when he said, *Timor mortis pejor quam ipsa mors* ['The fear of death is worse than death itself.']

shall I be with thee?' Cyprian could receive the cruellest sentence of death with a *Deo gratias;*[1] and holy Andrew saluted the cross on which he was to be crucified, saying, 'Take me from men, and restore me to my Master.' And so also Laurence Saunders, when he was come to the stake at which he was to be burnt, he kissed it, saying, 'Welcome the cross of Christ, welcome everlasting life.' But,

(12.) Twelfthly, *If God be the saints' portion, oh then let the saints still think of God, and look upon God under this notion.* A man that has God for his portion should always have very high, noble, sweet, and precious thoughts of God. It becomes not those that have God for their portion to be always looking upon God as an angry God, or as a displeased Father, or as an incensed judge, or as an enraged enemy, or as a bitter friend. When God would make known his name, his nature, his glory to Moses, he proclaims himself to be, 'The Lord God, merciful and gracious, longsuffering, and abundant in goodness and truth, keeping mercies for thousands, forgiving iniquity, transgression, and sin' (Exod. 34:6, 7). And certainly to keep up such precious thoughts and notions as these are of God, is that work of works that lies upon every man's hand that has God for his portion. O sirs! there is a very great aptness and proneness, even in those that have God for their portion, to have black, dark, hard, dismal, and dreadful thoughts and apprehensions of God, as you may see in Asaph, Heman, Job, David, *etc.*[2] By nature we are as full of hard thoughts of God, as hell is full of sin; and when the heart is not mightily overawed by the

[1] ['Thanks be to God.']

[2] Psa. 77; 88; Job 3; Psa. 73:11-14.

Spirit of God and overpowered by the grace of God, there all manner of dark and dismal apprehensions of God abounds. Besides, Satan knows very well that our corrupt natures are made up of sad and hard thoughts of God; and therefore he will use all his power and craft to blow up every spark, every hard thought of God, into a flame, especially when outward troubles and inward distresses are upon us. What says Satan? Do you think that God loves you? O Christian, when he deals thus sharply and severely with you, does he pretend kindness to you, and yet hide his face from you, and set you up as a mark to shoot at? How can he be your friend, who has cast you down at your enemies' feet, and given you up into their paws and jaws? How can you think that he has any pity and compassion towards you, who makes no better provision for you? What vanity is it to believe that he will give you a crown, that denies you a crust? And that he will give you a house not made with hands, and yet suffer you to be turned out of house and home? And that he will do so much for you in another world, who does so little for you in this world? *etc.* And thus Satan takes his opportunities to provoke corrupt nature and to kill the soul with hard thoughts of God.

And certainly that Christian is a very great stranger to his own heart, that is not able to say from experience that it is one of the highest and hardest works in this world to keep up good and gracious thoughts of God, to keep up honourable and noble thoughts of God, in a suffering condition or under dark and dismal dispensations. Oh, but now those that have God for their portion, they should abandon and abhor all hard thoughts of God, yea, however severe the dealings of God are towards them, yet it is their duty and their glory to keep up very sweet and precious thoughts of God, Psa. 73:1. O sirs! the more choice and honourable thoughts you keep up of God in your own souls, the more you will love the Lord, and the more you will delight in the Lord, and the more content and satisfaction you will take in the Lord. Such Christians that take a pleasure to be still representing God to themselves in the most hideous, terrible, and amazing shapes, they kill their love and their joy, and they create a hell of torments in their own souls.

Well, Christians! let me put a cluster of the grapes of Canaan into your hands at once, and that by telling of you, that the more glorious and blessed thoughts you keep up in your souls of God, the more spiritual, the more frequent, the more fervent, the more abundant, the more constant, and the more unwearied you will be in the work of the Lord, and the more all your graces will be acted, exercised, strengthened, and increased, yea, and the more your evidences for heaven will be cleared, your gracious experiences multiplied, your communion with God raised, your way to glory facilitated, and all your sufferings sweetened; and therefore never let noble and precious thoughts of God die in your souls. Though he frown upon you, O Christian, yet say, he is your portion; and though he chides you, yet say, he is your portion; and though he corrects you, yet say, he is your portion; and though he deserts you and carries it strangely towards you, yet say, he is your portion; and though he snatches many a mercy from you, yet say, he is your portion; and though he multiplies your burdens upon you, yet say, he is your portion; and though he writes bitter things against you, yet say, he is your portion; yea, though he should pass a sentence of death upon you, yet still say, he is your portion. O Christians, this would still raise a heaven in your hearts, if under all dispensations you would still look upon God as your portion, and live upon God as your portion. But,

(13.) Thirteenthly, *If God be a believer's portion, then never let a believer be afraid to die or unwilling to die.* Let them be afraid to die that have only the world for their portion here, and hell for their portion hereafter; but let not a saint be afraid of death, that has for his portion the Lord of life.[1] A man that has God for his portion should rather court death than tremble at it; he should rather sweetly welcome it than turn his back upon it; for death to such a one is but the way to paradise, the way to all heavenly delights, the way to those everlasting springs of pleasure that are at God's right hand, the way to life, immortality, and glory, and the way to a clear, full, constant, and eternal fruition of God, Psa. 16:11. Augustine upon those words, Exod. 33:20, 'Thou canst not see my face and live,' makes this short but sweet reply, 'Then, Lord, let me die, that I may see your face.' Death is a bridge that leads to the paradise of God. All the hurt that it can do is to bring a believer to a full enjoyment of his portion.[2] When Modestus, the emperor's lieutenant, threatened to kill Basil, he answered, If that be all, I fear not; yea, your master cannot more pleasure me than in sending me unto my heavenly Father, to whom I now live, and to whom I desire to hasten. Old Alderman

[1] See twenty arguments in my 'String of Pearls,' to move you to be willing to die.—G.

[2] Bernard says that he heard his brother Gerard, when just in dying, rejoice and triumphingly say, *Jam mors mihi non stimulus sed jubilus* [Now I find death a source of joy not of torment].

Jordan used to say that death would be the best friend he had in the world, and that he would willingly go forth to meet it; or rather say with holy Paul, 'O death, where is thy sting?' triumphing over it. What is a drop of vinegar put into an ocean of wine? what is it for one to have a rainy day, who is going to take possession of a kingdom? A Dutch martyr feeling the flame to come to his beard, 'Ah, said he, what a small pain is this, to be compared to the glory to come!'[1] Lactantius boasts of the braveness of that spirit that was upon the martyrs in his time. Our children and women, not to speak of men, says he, in silence overcome their tormentors, and the fire cannot so much as fetch a sigh from them. John Noyes took up a faggot at the fire and kissed it, saying, 'Blessed be the time that ever I was born, to come to this preferment.' Never did a neckerchief become me so well as this chain, said Alice Driver, when they fastened her to the stake to be burnt. Mr Bradford put off his cap, and thanked God, when the keeper's wife brought him word that he was to be burnt on the morrow. Mr Taylor fetched a frisk[2] when he was come near the place where he was to suffer. Henry and John, two Augustine monks, being the first that were burnt in Germany, and Mr Rogers, the first that was burnt in Queen Mary's days, did all sing in the flames; and 'Be of good cheer,' said the woman-martyr to her husband that was to suffer with her, 'for though we have but an ill dinner on earth, we shall sup with Christ in heaven.' And what said Justin Martyr to his

[1] [Foxe.] Acts and Mon., 813. [By 'Dutch' is meant High Dutch, *i.e.* German; Deutsch: cf. *sub voce*, in Foxe, by Townsend, vol. iv. pp. 282-284.—G.]

[2] [That is, began to dance.]

murderers, on behalf of himself and his fellow-martyrs? 'You may kill us, but you can never hurt us.'

Ah, Christians! how can you read over these choice instances and not blush, and not be ashamed to consider what a readiness, what a forwardness, and what a noble willingness there was in these brave worthies to die and go to heaven, and to be fully possessed of their God, of their portion, whilst you shrug at the very thoughts of death, and frequently put that day far from you, and had rather, with Peter, fall upon 'building of tabernacles,' Matt. 17:4, than, with Paul, 'desire to be dissolved, and to be with Christ,' Phil. 1:23. O Christians! how justly may that father be angry with his child that is unwilling to come home! and how justly may that husband be displeased with his wife who is unwilling to ride to him in a rainy day, or to cross the sea to enjoy his company! And is not this your case? is not this just your case, who have God for your portion, and yet are unwilling to die, that you may come to a full enjoyment of your portion? But,

(14.) Fourteenthly, and lastly, *If God be the saint's portion, then let all the saints give all diligence to make this clearly and fully out to their own souls, that God is their portion,* 2 Pet. 1:5-8. Next to a man's having God for his portion, it is the greatest mercy in this world for a man to know that God is his portion, and to be able groundedly to say with the church, 'The Lord is my portion,' says my soul. Now this is a work that may be done. I suppose there is never a believer on earth but may attain to this personal evidence and certainty of knowledge that God is his portion. Express promises speak out such a thing as this is: Zech. 13:9, 'They shall call on my name: and I will hear them; I will say, It is my people: and they shall say, It is my God'; so Ezek. 34:30, 'Thus shall they know that I the Lord their God am with them, and that they, even the house of Israel, are my people, saith the Lord'; Psa. 9:18, 'For the patient abiding of the meek shall not be forgotten for ever.' God will as soon put the faith of reliance and the faith of assurance to a blush, as he will put the faith of expectance to a blush:[1] Psa. 22:26, 'The meek shall eat and be satisfied: they shall praise the Lord that seek him: your heart shall live for ever.' First or last, such as seek him shall have such an answer of their prayers as shall turn their prayers into praises, and their petitions into thanksgivings: Psa. 84:11, 'The Lord will give grace and glory, and no good thing will he withhold from them that walk uprightly.' God will be a universal, all-sufficient, and satisfactory good to them that walk uprightly.

The Lord is as full of goodness as the sun is full of light, and he will as freely, and as fully, and as impartially communicate his goodness to them that walk uprightly, as the sun does her light both to the just and the unjust (Matt. 5:45). As under the name of no good thing will he withhold, all temporal good things are to be understood, so under the name of grace all spiritual good things are to be understood, and under the name of glory all eternal good things are to be understood. And now, if God will give all spiritual and all eternal good things to his people, how can he then but sooner or later give a clear and satisfactory evidence into his people's bosoms that he is their portion? And not

[1] Heb. 10:37: μικρὸν ὅσον ὅσον [*mikron hoson hoson*]. Here are two diminutives in the Greek, a little, little while, to note that God will not in the least delay his coming to his people.

only express promises, but also the graces of the Spirit and the testimony of the Spirit confirm the same thing. The language of every saving grace is this: The Lord is your portion, O believing soul; and the language and testimony of the Spirit is the same: Rom. 8:15, 'Ye have received the Spirit of adoption, whereby we cry, Abba, Father'; verse 16, 'The Spirit itself beareth witness with our spirit, that we are the children of God.' Shall an instinct in nature teach young ones to know their dams,[1] and shall not the Spirit of God, by a divine instinct, teach the saints to know God to be their God, and to be their portion also? Surely yes. Though this or that particular Christian may go to his grave without a satisfactory evidence in his own bosom that God is his portion, yet in an ordinary course, at first or last, God gives his people some assurance that he is their portion, yea, rather than they shall always live or die without assurance of their salvation, and that he is their portion, he will work a miracle to assure them of his love.

I have both heard and read of a rare story of Mrs Honywood, a famous professor of the gospel, and one that for many years together lay under the burden of a wounded spirit, and was much troubled in mind for want of assurance that God was her portion, and that she should be saved from wrath to come. At length there came a godly minister to her, who endeavoured to settle her faith and hope in Christ; and pressing many gospel promises upon her, she took it with a kind of indignation and anger that he should offer to present any promises to her, to whom, as she thought, they did not belong; and having a Venice glass in

---

[1] [That is, mothers.]

her hand, she held it up, and said, Speak no more to me of salvation, for I shall as surely be damned as this poor brittle glass shall be broke against the wall, throwing it with all her force to break it. But it so pleased God that, by a miraculous providence, the glass was preserved whole. The minister, beholding the miracle, took up the glass, and said to her, 'Behold, God must work a miracle before you, before you will believe.' And for ever after that day she had very strong assurance of her salvation, and that God was her portion; and so lived and died in a sweet and comfortable sense of the love and favour of God.

Now, to provoke you to labour with all your might to attain to a clear, personal, satisfactory evidence in your own bosoms that God is your portion, do but seriously consider and lay to heart the rare and singular advantages that will redound to your souls by this means. I shall only touch upon some, by which yourselves may guess at others.

[1.] First, By this means *your hearts will come to be fixed, settled, and established*. A man's soul never comes to be fixed and settled by knowing in the general that God is the saint's portion, but by a personal evidence and certainty of knowledge that he is his particular portion. Whilst a man's particular propriety is unsettled, all is unsettled in his soul; but when a man's particular propriety is settled, when he can say, This God is my God, and the Lord is my portion, then all is settled, then all is at peace in the soul, Psa. 57:7; 108:1; 112:7. A man that has God for his portion, if he do not know it, will still be like a ship at sea in the midst of a storm, tossed here and there, and now rolling on one side and then on the other, and never quiet, never lying still; but a man that has God for his portion, and knows it, he is like a ship in a good harbour, that lies quiet and still; yea, he is like mount Zion, that cannot be removed. But,

[2.] Secondly, A clear, personal evidence that God is a man's portion, will *rid his soul of all sinful doubts.* O Christians! now your hearts are as full of doubts as hell is full of darkness. One day you doubt whether your graces are true, and another day you doubt whether your comforts are true. Now, you doubt of your saintship, and anon of your sonship, and then of your heirship. Sometimes you doubt of your communion with God, sometimes you doubt of your acquaintance with God, and sometimes you doubt of your acceptance with God. One hour you doubt of the favour of God, and the next hour you doubt of your access to God. And as it is thus with you, so it will be thus with you till you come to have some clear satisfaction in your own spirits that God is your portion. O Christians! had you but once a personal evidence in your own bosoms that God is your portion, all those doubts that are bred and fed by ignorance and unbelief, and that rob the soul of all joy, comfort, and content, and that render men babes in Christianity, and that cast reproach upon God, Christ, and the promises, and that most gratify and advantage Satan to tempt and try your souls, would vanish and disperse as the clouds do before the sun when it shines in its brightness.

Till a Christian's eyes be opened to see God to be his portion, his heart will be full of doubts and perplexities. Though Mary Magdalene was very near to Christ, yet she stands sighing, mourning, and complaining, that 'they had stolen away her Lord,' John 20:13-16. A Christian may have God for his portion, yet till he comes to see God to be his portion, he will spend his days in sighing, mourning, and complaining. O Christians! till you come to see God to be your portion, your doubts will lie down with you and rise with you, they will talk with you and walk with you, till they make your lives a very hell. It was an excellent speech of Luther, 'The whole Scripture,' says he, 'principally aims at this thing, that we should not doubt, but that we should hope, trust, and believe that God is a merciful, bountiful, and gracious God to his people.' And what will bring a man's heart over to answer to this blessed aim of the Scripture? Certainly nothing below an assurance that God is his portion. It was a noble resolution of blessed Bradford, who, in one of his epistles, says thus: 'O Lord, sometimes I think I feel it so with me, as if there were no difference between my heart and the hearts of the wicked. My mind is as blind as theirs, and my will as stout, stubborn, and rebellious as theirs; and my affections are as much disordered as theirs, and my conscience as much benumbed and stupefied as theirs, and my heart as hard and flinty as theirs; shall I therefore conclude that you are not my Father? Nay, I will reason otherwise,' says he; 'I do believe you are my Father; I will come to you, that you may enlighten this blind mind of mine, and bend and bow this stout and stubborn will of mine; and that you may put order into these disordered affections of mine, and that you may put life and quickness into this stupefied and benumbed conscience of mine, and that you may put softness and tenderness into this hard and flinty heart of mine.' And thus he nobly reasoned himself, and believed himself, out of all his fears and doubts. There is no such way for a man to be rid of all his fears and doubts, as to live in the sight and faith of this truth, that God is his portion.

Plutarch reports of one, who would not be resolved of his doubts, because he would not lose the pleasure in seeking for resolution, like to him that would not have his physician to quench the thirst he felt in his ague,[1] because he would not lose the pleasure of drinking; and like those that would not be freed from their sins, because they would not lose the pleasure of sinning. But I hope better things of all those that have God for their portion, than to find them in love with their doubts, or to be unwilling to be rid of their doubts. Next to a man's going to hell, it is one of the greatest afflictions in the world for a man always to live in doubts about his going to heaven. Next to damnation, it is one of the greatest troubles that can attend a Christian, to be always exercised and perplexed with doubts about his salvation. Next to being damned, it is the hell of hells to live in continual fears of damnation. Now the only way to prevent all this, is to know that God is your portion. But,

[3.] Thirdly, A clear, personal evidence that God is a man's portion, *will exceedingly sweeten all the crosses, losses, and changes that shall attend him in this world.* Habakkuk knew that God was the God of his salvation; and that he was his portion; and therefore he rejoices: 'Though the fig tree did not blossom, and though there were no fruit in the vines; and though the labour of the olive did fail, and the fields did yield no meat, and the flocks were cut off from the fold, and there were no herd in the stalls,' Hab. 3:17, 18. And the same noble temper was upon those worthies in Heb. 10:34, 'They took joyfully the spoiling of their goods, knowing in themselves that they had in heaven a better and an enduring substance.' They took joyfully the spoiling of

[1] [That is, fever.]

their earthly portions, being well assured in their own souls that they should enjoy a heavenly portion, an everlasting portion. And so the apostles knew that they had 'an house not made with hands, eternal in the heavens,' 2 Cor. 5:1; and this carried them bravely through honour and dishonour, through evil report and good report, and through all weaknesses, sicknesses, distresses, wants, dangers, and death; and this made their heavy afflictions light, and their long afflictions short, and their bitter afflictions sweet, 2 Cor. 4:16-18. This was that tree which, being cast in the waters of Marah, made them sweet, Exod. 15:23-25; and this was that which did unsting all their crosses, losses, and reproaches, and that made them rejoice and sing under those very burdens and trials that would have broke the necks, backs, and hearts of others, Acts 5 and 16.

When a man has a clear personal evidence that God is his portion, then no outward changes will make any considerable change in him. Though Laban had changed Jacob's wages ten times, yet Jacob was Jacob still, Gen. 31:7. Let times change, and men change, and powers change, and nations change, yet a man that has God for his portion, and knows it, will never change his countenance, nor change his Master, nor change his service, nor change his works, nor change his ways. Under all changes he will still be *semper idem*, always the same. Many great and dreadful changes passed upon Joseph, but yet, under all, Joseph's bow 'abode in strength,' Gen. 49:23, 24. When a man knows that God is his portion, whatever changes may pass upon him, yet his bow will still abide in strength. Marcellus the pope would not change his name, according to the custom of other popes, to show his immutability, and that he was no changeling;[1] but how many are there in these days, who were looked upon as better men, who have changed their names, their notes, their coats, their principles, their practices, and all for worldly advantages. These changelings, that change from better to worse, and from naught[2] to be very naught, yea, stark naught, are the worst and the naughtiest of men, and deserve to be hanged in chains; and certainly, when the wrath of God breaks forth, these changelings shall be as stubble before it, Mal. 4:1; Heb. 10:38. God abhors none as he does those who run from him to serve other lords, and who gad about to change their way: Jer. 2:36, 37, 'Why gaddest thou about so much to change thy way? thou also shalt be ashamed of Egypt, as thou wast ashamed of Assyria. Yea, thou shalt go forth from him, and thine hands upon thine head: for the Lord hath rejected thy confidences, and thou shalt not prosper in them.' There is nothing that will keep a man from apostasy, and from making a defection from God, his ways, his worship, his glory, *etc.*, like a blessed persuasion that God is his portion, 2 Pet. 1:5-11. But,

[4.] Fourthly, A clear personal evidence that God is a man's portion, will *exceedingly raise and advance the comfort and joy of a man's heart*. It is not merely my having of God for my portion, but it is my seeing, it is my knowing, it is my fruition of God as my portion, that is the true spring of all delight, comfort, and consolation. When a man's interest in God is clear, then all the precious promises will be full wells of salvation, and full breasts of consolation to him, but till then they will be but as dry breasts, as barren heaths,

---

[1] Qu. Marcellus II., who was pope only twenty-three days.—G.
[2] [That is, bad, wicked, sinful.]

as a fruitful wilderness, and as empty wells.[1] Whilst a man is doubtful whether God be his God, it is certain that the spring of joy and comfort will run low in his soul; whilst a man lives in fear that his title and interest is not good, how can he rejoice? When a man's interest in God is clear, then his heaven of joy begins. A man that has God for his portion, and knows it, cannot but live in a paradise of joy, and walk in a paradise of joy, and work in a paradise of joy, and eat in a paradise of joy, and recreate himself in a paradise of joy, and rest in a paradise of joy; he cannot but have a heaven of joy within him, and a heaven of joy about him, and a heaven of joy over him. All his looks will speak out joy within, and all his words will speak out joy within, and all his works will speak out joy within, and all his ways will speak out joy within.

I remember a notable saying of one, How sweet was it to me of a sudden to be without those sweet vanities! and those things which I was afraid to lose, with joy I let go; for you, who are the true and only sweetness, cast out those from me, and instead of them entered in yourself, who are more delightful than all pleasure, and more clear than all light.[2] When a man's interest in God is clear, his joy will be full, John 16:24; when a man is happy, and knows it, he cannot but rejoice; when a man has God for his portion, and knows it, all the world cannot hinder the strong consolations of God from rising high in his soul.

Why have the saints in heaven more joy and delight than the saints on earth, but because they have a clearer and a

---

[1] 2 Pet. 1:4; Isa. 12:3; 66:2. Without delight the soul cannot live: take away all delight, and the soul dies, says Augustine.

[2] Augustine in his Confessions.

fuller knowledge of their interest and propriety in God than the others have? The knowledge of a man's propriety[1] in God is the comfort of comforts. Propriety makes every comfort a pleasurable comfort, a delightful comfort. When a man walks in a fair meadow, and can write *mine* upon it, and into a pleasant garden, and can write *mine* upon it, and into a fruitful cornfield, and can write *mine* upon it, and into a stately habitation, and can write *mine* upon it, and into a rich mine, and can write *mine* upon it, oh how it pleases him! how it delights him! how it joys and rejoices him! Of all words this word *meum*[2] is the sweetest and the comfortablest. Ah! when a man can look upon God, and write *meum*; when he can look upon God, and say, This God is my God for ever and ever; when he can look upon God, and say, This God is my portion; when he can look upon God, and say with Thomas, 'My Lord and my God,' John 20:28, how will all the springs of joy rise in his soul! Oh, who can but joy to be owner of that God that fills heaven and earth with his fulness? who can but rejoice to have him for his portion, in having of whom he has all things, in having of whom he can want nothing?

The serious thoughts of our propriety in God will add much sweet to all our sweets, yea, it will make every bitter sweet. When a man seriously thinks, It is my God that cheers me with his presence, it is my God that supports me with his power, it is my God that guides me by his counsel, it is my God that supplies me with his goodness, and it is my God that blesses all my blessings to me; it is my God that afflicts me in love, it is my God that has broken me

[1] 'Property' = 'interest.'—G.
[2] 'mine.'

in my estate and in my credit, it is my God that has sorely visited such a child, it is my God that has passed a sentence of death upon such a friend, it is my God that has thus straitened me in my liberty, and it is my God that has thus cast me down at my enemies' feet, *etc.*, how these thoughts cheer up the spirit of a man, and make every bitter sweet, and every burden light unto him.

A beautiful face is at all times pleasing to the eye, but then especially when there is joy manifested in the countenance. Joy in the face puts a new beauty upon a person, and makes that which before was beautiful to be exceeding beautiful; it puts a lustre upon beauty. And so holy joy puts a divine beauty and lustre upon all the ways of God, and upon all the people of God. And therefore, it highly concerns all Christians, as they would have a heavenly beauty, lustre, and glory upon them, to rejoice; and that they may rejoice, it as highly concerns them to know their interest and propriety in God. But,

[5.] Fifthly, A clear personal evidence that God is a man's portion *will very much raise him in his communion with God, and exceedingly sweeten his fellowship with God.*[1] There are no Christians on earth that have such high, such choice, such free, such full, such sweet, and such uninterrupted communion with God, as those that have a clear sight of their interest and propriety in God. The spouse, in that book of Solomon's Song, again, and again, and again sings and sounds out her propriety and interest in Christ: Song

---

[1] 1 John 1:1-4; 2 Cor. 13:14. Man's *summum bonum* [greatest good] stands in his communion with God, as Scripture and experience evidences, Psa. 144:15. My God and I am good company, said famous Dr Sibbes.

of Sol. 2:16, 'My beloved is mine, and I am his.' Song of Sol. 6:8, 'I am my beloved's, and my beloved is mine.' Song of Sol. 7:10, 'I am my beloved's, and his desire is towards me.' Now, mark, how does the sense of this propriety of hers in Christ work? Why, it works very highly, very strongly, very inflamingly, very affectionately: Song of Sol. 1:2-4, 'Let him kiss me with the kisses of his mouth:, for thy love is better than wine. Because of the savour of thy good ointments, thy name is as ointment poured forth, and therefore do the virgins love thee. Draw me, we will run after thee: the king hath brought me into his chambers: we will be glad and rejoice in thee, we will remember thy love more than wine: the upright love thee.' Verse 13, 'A bundle of myrrh is my beloved unto me; he shall lie all night betwixt my breasts.' Song of Sol. 2:3-6, 'As the apple tree among the trees of the wood, so is my beloved among the sons. I sat down under his shadow with great delight, and his fruit was sweet unto my taste. He brought me to the banqueting house, and his banner over me was love. Stay me with flagons, comfort me with apples: for I am sick of love. His left hand is under my head, and his right hand doth embrace me.' And Song of Sol. 7:5, 'The king is held in the galleries.' The spouse had a clear sight and a deep sense of her interest and propriety in Christ; and oh, how high, how close, how full, how sweet, is she in her communion and fellowship with Christ! It is the sight and sense of propriety and interest that heightens and sweetens that communion that is between husband and wife, father and child, brother and sister, and friend and friend; so it is the sight and sense of a man's propriety and interest in God that heightens and sweetens his communion and fellowship with God.

A clear sight of a man's interest and propriety in God will exceedingly sweeten every thought of God, and every appearance of God, and every taste of God, and every smile of God, and every communication of God, and every ordinance of God, and every work of God, and every way of God; yea, it will sweeten every rod that is in the hand of God, and every wrinkle that is in face of God, Psa. 139:17, 18. A man that sees his interest in God, will hang upon him, and trust in him, though he should never write such bitter things against him, and though he should never deal so severely with him, yea, though he should slay him, as you may see in Job 13:15. He hit it who said, A man whose soul is conversant with God shall find more pleasure in the desert and in death, than in the palace of a prince. Urbanus Regius, having one day's converse with Luther, said, It was one of the sweetest days that ever he had in all his life. But if one day's communion with Luther was so sweet, oh how sweet must one day's communion with God be. And therefore, as ever you would have high, and full, and sweet communion with God, keep up a clear sight, a blessed sense of your interest and propriety in God. But,

[6.] Sixthly, A clear personal evidence that God is a man's portion, is *a man's all in all*. O sirs! this is the life of your lives, and the life of your prayers, and the life of your praises, and the life of your confidences, and the life of your mercies, and the life of your comforts, and the life of your hopes. A clear sight of your propriety in God is the very life of promises, the life of ordinances, the life of providences, the life of experiences, and the life of your gracious evidences. It is a pearl of price; it is your paradise; it is manna in a wilderness, it is water out of a rock, it is a cloud by day, and a pillar of fire by night; it is Jacob's ladder; it is a salve for every sore, it is medicine for every disease, it is a remedy against every malady; it is an anchor at sea, and a shield on shore; it is a star to guide you, a staff to support you, a sword to defend you, a pavilion to hide you, a fire to warm you, a banquet to refresh you, a city of refuge to secure you, and a cordial to cheer you; and what would you have more? But,

[7.] Seventhly, and lastly, A clear personal evidence that God is a man's portion will *exceedingly sweeten the thoughts of death, and all the approaches of death, and all the warnings and forerunners of death unto him*. It will make a man look upon his last day as his best day, Eccles. 7:1; it will make a man look upon the king of terrors as the king of desires, Job 18:14; it will make a man laugh at the shaking of the spear, at the sounding of the trumpet, at the confused noise of the battle, at garments rolled in blood, at the sighs and groans of the wounded, and at the heaps of the slain. It was the martyrs' clear sight of their interest and propriety in God that made them compliment with lions, and dare their persecutors, and to kiss the stake, and to sing and clap their hands in the midst of the flames, and to tread upon hot burning coals as upon beds of roses, and divinely to triumph over their tormentors. It was this that made the primitive Christians ambitious of martyrdom, and that made them willingly and cheerfully lay down their lives, that they might, Elijah-like, mount to heaven in fiery chariots. A man that sees his propriety in God, knows that death shall be the funeral of all his sins, sorrows, afflictions, temptations, desertions, oppositions, vexations, oppressions, and persecutions; and he knows that death shall be the resurrection of his hopes, joys, delights, comforts, and contentments, and that it shall bring him to a more clear, full, perfect, and constant enjoyment of God: and this makes him sweetly and triumphantly to sing it out, O death! where is thy sting? O grave! where is thy victory? 1 Cor. 15:35-37. And oh that these seven considerations might prevail with all your souls to be restless, till you have in your own bosoms clear and full satisfaction that God is your portion.

Now this last inference leads me by the hand to a use of trial and examination. O sirs! if God be the saint's portion, the believer's portion, how highly it concerns every one that looks upon himself as a saint or as a believer, to search, try, and examine whether God be his portion or no?

Question 1:
How Shall We Know If God Be Our Portion?

Quest. But you will say, How shall we know whether God be our portion or no? Oh! were all the world a lump of gold, and in our hands to dispose of, we would give it to know that God is our portion! Oh! the knowledge of this would be as life from the dead; it would create a heaven in our hearts on this side heaven; it would presently put us into a paradise of pleasure and delight; but still the question is, How shall we know it? It is an easy thing to say that God is our portion; but how shall we come infallibly to know that God is our portion?

Now, to give clear and full satisfaction to this great and weighty question, I shall give in these following answers, by which you may certainly and undoubtedly know, whether God be your portion or not:

(1.) First, If God be your portion, then *you have very sweet, precious, high, and honourable thoughts of God*; then your thoughts will still be running out after God, and your meditations of him will be sweet.[1] A man that has God for his portion, is always best when his thoughts and

---

[1] Lord, says Augustine, the more I meditate on you, the sweeter you are to me. Jerome calls meditation his paradise, and Theophylact calls it the very gate and portal by which we enter into glory. To think is to live, says Cicero.

meditations are running out most after God: Psa. 104:34, 'My meditations of him shall be sweet: I will be glad in the Lord'; Psa. 63:5, 6, 'My soul shall be satisfied as with marrow and fatness; and my mouth shall praise thee with joyful lips: when I remember thee upon my bed (or beds, as the Hebrew has it; David never bedded at home nor abroad, here nor there, but still his thoughts were running out to God), and meditate on thee in the night watches'; Psa. 139:17, 18, 'How precious also are thy thoughts unto me, O God! how great is the sum of them! If I should count them, they are more in number than the sand: when I awake, I am still with thee.' The psalmist had very frequent, high, precious, and honourable thoughts of God; he valued nothing at so high a rate as sweet and noble thoughts of God, and of his power, wisdom, goodness, faithfulness, and graciousness, *etc.*

David had such precious thoughts of God, and such great and glorious thoughts of God, and such infinite and innumerable thoughts of God, that he was as well able to number the sands of the sea, as he was able to number them up: 'And when I awake I was still with thee.' He was still contemplating upon God; he fell asleep with precious thoughts of God, and he awoke with precious thoughts of God; he rose up with precious thoughts of God, and he lay down with precious thoughts of God; he went forth with precious thoughts of God, and he returned home with precious thoughts of God. Take a Christian when he is himself, when he is neither under sad desertions, nor black temptations, nor great afflictions, and he can as soon forget his own and his father's house, the wife of his bosom, the fruit of his loins, yea, he can as soon forget to eat his bread, as he can forget his God.

When Alexander the Great had overthrown Darius, king of Persia, he took among the spoils a most rich cabinet, full of the choicest jewels that were in all the world; upon which there rose a dispute before him, to what use he should put the cabinet; and every one having spent his judgment according to his fancy, the king himself concluded, that he would keep that cabinet, to be a treasury to lay up the books of Homer in, which were his greatest joy and delight. A sanctified memory is a rich cabinet full of the choicest thoughts of God;[1] it is that rich treasury in which a Christian is still laying up more and more precious thoughts of God, and more and more high and holy thoughts of God, and more and more honourable and noble thoughts of God, and more and more awful[2] and reverent thoughts of God, and more and more sweet and comfortable thoughts of God, and more and more tender and compassionate thoughts of God, *etc.* Take a Christian in his ordinary course, and you shall find that wherever he is, his thoughts are running out after God; and about whatever he is, his thoughts are still running out after God; and into whatever company he is cast, whether they are good or bad, yet still his thoughts are running out after God.

Look, as an earthly-minded man has his thoughts and meditations still exercised and taken up with the world, as you may see in Haman, whose heart and thoughts were taken up with his honours, preferments, riches, wife, children, and friends, *etc.*:[3] Esther 5:10-12, 'Nevertheless Haman

---

[1] Psa. 25:1; 86:4; 143:8; Basil calls meditation on [God] the treasury, where all graces are locked up.

[2] [That is. full of awe; awesome.]

[3] The thoughts and hearts of the people of Constantinople were

refrained himself: and when he came home, he sent and called for his friends, and Zeresh his wife. And Haman told them of the glory of his riches, and the multitude of his children, and all the things wherein the king had promoted him, and how he had advanced him above the princes and servants of the king. Haman said moreover, Yea, Esther the queen did let no man come in with the king unto the banquet that she had prepared but myself; and tomorrow am I invited unto her also with the king.'

And the same spirit you may see working in those that had made gold their god, in Psa. 49:10, 11, 'For he seeth that wise men die, likewise the fool and the brutish person perish, and leave their wealth to others. Their inward thought is, that their houses shall continue for ever, and their dwelling places to all generations; they call their lands after their own names.' The Hebrew runs thus: 'Their inwards are their houses for ever,' as if their houses were got within them. Not only the thoughts, but the very inmost thoughts, the most retired thoughts and recesses of world-lings' souls, are taken up about earthly things; and though they care not whether their names are written in heaven or not, yet they do all they can to propagate and immortalize their names on earth.

And the rich fool was one in spirit with these the psalm-ist speaks of, as you may see in Luke 12:16, 22, 'And he spake a parable unto them, saying, The ground of a certain

---

so extremely set upon the world, and running out after the world, that they were buying and selling in their shops even three days after the Turks were within the walls of their city; and that was the reason that the streets run down with their blood, and the blood of their wives and children.

rich man brought forth plentifully: and he thought within himself (the Greek word διελογίζετι, *dielogizeti*, is a marvellous proper word for the purpose; it signifies to talk with a man's self, or to reason with a man's self. This foolish worldling was much in talking to himself, and in reasoning with himself about his goods and barns, *etc.*, as the usual manner of men is that are of a worldly spirit), saying, What shall I do, because I have no room where to bestow my fruits? And he said, This will I do: I will pull down my barns, and build greater; and there will I bestow all my fruits and my goods. And I will say to my soul, Soul, thou hast much goods laid up for many years; take thine ease, eat, drink, and be merry.' Among all his worldly thoughts, there is not one thought of God, of Christ, of grace, of heaven, of holiness, of eternity, to be found. His thoughts were so taken up with his bags, and his barns, and his buildings, and his ease, and his belly, that he had no time to think of providing for another world; and therefore God quickly despatches him out of this world, and throws him down from the highest pinnacle of prosperity and worldly glory into the greatest gulf of wrath and misery, verse 20. And this foolish worldling puts me in mind of another, who, being offered a horse by his fellow upon condition that he would but say the Lord's prayer, and think upon nothing but God, which proffer[1] being accepted, he began: 'Our Father which art in heaven, hallowed be thy name.' But I must have the bridle too, said he. No, nor the horse neither, said the other; for you have lost both already.

When worldlings should most think of God, and be most struck with the dread and majesty of God, and be most afflicted and taken up with the glory of God, yet then their

[1] [Or proposal.]

thoughts and hearts will be gadding and running after the world, as you may see in Ezekiel's hearers; Ezek. 33:30-32, and in Paul's, Phil. 3:18, 19. When Queen Mary was dying, she said that if they did but open her when she was dead, they should find Calais lying at her heart. Ah! how often do stinking lusts and rotten towns, and moth-eaten bags, and other trifling vanities, lie near those hearts where God, and Christ, and the Spirit, and grace, and ordinances, and saints, and heaven should lie! Look, as the thoughts of the men of the world mainly run out after the world, after their earthly portions, so the thoughts of those that have God for their portion mainly run out after God, and they are never so well as when they are most thinking and musing on God. But,

(2.) Secondly, If God be your portion, then *in all your straits, trials, troubles, and wants, you will run to your God, you will fly to the Lord, as to your only city of refuge:*[1] 1 Sam. 30:6, 'And David was greatly distressed; for the people spake of stoning him, because the soul of all the people was grieved (or bitter), every man for his sons and for his daughters: but David encouraged himself in the Lord his God.' When a shower of stones were coming about David's ears, he runs and shelters himself under the wings of his God. Though David was an exile in a heathenish country, though Ziklag, the place of his habitation, was burnt, though he had neither house nor home to flee to, though his wives were in his enemies' hands, and though his friends and followers were desperately incensed, enraged, exasperated, and provoked against him, and took counsel together

[1] Psa. 28:1; 31:2, 3; 61:2; 62:2, 6, 7; 92:15; 94:22; Isa. 32:1, 2.

about stoning him, looking upon him as the author of all their crosses, losses, calamities, and miseries; yet now he comforts and encourages himself in the Lord his God: Psa. 142:4, 'I looked on my right hand, and beheld, but there was no man that would know me: refuge failed me; but no man cared for my soul.' But what does the psalmist do in this case? Does he despair or despond? No. Does he cast away his hope and confidence in God? No. Why, what does he do then? Why, when all outward comforts fail him, he runs to God as to his last refuge: ver. 5, 6, 'I cried unto thee, O Lord: I said, Thou art my refuge and my portion in the land of the living. Attend unto my cry, for I am brought very low: deliver me from my persecutors; for they are stronger than I.' He does not run in his straits from God to the creatures, for that had been to run from the fountain of living waters to broken cisterns, Jer. 2:12, 13, John 6:68; Isa. 33:16, from the light of the sun to the light of a farthing candle, and from the Rock of ages to a leaf driven about with the wind, and from paradise into a howling wilderness.

But where does he run to then? Why, he runs to God; he knew that God was his light, his life, his love, his peace, his joy, his strength, his shelter, his safety, his security, his crown, his glory, and therefore he runs to his God. And, indeed, in times of danger, where should the child run to shelter himself but to his father? and where should the wife run but to her husband? and the servant but to his master? and the soldier but to his stronghold? and a Christian but to his God? Prov. 18:10, 'The name of the Lord is a strong tower: the righteous runneth into it, and is safe.' Sometimes by *the name of the Lord* we are to understand God himself, but most commonly God's attributes are called his name, because by them he is known, as a man is by his name; and here by the name of the Lord we are to understand the power of the Lord, for by that God is known, as men are known by their names. Now God himself is a strong tower, and the power of God is a strong tower, yea, it is a tower as high as heaven, and as strong as strength itself; it is a tower so deep no pioneer[1] can undermine it, so thick no cannon can pierce it, so high no ladder can scale it, so strong that no enemy can assault it or ever be able to stand before it, and so well furnished and provided for all purposes and intents, that all the powers of darkness can never distress it, or in the least straiten it.

Now to this impregnable and inexpugnable[2] tower the righteous in all their distresses and dangers run. All creatures run to their refuges when they are hunted and pursued, and so do righteous souls to theirs. But what does the righteous man gain by running to his strong tower? Why, he gains safety; he is safe, says the text, or rather according to the Hebrew נשגב, *exaltatur*,[3] he is exalted, he is set aloft, he is a soul out of gunshot, he is a soul out of all hazard and danger, he is safe in everlasting arms, he is safe in his strong tower of defence, he can easily overlook all hazards, yea, he can look upon the greatest dangers with a holy neglect.

And when the burning fiery furnace was heated seven times hotter than at first, where do Shadrach, Meshech,

[1] [That is, one of a group of foot soldiers detailed to prepare the way in advance of the main body of the army.]

[2] [That is, not able to be taken by assault.]

[3] The Hebrew word is from *Sagab*, that signifies to exalt, or to set aloft.

and Abednego run? Why, they run to God: Dan. 3:16-18, 'Shadrach, Meshech, and Abednego, answered and said to the king, O Nebuchadnezzar, we are not careful to answer thee in this matter. If it be so, our God, whom we serve, is able to deliver us from the burning fiery furnace, and he will deliver us out of thy hand, O king. But if not, be it known unto thee, O king, that we will not serve thy gods, nor worship the golden image which thou hast set up.'

And so Moses in Psa. 90:1, 'Lord, thou hast been our dwelling place in all generations'; or as the Hebrew has it, you have been our refuge-place in generation and generation. By this Hebraism, generation and generation, the prophet sets forth all generations, to show that there has been no generation in which God has not been the refuge of his people. God was a refuge to his people before the flood, and he has been a refuge since the flood, and he will be a refuge to his people, whilst he has a people in the world. All the time that Moses and the people of Israel were travelling up and down in that terrible howling wilderness, in which they were compassed about with dreadful dangers on all hands, God was a refuge and a dwelling-place to them. In all their troubles and travels for four hundred years together, God was a shelter, a refuge, and a house of defence to them. Every man's house is his strong castle, and to it he retreats when dangers come; and thus did the people of God in the text. When dangers threatened them, they still run to their God, they still made their retreat to the Holy One of Israel.

A man that has God for his portion, when he is at worst can never be houseless nor harbourless. As long as God lives, he can never lack a house, a mansion-house to hide his head in. All the powers on earth and all the powers of hell can never unhouse, nor never unharbour, nor never unshelter that man that has God for his portion. It was a witty saying of that learned man Picus Mirandula, 'God created the earth for beasts to inhabit, the sea for fishes, the air for fowls, and heaven for angels and stars, so that man has no place to dwell and abide in but God alone.' And certainly he that by faith dwells in God, dwells in the best, the noblest, the safest, and the strongest house that ever was dwelt in. And so Psa. 91:1, 2, 'He that dwelleth in the secret place of the most High, shall abide under the shadow of the Almighty. I will say of the Lord, He is my refuge, and my fortress: my God; in him will I trust.' In this whole psalm the safety of a saint is set forth to the life; to abide under the shadow of the Almighty, notes the defence and protection of God. Those words, 'shall abide under the shadow of the Almighty,' are a metaphor taken from a bird or a hen, that hides her young ones under her wings, and so secures them from the kite, or any other birds of prey. God never lacks a wing to hide his children under; and look, as little chickens run under the wings of the hen when danger is near, so the people of God commonly run under the wings of God when danger is near. And certainly, that Christian may well bid defiance to all dangers, and easily and sweetly sing away all cares and fears, who can by faith shelter himself and lodge himself under the shadow of Shaddai.

Look, as the worldling in all his straits, troubles, trials, dangers, and wants, still runs to his bags, to his earthly portion for succour, for comfort, for support, for relief, for shelter, for protection,[1] Prov. 18:11; Matt. 19:24; 1 Tim.

---

[1] I have read of a wretched worldling, who being sick to death, called for one of his bags of gold, and laid it to his heart, and then

6:17, so a Christian in all his troubles, trials, and distresses, still runs to his God for shelter, comfort, and support: Psa. 31:1-3, 'In thee, O Lord, do I put my trust; let me never be ashamed: deliver me in thy righteousness. Bow down thine ear to me; deliver me speedily: be thou my strong rock, for an house of defence to save me. For thou art my rock and my fortress: therefore, for thy name's sake lead me, and guide me.' Psa. 61:2, 3, 'From the end of the earth will I cry unto thee, when my heart is overwhelmed: lead me to the rock that is higher than I. For thou hast been a shelter for me, and a strong tower from the enemy.' Psa. 94:21, 22, 'They gather themselves together against the soul of the righteous, and condemn the innocent. But the Lord is my defence; and my God is the rock of my refuge.' Psa. 57:2, 'I will cry unto God most High; unto God that performeth all things for me.' Isa. 25:9, 'And it shall be said in that day, Lo, this is our God; we have waited for him, and he will save us: this is the Lord; we have waited for him, we will be glad and rejoice in his salvation.' Mic. 7:7, 'Therefore I will look unto the Lord; I will wait for the God of my salvation: my God will hear.' Thus you see that the saints in all their straits and trials still run to God. They know that that God that is their portion is an all-sufficient God, and that he is a sun and a shield to them that walk uprightly; and therefore they delight to be still running under his shadow.

A man that has God for his portion, may truly say in his greatest distresses and troubles, Well, though I have no riches to fly to, nor no friends to shelter me, nor no relations to stand by me, nor no visible power on earth to protect

---

cried out, Oh it will not do, it will not do; and then called for another, and still cried out, Oh it will not do, it will not do.

me, yet I have a God for my portion that is always willing to supply me, and able to secure me: Psa. 18:1, 2, 'I will love thee, O Lord, my strength,' or as the Hebrew has it, 'I will dearly love the Lord,' or 'I will love him with inmost bowels of affections,' as a tender-hearted mother loves her dearest babe with the inmost bowels of affections. 'The Lord is my rock, and my fortress, and my deliverer; my God, my strength, in whom I will trust; my buckler, and the horn of my salvation, and my high tower.' In this verse you have nine several expressions to discover what an all-sufficient refuge God is to his people in their greatest distresses. When a Christian is at worst, yet he has bread celestial, bread to eat that the world knows not of. The grand policy of a Christian to secure himself against all dangers is to run to God. But,

(3.) Thirdly, If God be your portion, then you *will hold fast your portion, and rather part with anything than part with your portion.* Naboth would not upon any terms part with his inheritance; he would rather let all go, yea, his very life go, than let his inheritance go, his portion go: 1 Kings 21:3, 'And Naboth said to Ahab, The Lord forbid it me, that I should give the inheritance of my fathers unto thee'; or, as the Hebrew has it, This be abomination to me from the Lord; that is, The Lord keep me from this as from an abominable thing. To alter or alienate the property of inheritances was expressly forbidden by God in his law, Lev. 25:23; Num. 36:7; Ezek. 46:18; and therefore Naboth looks upon Ahab's offer and motion as a detestable and an abominable thing, and resolves to hold fast his inheritance, whatever it cost him.

So a Christian will hold fast his God, whatever comes on it; he will let anything go, rather than let his God go or his

Christ go: Song of Sol. 3:4, 'It was but a little that I passed from them, but I found him whom my soul loveth: I held him, and would not let him go, until I had brought him into my mother's house, and into the chamber of her that conceived me.'[1] The Hebrew word that is here rendered held is from *achaz*, which signifies to hold, as a man would hold his possession, his inheritance. The word signifies to hold with both hands, to hold with all one's might and with all one's strength; and thus the spouse held the Lord Jesus; she held him with both hands; she held him with all her might and with all her strength; she held him with a holy violence, with a holy force; she held him as a man would hold his prisoner that had a mind to escape, or as a man would hold his sword or buckler when his life is in danger.

So Jacob, Gen. 32:26, 'And he said, Let me go, for the day breaketh. And he said, I will not let thee go, except thou bless me.' When Jacob was all alone, and in a dark night, and upon one leg, and when his joints were out of joint, and he very much overmatched, yet then he holds God fast, he wrestles and weeps, and weeps and wrestles, he tugs and sweats, and sweats and tugs, and will not let go his hold, till, like a prince, he had prevailed with God, Hos. 12:4.

Ruth, you know, was so glued to her mother Naomi, that no arguments could prevail with her to leave her mother-in-law. She was fully resolved in this, that where her mother-in-law went she would go, and where her mother-in-law lodged she would lodge, and that her mother-in-law's people should be her people, and her mother-in-law's God her God, and that where her mother-in-law died there she

---

[1] The motto of a Christian, whilst he is in the wilderness of this world, is self-diffidence and Christ-dependence, Song of Sol. 8:5.

would die, and there would she be buried, Ruth 1:14-18. So a man that has God for his portion is so glued to his God, that nothing can take him off from following of God and from cleaving to God.

When David was in his wilderness condition, yet then his soul followed hard after God, then his soul stuck close to God: Psa. 63:1, 2, 'O God, thou art my God; early will I seek thee: my soul thirsteth for thee, my flesh longeth for thee in a dry and thirsty land, where no water is.' Verse 8, 'My soul followeth hard after thee'; or, as the words may be read, 'My soul cleaves after you.' David's enemies did not follow harder after him than he followed hard after God. The wife in a man's bosom could not cleave so close to him as David's soul cleaved close to God when he was in a wilderness estate, when he was in an afflicted condition. It is nothing to follow God in a paradise, but it is rare to follow God in a wilderness; it is nothing to follow God when the way is strewn with rosebuds, but it is the glory of a Christian to follow God when the way is strewn with thorns and briars; it is nothing to follow God in a crowd, or with the crowd, but it is the excellency of a Christian to follow God in a wilderness, where few or none follows after him; it is nothing to follow God in the midst of all encouragements, but it is wonderful to follow God in the midst of all discouragements. Oh the integrity! oh the ingenuity! oh the strong intention! oh the deep affection! oh the noble resolution, of that Christian that hangs upon God in a wilderness, and that cleaves to God in a wilderness, and that follows hard after God in a wilderness!

Look, as Shechem's soul did cleave to Dinah, and as Jacob's soul did cleave to Rachel, and as Jonathan's soul did cleave to David in the very face of all hazards, dangers, difficulties, troubles, trials, and distresses, so the very soul of a man that has God for his portion will cleave to God in the very face of all hazards, dangers, difficulties, troubles, trials, and distresses that he meets with, Psa. 44:8-23. It is neither the frowns of men, nor the reproaches of men, nor the scorns of men, nor the contempts of men, nor the oppositions of men, nor the treacheries of men, nor the combinations of men, that will work him to let go his hold of God. A man that has God for his portion knows that, whilst he holds his God, he holds his life; and that, whilst he holds his God, he holds his comfort, his crown, his heaven, his all; and therefore he will rather let all go, than let his God go.

And so much the several *leave nots* that are scattered up and down in the blessed Scripture clearly evidence; as in 1 Kings 8:57, 'The Lord our God be with us, as he was with our fathers: let him not leave us, nor forsake us'; and Psa. 27:9, 'Hide not thy face far from me; put not thy servant away in anger: thou hast been my help; leave me not, neither forsake me, O God of my salvation.' And so Psa. 119:121, 'I have done judgment and justice: leave me not to mine oppressors.' And so Psa. 141:8, 'But mine eyes are unto thee, O God the Lord: in thee is my trust; leave not my soul destitute,' or leave not my soul naked, as the Hebrew word signifies. And so in Jer. 14:9, 'Why shouldest thou be as a man astonied,[1] as a mighty man that cannot save? yet thou, O Lord, art in the midst of us, and we are called by thy name; leave us not.' Now in these five scriptures you have five *leave us nots*, and what do they import? Certainly

---

[1] [That is, dazed; bewildered; filled with consternation.]

nothing less than a marvellous unwillingness in the people of God to part with God, or to let go their hold of God.

I have read of Cynaegirus, an Athenian captain, who, in the Persian wars, pursuing his enemy's ship, which was laden with the rich spoils of his country, and ready to set sail, how he first held it with his right hand till that was cut off, and then with his left hand till that was cut off, and then with his stumps till his arms were cut off, and then he held it with his teeth till his head was cut off; as long as he had any life or strength left in him, he would not let go his hold. So a man that has God for his portion will rather die at the foot of God than he will let go his hold of God: Job 13:15, 'Though he slay me, yet will I trust in him.' But,

(4.) Fourthly, If God be your portion, then *you live upon God as upon your portion*. Look, as the men of the world live upon their earthly portions, so a man that has God for his portion lives upon his God, as you may plainly see by comparing the scriptures in the margin together.[1] Look, how the poor man lives upon his labours, the covetous man upon his bags, the ambitious man upon his honours, the voluptuous man upon his pleasures, *etc.*, so a Christian lives upon his God. In all his duties he lives upon God, and in all his mercies he lives upon God, and in all his wants he lives upon God, and in all his straits and trials he lives upon God, and in all his contentments and enjoyments he still lives upon God for his justification: Rom. 8:33, 'It is God that justifieth,' and he still lives upon God for the perfecting of his sanctification; Phil. 1:6, 'Being confident of this very

[1] 1 Sam. 30:6; Hab. 3:17, 18; Psa. 73:26; Rom. 14:7, 8; Gal. 2:20; Phil. 1:21.

thing, that he which hath begun a good work in you, will perform it until the day of Jesus Christ'; and he lives upon God for the maintaining and increasing of his consolation, 2 Cor. 1:3-5. When he is under the frowns of the world, then he lives upon the smiles of God; when he is under the hatred of the world, then he lives upon the loves of God; and when he is under the reproaches of the world, then he lives upon his credit with God; when he is under the threatenings of the world, then he lives upon the protection of God; and when he is under the designs and plottings of the world, then he lives upon the wisdom and counsel of God; when he is under the slightings and neglects of the world, then he lives upon the care of God; and when he is under the crosses and losses of the world, then he lives upon the fulness and goodness of God, *etc.* Alexander told his soldiers, I wake that you may sleep. Most sure I am, that he that is the saint's portion never slumbers nor sleeps, Psa. 121:3, 4. God is always watchful and wakeful to do his people good; he never wants skill or will to help them, he never wants a purse, a hand, or a heart to supply them, *etc.*

O sirs! Every man singles out something to live upon. Some single out one thing, some another. Says the wife, I must live upon my husband; says the child, I must live upon my father; says the servant, I must live upon my master; says the old, We must live upon the labours of the young; says the poor, We must live upon the charity of the rich; and why then shall not a Christian live upon his God? A Christian that has God for his portion may say, when he is at worst, Well, though I have not this nor that nor the other outward comfort to live upon, yet I have the power of a God to live on, and I have the providence of a God to live on, and

I have the promise of a God to live on, and I have the oath of a God to live on, and I have the love of a God to live on, and I have the bounty of a God to live on, and I have the fulness of a God to live on, and I have the care of a God to live on; and what can I desire more?

John of Alexandria, surnamed the Almoner, used yearly to make even his revenues, and when he had distributed all to the poor, he thanked God that he had now nothing left to live upon but his Lord and Master Jesus Christ. When all is gone, yet a Christian has his God to live upon as his portion, and that is enough to answer to all other things, and to make up the want of all other things. Look, as he has nothing that has not God for his portion, so he wants nothing that has God for his portion. It was a weighty saying of one [Cajetan], 'The spiritual good of a man consists in this, that a man has friendship with God, and consequently that he lives for him, to him, with him, in him; that he lives for him by consent, to him by conversation, with him by cohabitation, and in him by contentation. Old godly Similes said that he had been in the world sixty years, but had lived but seven, counting his life not from his first birth, but from his new birth. A man lives no longer than he lives upon God as his portion: when a man begins to live upon God as his portion, then he begins to live indeed, and not till then. But,

(5.) Fifthly, If God be your portion, then *he carries your heart from all other things* (Psa. 42:1, 2). The portion always carries the heart with it.[1] Matt. 6:20, 21, 'But lay up for yourselves treasures in heaven, where neither moth nor

---

[1] Bernard well observes, that a wise man's heart is with the Lord.

rust doth corrupt, and where thieves do not break through nor steal: for where your treasure is, there will your hearts be also.' Psa. 63:1, 'O God, thou art my God; early will I seek thee' (or, I will diligently seek you, as merchants do precious stones that are of greatest value), 'my soul thirsteth for thee.' He does not say, my soul thirsts for water, but my soul thirsts for you; nor he does not say, my soul thirsts for the blood of my enemies, but my soul thirsts for you; nor he does not say, my soul thirsts for deliverance out of this dry and barren wilderness, but my soul thirsts for you in a dry and thirsty land, where no water is; nor he does not say, my soul thirsts for a crown, a kingdom, but my soul thirsts for you, 'my flesh longeth for thee.' These words are a notable metaphor, taken from women with child, to note his earnest, ardent, and strong affections towards God.

And so Psa. 84:2, 'My heart and my flesh crieth out for the living God.' The word that is here rendered *crieth*, is from *Ranan*, that signifies to shout, shrill, or cry out, as soldiers do at the beginning of a battle, when they cry out, Fall on, fall on, fall on, or when they cry out after a victory, Victory, victory, victory! The Hebrew word notes a strong cry, or to cry as a child cries when it is sadly hungry, for now every whit[1] of the child cries, hands cry, and face cries, and feet cries; and so Psa. 119:20, 'My soul breaketh for the longings it hath unto thy judgments at all times.' Look, as the stone will still be rolling towards its centre, its place, though it break itself into a thousand pieces; so a soul that has God for his portion cannot rest till he comes to God, till he comes to his centre. It is very observable, that when the God of glory appeared to Abraham, he made nothing

[1] [That is, part.]

of leaving his father's house, his kindred, and his country, Acts 7:1-5; Gen. 12:1. A glimpse of that glory works him to give up all easily, readily, and quietly. A man that can look upon the God of glory to be his portion, he cannot but look upon the greatest, the nearest, and the dearest enjoyments of the world, as nothing; he cannot but look upon honour as a bubble, and worldly pomp as a fancy, and great men as a lie, and poor men as vanity. He cannot but look upon his nearest and his dearest relations, his highest and his noblest friends, his choicest and his sweetest comforts, but as a dream and a shadow that soon vanishes away.

It is observable in the courts of kings and princes, that children and the ruder sort of people are much taken with pictures and rich shows, and feed their fancies with the sight of rich hangings and fine showy things; whereas such as are great favourites at court, pass by all those things as things that are below them, and as things that are not worthy of their notice, who have business with the king, and who have the eye, the ear, the hand, and the heart of the king to take pleasure and delight in; so most men admire the poor low things of the world, and are much taken with them as things that have a great deal of worth and excellency in them; but a man that has God for his portion, the King of kings for his portion, and all that he has, he passes by all the showy and fashionable things of the world, as things below him, as things not worthy of him. His business is with his God, and his thoughts, his heart, and affections are taken up with his God.

Naturalists tell us that the loadstone will not draw in the presence of the diamond. O sirs! whilst a man can eye God as his portion, all the pride, pomp, bravery, glory, and gallantry in the world will never be able to draw him from God, Heb. 11:24-27, 35. It is reported that when the tyrant Trajan commanded Ignatius to be ripped up and unbowelled, they found *Jesus Christ* written upon his heart in characters of gold. Here was a heart worth gold indeed; Christ carried away his heart from all other things. So if God be your portion, he will certainly carry your heart away from all earthly things. Look, as earthly portions carry away worldly hearts from God, Ezek. 33:31, 32; Luke 12:16-21; so when God once comes to be a man's portion, he carries his heart away from the world, the flesh, and the devil. All the world cannot keep a man's interest and his heart apart. If a man make sin his interest, all the world cannot keep sin and his heart apart. If a man make the world his interest, all the power on earth cannot keep the world and his heart apart. And so if a man make God his interest, all the world cannot keep God and his heart apart: no sword, no prison, no racks, no flames can keep a man's interest and his heart apart. A man's heart will be working towards his interest, even through the very fire, as you may see in the three children, Dan. 3:17, 18.

Look, as the needle's point in the seaman's compass never stands still, but quivers and shakes till it come right against the north pole; and as the wise men of the east never stood still till they were right against the star which appeared to them; and as the star itself never stood still till it came right against that other star, which shone more brightly in the manger than the sun did in the firmament; and as Noah's dove could find no rest for the sole of her foot all the while she was fluttering over the flood, till she returned to the ark with an olive branch in her mouth: so the heart of a

Christian that has God for his portion can never rest, can never be at quiet, but in God. But,

(6.) Sixthly, If God be your portion, then *you will own your God, and stand up courageously and resolutely for your God.*[1] Every man will own his portion, and stand up stoutly and resolutely for his portion, and so will every Christian do for his God: Psa. 119:46, 'I will speak of thy testimonies before kings, and will not be ashamed.' David was resolved upon a noble and resolute owning of God and his testimonies before the greatest and the highest of men; and this he would do and not blush, this he would do and not be ashamed, this he would do and not be daunted.[2] It was neither the majesty or authority of princes, it was neither the power or dread of princes, that could hinder David from giving in his testimony on God's side, or on truth's side.

Joshua 24:18, 'We will serve the Lord; for he is our God': vers. 21, 22, 'And the people said unto Joshua, Nay, but we will serve the Lord; and Joshua said unto the people, Ye are witnesses against yourselves, that ye have chosen you the Lord to serve him; and they said, We are witnesses.' Verse 24, 'And the people said unto Joshua, The Lord our God will we serve, and his voice will we obey.' They had chosen God to be their God, as God had chosen them to be his peculiar people above all the nations of the earth; and therefore, notwithstanding all that Joshua had objected, they were fully resolved to own the Lord, and to cleave to the Lord,

---

[1] Histories abound with instances of this nature.

[2] A man of no resolution, or of a weak resolution, will be won with a nut, and lost with an apple; but a man of a noble resolution will own God in the face of the greatest majesty on earth.

and to obey the Lord, and wholly to devote themselves to the service of the Lord. Having taken the Lord to be their God, they were firmly resolved to own the Lord really, and to own him fully, and to own him primarily, and to own him only, and to own him everlastingly.

And so Deut. 26:17, 'Thou hast avouched the Lord this day to be thy God, and to walk in his ways, and to keep his statutes, and his commandments, and his judgments, and to hearken unto his voice.' They had avouched[1] God to be their God, and therefore they were resolved upon all those holy ways and means by which they might evidence to the world their owning of God to be their God.

And so in 2 Chron. 30:8, 'They yield themselves unto the Lord,' or, as the Hebrew has it, 'They give the hand unto the Lord.' You know when men make covenants or agreements to own one another, or to stand by one another, they commonly strike hands, or take one another by the hand. Certainly all those that have the Lord for their portion, have given their hands to the Lord, that they will own him, and stand by him, and cleave to him, as Jonathan did to David, or as Ruth did to Naomi. How stoutly and courageously did the three young men own the Lord, and stand by the Lord in the face of the fiery furnace, Dan. 3:17, 18; and Daniel will, upon choice, be rather cast into the den of lions than that the honour of God should in the least be clouded, or his glory darkened by any neglects or omissions of his, Dan. 6.

And so did all those worthies, 'of whom this world was not worthy,' Heb. 11:38. Oh, how did they own God, and stand up for God, notwithstanding the edge of the sword,

---

[1] [That is, affirmed.]

the violence of fire, the cruel mockings and scourgings, the bonds and imprisonments, the stoning and sawing asunder, the temptings and wanderings about in sheepskins and goatskins, and all other trials and torments that did attend them. Basil affirms that the primitive Christians did so courageously and resolutely own God, and stand up for God in the face of the most dreadful sufferings, that many of the heathens, seeing their heroic zeal, courage, magnanimity, and constancy, turned Christians. Domitian raised the second persecution against the Christians because they would not give the title of Lord to any but Christ, nor worship any but God alone. Among the many thousand instances that might be given, let me only give you a few of a later date, by which you may see how courageously and resolutely the saints have stood up for God, and owned God, in the face of the greatest dangers that has attended them.

Luther owned God and stood up resolutely for God against the world.[1] And when the emperor sent for him to Worms, and his friends dissuaded him from going, as sometimes Paul's did him, Go, said he, I will surely go since I am sent for in the name of our Lord Jesus Christ; yea, though I knew that there were as many devils in Worms to resist me as there be tiles to cover the houses, yet I would go: and when he and his associates were threatened with many dangers from opposers on all hands, he lets fall this heroic and magnanimous speech, 'Come, let us sing the forty-sixth Psalm, and then let them do their worst.' And indeed it was a brave courageous speech of the same author, who, when one demanded where he would be when the emperor should, with all his forces, fall upon the elector of Saxony,

---

[1] Acts et Mon. 776. [*Sub Worms* in Foxe, by Townsend.—G.]

who was the chief protector of the Protestants, answered, *Aut in coelo aut sub coelo*, either in heaven or under heaven.

William Flower, the martyr, said that the heavens should as soon fall as he would forsake his profession, or budge in the least degree from it.

Apollonius, as Philostratus reports, being asked, if he did not tremble at the sight of the tyrant, made this answer, God, who has given him a terrible countenance, has given also to me an undaunted heart.

When the persecutors by their dreadful threatenings laboured to terrify one of the martyrs, he replied, that there was nothing of things visible, nor nothing of things invisible, that he was afraid of. I will, says he, stand to my profession of the name of Christ, and 'contend earnestly for the faith once delivered to the saints.'

When Bishop Gardiner asked Rowland Taylor if he did not know him, he answered, Yea, I know you, and all your greatness, yet you are but a mortal man; and if I should be afraid of your lordly looks, why do you not fear God, the Lord of us all?

The executioner kindling the fire behind Jerome of Prague, he bade him kindle it before his face, for, he said, if I had been afraid of it, I had not come to this place, having had so many opportunities offered me to escape it; and at the giving up of the spirit, he said, This soul of mine in flames of fire, O Christ, I offer to you.

The German knight, in his apologetical letter[1] for Luther against the pontifical clergy, says, I will go through what I have undertaken against you, and will stir up men to seek their freedom; I neither care nor fear what may befall

[1] [That is, letter of defence.]

me, being prepared for either event, either to ruin you, to the great benefit of my country, or else to fall with a good conscience.

When Dionysius was given up to the executioner to be beheaded, he remained resolute, courageous, and constant, saying, 'Come life, come death, I will worship none but the God of heaven and earth.' Thus you see by these instances that men that have God for their portion will courageously own God, and bravely and resolutely stand up for God, whatever comes on it.

The blood that has been shed in most nations under heaven clearly evidences this, that men will own their earthly portions, and that they will stand up stoutly, resolutely, and courageously in the defence of them; and so certainly will all those own God, and stand up in the defence of God, his glory, and truth, who have God for their portion. Take a true bred Christian, when he is himself, take a Christian in his ordinary course, and he cannot but own his God, and stand up stoutly and courageously for his God in the face of all difficulties and dangers. But,

(7.) Seventhly, If God be your portion, then *you will look upon all things below your God as poor, low, mean, and contemptible things*, Psa. 73:24, 25. A worldly man looks upon all things below his earthly portion as contemptible; and so does a Christian look upon all things below his God as contemptible: Phil. 3:7, 8, 'But what things were gain to me, those I counted loss for Christ. Yea, doubtless, and I count all things but loss for the excellency of the knowledge of Christ Jesus my Lord: for whom I have suffered the loss of all things, and do count them but dung' (the Greek word σκύβαλα, *skubala*, properly signifies such sordid, coarse, and contemptible things, which are either cast forth by dogs, or cast before dogs),[1] 'that I may win Christ.' And it is very observable, that after this great apostle had been in the third heaven, and had been blessed with a glorious sight of God, he looked upon the world as a poor, mean, low, contemptible thing, 2 Cor. 12:1 -3: Gal. 6:14, 'God forbid that I should glory, save in the cross of our Lord Jesus Christ, by whom the world is crucified unto me, and I unto the world.' Paul scorned, despised, and rejected the world, and the world scorned, despised, and rejected him. Paul cast off the world, and the world cast off him; he disregarded the world, and the world disregarded him; he was dead to the world, and the world was dead to him. The world and Paul were well agreed; the world cared not a pin for Paul, and Paul cared not a straw for the world.

And so when Moses had seen him that was invisible, when he had taken a full prospect of that other world, and when he had beheld God as his portion, oh, how he slights, scorns, and tramples upon all the honours, preferments, profits, pleasures, delights, and contentments of Egypt, as things below him, and as things that in no respects were worthy of him, Heb. 11:24-27. It is a Rabbinical conceit, that Moses being a child had Pharaoh's crown given him to play with, and he made no better than a football of it, and cast it down to the ground, and kicked it about, as if it were a sign of his future vilifying and contemning[2] of temporal things. I shall not much trouble my head about what Moses did when he was a child; but of this I am sure, having the word

---

[1] Dogs' dung, some interpret the word.

[2] [That is, despising, treating with contempt.]

of God for it, 'That when he was come to years' (Heb. 11:24), or as the Greek has it, μέγας γενόμενος [*megas genomenos*], being grown big, or being grown a great one, and so sufficiently understood himself, and knew very well what he did,[1] he did little less than make a football of Pharaoh's crown. Witness his refusing with a holy scorn and disdain to be called the son of Pharaoh's daughter, and so to succeed Pharaoh in the throne.

And so in Rev. 12:1, 2, 'And there appeared a great wonder in heaven, a woman clothed with the sun, and the moon under her feet, and upon her head a crown of twelve stars.' The church here is compared to a woman for her weakness, fruitfulness, and loveliness; and it is observable, that she is clothed with the sun, that is, with Christ's own comeliness and righteousness, which resembles the sun in its several properties and effects, not now to be insisted on. Now this woman, the church, is said to have the moon under her feet. By the moon we are to understand all temporary and transitory things. Now the church treads upon all these things as trash and trumpery that were much below her, and despised by her. Look, as the great men of the world commonly look upon all portions that are below their own with an eye of scorn, disdain, and contempt, as Haman did, Esther 5:9-14; and as those bold daring sinners did, Psa. 73:4-14, so those that have God for their portion look upon all things below their God with an eye of scorn and disdain. I have read of Lazarus, that after his resurrection from the dead he was never seen to laugh; his thoughts, his heart, his affections were so fixed upon God, and so taken up with God, with his portion, that he was as a dead man to all the

---

[1] Some conclude he was forty years old now from Acts 7:23.

gay and gallant things of the world, he saw nothing in them worthy of a smile.

And so when once Galeacius, that famous Italian marquis, came to understand that God was his portion, in the face of the highest offers imaginable, of honour, favour, profit, and preferment, he cried out, Cursed be he that prefers all the glory of the world to one day's communion with God.

The old Grecians, who had altogether fed on acorns before, when bread came in among them, they made no reckoning of their mast,[1] but reserved it only for their swine. And the Lacedaemonians despised their iron and leather money, when gold and silver came in use among them. So when a man comes once to experience God to be his portion, ah, at what a low rate will he value the swelling honours, the deceitful riches, and the vanishing pleasures of this beggarly world (John 4:14). Christians are compared to eagles,[2] Matt. 24:28. Now the eagle is a kingly, a princely bird; it is a bird of a sharp piercing sight, and of a swift and lofty flight; it flies high and sets light by things below, except it be when necessity compels her: and so it is with those that have God for their portion; they fly high and they live high, in God, and therefore they cannot but set light by the toys and trifles of the world. But,

(8.) Eighthly, If God be your portion, then *your God is most precious to you, then you set the highest price and value imaginable upon your God*. Every man sets the highest price upon his portion. Though a man may set a good price upon

---

[1] [That is, nuts (such as acorns) accumulated on the forest floor and often serving as food for animals.]

[2] Query?—G.

his delightful gardens, his pleasant walks, his delicate fish ponds, his fruitful trees, his sweet flowers, *etc.*, yet it is no price to that which he sets upon his portion. Well, says a man, though here be a hundred things to delight my eye, and to please my fancy, and to satiate my appetite, yet I infinitely value my portion above them all. And who but a fool in folio[1] will value a thousand a year above a few accommodations that are only for pleasure and delight? So though a Christian may set a considerable value upon all his outward comforts and contentments, yet it is no value to that he sets upon his God, upon his portion. This and that is precious to me, says a Christian, but my God is infinitely more precious than all, Psa. 73:25, 26; 4:6, 7.

A Christian sets up God above his goods, Heb. 10:34; and above his lusts, Gal. 5:24; and above his relations, 1 Sam. 30:1-7; yea, and above his very life: Rev. 12:11, 'And they overcame him by the blood of the Lamb, and by the word of their testimony; and they loved not their lives unto the death: Psa. 63:3, 'Thy lovingkindness is better than life.' The Hebrew is *chaiim*, *lives*. Put many lives together, yet there is more excellency and glory in the least beam, in the least discovery of divine love, than there is in them all. A man may be weary of life, but never of divine love. Histories tell us of many that have been weary of their lives, but no histories can furnish us with an instance of anyone that was ever weary of divine love. Look, as the people prized David above themselves, saying, 'Thou art worth ten thousand of us,' 2 Sam. 18:3, so they that have indeed God for their portion, oh how do they prize God above themselves, and above everything below themselves! and doubtless they

[1] [That is, a fool of the largest kind; the biggest fool.]

that in a course do not lift up God above all, they have no interest in God at all.

Whatever a man eyes as his greatest interest, that he sets up above all, and before all other things in the world. Now if a man eyes God as his greatest interest, he cannot but set God on top of all. I have not faith enough to believe that ever such did truly love God who love anything more than God, or who set up anything above God, Luke 14:26. Look, as Darius set up Daniel over all, and as Pharaoh set up Joseph above all, so a man that has God for his portion, he sets up God over all, and he sets up God above all. One [Augustine] set so high a price upon Christ, that he has long since told us that he would willingly go through hell to Christ; and says another [Bernard], I had rather be in my chimney corner with Christ, than in heaven without him. When one of the martyrs was offered riches and honours if he would recant, he made this excellent answer, Do but offer me some thing that is better than my Lord Jesus Christ, and you shall see what I will say to you. And I have read of another, that set so high a price upon the Lord Jesus, that whenever he did but mention the name of Jesus, his eyes dropped tears. Were every star in the firmament a sun, yet a man that has God for his portion would prize him above them all.

Do you ask me where are my jewels? My jewels are my husband, said Phocion's wife. Do you ask me where are my ornaments? My ornaments are my two sons, brought up in virtue and learning, said the mother of the Gracchi. Do you ask me where are my treasures? My treasures are my friends, said Constantius, the father of Constantine. So if you ask a Christian that has God for his portion where his jewels, his ornaments, his treasures, his comforts, and the delights of his soul are, he will answer you that they are all in God, he will tell you that God is his portion, and that God is his great all, and that he enjoys all in God, and God in all, and therefore he cannot but prize God above all. But to prevent mistakes in this weighty case, let me give you a few brief hints; as,

[1.] First, If God be truly precious to you, then *all of God is precious to you*; his name is precious to you, his honour is precious to you, his ordinances are precious to you, his Sabbaths are precious to you, his promises are precious to you, his precepts are precious to you, his threatenings are precious to you, his rebukes are precious to you, his people are precious to you, and all his concernments are precious to you. Look, as every sparkling stone that is set round about a rich diamond is precious in the eyes of the jeweller, so is every sparkling excellency in God precious in his eyes that sets a high value upon God. Look, as all of the newborn babe is precious in the eyes of the tender mother,[1] as head, face, hands, arms, body, feet, *etc.*, so all of God is very precious in his eyes that has any tender regard of God; and look, as all of a husband is precious in the eyes of a loving wife, *viz.*, his person, name, credit, honour, estate, liberty, life, *etc.*, so all of God is very precious in his eyes that loves God with a real love, with a superlative love. But,

[2.] Secondly, If God be most precious to you, then *all the dishonours that are done to God, his truth, his worship, his ways, his ordinances, his institutions, his government, his people, are most grievous and burdensome to you.* 'The reproaches of them that reproached thee are fallen upon

[1] It was a harlot that would have the child divided, 1 Kings 3:25, 26.

me,' Psa. 69:9; 'I beheld the transgressors, and was grieved;
because they kept not thy word,' Psa. 119:158. The word that
is here translated *grieved* is from *katat*, that signifies to
loathe, abhor, and contend: I beheld the transgressors, and
I loathed them; I beheld the transgressors, and I abhorred
them; I beheld the transgressors, and I contended with
them; but not so much because they were my enemies,
as because they were yours. It is just between God and all
those that have a precious esteem of him, as it is between
two lute strings that are tuned one to another; no sooner
one is struck but the other trembles. A saint cannot see God
struck but his heart will tremble (Jer. 9:1-4).

A father, lying upon his deathbed, called three children to him which he kept, and told them that only one
of them was his natural son, and that the other two were
only brought up by him; therefore to him only he gave all
his goods; but which of those three was his own son he
would not in any wise declare. When he was dead, every
one pleaded his birthright, and the matter being brought to
trial, the judge, for the making, if possible, a true discovery,
took this course. He caused the dead corpse of the father
to be set up against a tree, and commanded the three sons
to take bows and arrows to shoot at their father, to see who
could come nearest to his heart. The first and second did
shoot and hit him, but the third was very much angry and
displeased with them both, and through the natural affection of a child to a father, threw away his bow and arrows,
and would not shoot at all. This being done, the judge
gave this sentence, *viz.*, that the first two that shot at their
supposed father's heart were no sons, but that the third
son, that would not shoot at all, and that was very much

displeased with those that did shoot, was the true son, and that he should have the goods.

O sirs! every bitter word is an arrow shot at the heart of God, and every bloody oath is an arrow shot at the heart of God, and every heavy curse is an arrow shot at the heart of God, and every superstitious custom is an arrow shot at the heart of God, and every snare that is laid for the righteous is an arrow shot at the heart of God, and every yoke that is laid upon the people of God is an arrow shot at the heart of God, and every affront that by debauched persons is given to God is an arrow shot at the heart of God, *etc.* And what true bred sons, what ingenuous sons, can see such arrows every hour in the day shot at the heart of God, and hear of such arrows that are shot a thousand thousand times in a day at the heart of God, and not grieve and mourn, and not be afflicted, troubled, displeased, and astonished to see men and to hear of men that were once made in the image of God to be turned into such incarnate devils, as thus to deal with God, yea, with such a God as can speak them into hell at his pleasure. But,

[3.] Thirdly, If God be most precious to you, then *you will part with anything for God, then you will let go anything, that you may hold your God, and enjoy your God*, Phil. 3:7, 8; Matt. 13:46; then your Isaac shall be made a sacrifice, if God will have it so, Gen. 22, and your Benjamin shall be sent into Egypt, if God will have it so, Gen. 43; then your Jonah shall be cast overboard, if God will have it so, Jon. 1; then out goes the right eye, and off goes the right hand, upon a divine command; then you will never cry out, Oh! this mercy is too near to me to part with for God, and that comfort is too dear to me to part with for God. Oh no; but then you will say, as the king of Sodom said to Abraham, 'Give me the persons, and take the goods to thyself,' Gen. 14:21. So you will say, 'Give us God, oh give us God, and let who will take the goods, let who will take the honours, and the profits, and the pleasures of this world; it is enough that Joseph is alive; it is enough if we may but enjoy our God.' A prince will part with anything rather than he will part with his crown jewels; and so will a Christian rather part with anything, than, upon choice, to part with his God, whom he values above all the crown jewels in the world. But,

[4.] Fourthly, If God be most precious to you, then *you can never have enough of God*; you can never have enough of communion with God; you can never have enough of the presence of God; you can never have enough of the Spirit of God; you can never have enough of the discoveries of God; you can never have enough of the assistance of God; you can never have enough of the secret influences and incomes of God; you can never have enough of the comforts and strong consolations of God, *etc.*[1] The grave, the barren womb, the mammonist,[2] the pope, the Turk, the devil, and hell, will be as soon satisfied as you can be satisfied without clearer, further, and fuller enjoyments of God. 'No man,' says God to Moses, 'can see my face, and live,' Exod. 33:20; upon which words Augustine makes this short but sweet reply, 'Then, Lord, let me die, that I may see your face.' It is impossible that ever a man's heart should rest satisfied till he comes to a full and perfect enjoyment of that which he has set up as his grand interest, as his great all. But,

---

[1] Psa. 27:4; 84:1, 2; 42:1, 2; 63:1-3; Song of Sol. 8:14; Rev. 22:20.
[2] [That is, one devoted to the ideal or pursuit of wealth.]

[5.] Fifthly and lastly, If God be most precious to you, then *you will give up yourself wholly to God without any reservation*. Whatever a man sets up as his great interest, to that he devotes himself, to the service of that he wholly gives up himself; so when a man eyes God as his most precious interest, and sets up God as his most precious interest, he cannot but devote himself wholly to God, he cannot but give up himself wholly to God:[1] Psa. 119:94, 'I am thine, save me.' I am not my own, nor sin's, nor Satan's, nor the world's, nor friends', nor relations', but 'I am thine,' I am really yours, I am wholly yours, I am only yours, I am always yours, I am yours to be sanctified, and I am yours to be saved; I am yours to be commanded, and I am yours to be ruled. Lord, I am your own, and therefore do with your own as you please, and dispose of your own as you please. I am at your foot, willing in some measure to be anything or nothing, as shall seem best in your own eyes. When the keys of the whole house, and of every room in the house, are given up to the king to be at his disposal, at his service, then he is entertained as a king, and honoured as a king, and valued and prized as a king; and so when all the keys of the soul, and every room in the soul, and every faculty of the soul, are given up to God to be at his disposal, at his service, then God is entertained as a God, and honoured as a God, and valued and prized as a God, but not till then.

And by these five hints, if you will not put a cheat upon your own souls, you may know whether God sits in the uppermost room of your hearts or not, and whether God be set up in your hearts above all, and whether he be indeed your great all, or your all in all. But,

[1] Song of Sol. 2:16; Acts 7:2-4; 13:22; Luke 5:5-7.

(9.) Ninthly, If God be your portion, then *there is no loss in all the world that lies so hard and so heavy upon you as the loss of your God*. There is no loss under heaven that so affects and afflicts a man that has God for his portion as the loss of his God. David met with many a loss, but no loss made so sad and so great a breach upon his spirit as the loss of the face of God, the loss of the favour of God: Psa. 30:6, 7, 'In my prosperity I said, I shall never be moved. Lord, by thy favour thou hast made my mountain to stand strong: thou didst hide thy face, and I was troubled.' The Hebrew word *bahal* signifies to be greatly troubled, to be sorely terrified, as you may see in 1 Sam. 28:21, 'And the woman came unto Saul, and saw that he was sore troubled.' Here is the same Hebrew word *bahal*.[1] Saul was so terrified, affrighted, and disanimated with that dreadful news that the devil in Samuel's likeness told him, that his very vital spirits so failed him that he fell into a deadly swoon.

And it was even so with David upon God's hiding of his face. David was like a withered flower that had lost all its sap, life, and vigour, when God had wrapped up himself in a cloud. The life of some creatures lies in the light and warmth of the sun; and so the life of the saints lies in the light and warmth of God's countenance. And as in an eclipse of the sun there is a drooping in the whole frame of nature, so when God hides his face, gracious souls cannot but droop and languish, and bow down themselves before him. Many insensible creatures, some by opening and shutting,

---

[1] And so this Hebrew word *bahal* you have again in Dan. 5:9, to express the greatness of Belshazzar's trouble and terror when he saw the handwriting upon the wall, and when none of his wise men could read the writing, *etc.*

as marigolds and tulips, others by bowing and inclining the head, as the solsequy[1] and mallow flowers are so sensible of the presence and absence of the sun, that there seems to be such a sympathy between the sun and them, that if the sun be gone or clouded, they wrap up themselves, or hang down their heads, as being unwilling to be seen by any eye but his that fills them; and just thus it was with David when God had hid his face in a cloud.

And it is very observable that Job did bear up very sweetly, bravely, patiently, and nobly under all his great losses of children, estate, *etc.*; but when the arrows of the Almighty were got within him, then he complains that his grief was heavier than the sands of the sea, Job 6:1-5; and when the face of God was hidden from him, how sadly he laments and bewails the withdrawings of God: 'Behold, I go forward, but he is not there; and backward, but I cannot perceive him: on the left hand, where he doth work, but I cannot behold him: he hideth himself on the right hand, but I cannot see him,' Job 23:8, 9. You know there is no pain more grievous and tormenting than that of breaking the bones. Now David again and again pitches upon this, to hint to you that dreadful smart and pain that his soul was under when he had lost his communion with God, and when his God was withdrawn from him, and had hid his face from him, Psa. 38:8; 51:8.

And so the church sadly laments the loss of her beloved in Song of Sol. 5:6, 'I opened to my beloved; but my beloved had withdrawn himself, and was gone: my soul failed when he spake,' or, 'he was gone, he was gone.' Now this passionate

[1] The early name of the 'sunflower.' The *solsequium* of Linnaeus.—G.

duplication speaks out her very great grief and trouble. Like a sad widow, she sits down and wrings her hands, and cries out, 'He is gone, he is gone'; 'My soul failed me'; or, as the Hebrew has it, *Naphshi jatsa*, 'my soul went out of me.' I was even as an astonished creature, I was even as a dead creature, to note how greatly and how deeply she was troubled and perplexed upon the account of his withdrawing from her. Oh! the fear, the terror, the horror, the dread, the grief, the sorrow that fell upon the spouse's heart when her beloved had turned his back upon her.

And so it was with Mary: John 20:11-13, 'But Mary stood without at the sepulchre weeping: and as she wept, she stooped down, and looked into the sepulchre, and seeth two angels in white sitting, the one at the head, and the other at the feet, where the body of Jesus had lain. And they said unto her, Woman, why weepest thou? She saith unto them, Because they have taken away my Lord, and I know not where they have laid him.' Of all losses, Mary was least able to bear the loss of her Lord. The loss was so great, and so heavy the loss, that she was not able to stand under it with dry eyes. Mary's mourning for the loss of her Lord was like that of Hadadrimmon in the valley of Megiddon, Zech. 12:11. There is no loss that comes so near to a Christian's heart as the loss of his Lord. A Christian can a thousand times better bear the loss of his name, which next to his soul and his grace is the best jewel that he has in all the world, the loss of his estate, the loss of his liberty, the loss of his nearest and dearest relations, yea, the very loss of his life, than he can bear the loss of his God.

You see how sadly Micah takes on for the loss of his wooden gods, in Judg. 18:23, 24, 'And they cried unto the children of Dan. And they turned their faces, and said unto Micah, What aileth thee, that thou comest with such a company? And he said, Ye have taken away my gods which I made, and the priest, and ye are gone away: and what have I more? and what is that ye say unto me, What aileth thee?' Now if Micah was so affected and afflicted upon the loss of his idol gods, his wooden gods, what cause then have Christians to be deeply affected and afflicted when they come to lose their God, which is the true God, the living God, the only God, and the God of gods! You know that when Samson's locks were cut off, his strength was gone, Judg. 16:19-21; and therefore, though he thought to go out, and do as great things as he had formerly done, yet he found by woeful experience that he could not; for now he was become as another man. And it is just so with the choicest saints: when their God is gone, then locks are cut, and their strength is gone, their doing strength, and their suffering strength, and their bearing strength, and their wrestling strength, and their prevailing strength, *etc.*, is gone when their God is gone; yea, when God goes, all goes. When the king removes, all his train follows; when God goes, comforts go; when God goes, joys go; when God goes, peace goes; when God goes, prosperity goes; when God goes, friends go; when God goes, all content and satisfaction goes; and therefore it is no wonder to see a Christian better bear any loss than the loss of his God, for in losing of him he loses all at a clap.[1] A Christian counts it his only happiness to enjoy his God, and his only unhappiness to be deprived of him. The constant language of a Christian is,

---

[1] *Qui te non habet, Domine Deus, totum perdidit* [He, who does not have you, O Lord God, has lost all].—Bernard.

'None but God, none but God'; as it was once the language of the martyr, 'None but Christ, none but Christ.'

Outward losses to some men have been unsufferably afflictive. One being turned out of his estate runs out of his wits, another hangs himself with the same hands with which he had formerly told his portion. Menippus of Phoenicia having lost his goods, strangled himself. Dinarcus Phidon, at a certain great loss, cut his own throat, to save the charge of a cord. When Henry II heard that his city Mentz was taken, he let fall this blasphemous speech: I shall never, said he, love God any more, that has suffered a city so dear to me to be taken away from me. And Augustus Caesar [Suetonius], in whose time Christ was born, was so troubled and astonished at the loss and overthrow that Varus gave him, that for certain months together he let the hair of his head and beard grow without cutting, and sometimes he would run his head against the very doors, and cry out, Quintilius Varus, deliver up my legions again; Quintilius Varus, deliver up my legions again. I might give you many sad instances nearer home, but that I love not to harp upon so sad a string.

But certainly no outward losses can lie so heavy upon the spirit of a worldling, as the loss of God lies upon the spirit of a saint.[1] I have read of a religious woman, who having brought forth nine children, professed that she had rather endure all the pains of those nine travails at once than endure the misery of the loss of God's presence. A man can better bear any loss than the loss of his box of jewels, and than the loss of his writings and evidences that he has to show for his estate; and therefore, when his house is on

[1] Compare the 77th and the 88th Psalms together.

fire, he does not cry out, Oh save that bed, or that chest, or that dish, or that stool, *etc.*; but he cries out, Oh save my box of jewels! oh save my writings! I care not though all be consumed, so my box of jewels and my evidences be but saved. Now God is a Christian's box of jewels, he is a Christian's grand evidence that he has to show for another world; and therefore his greatest fear is of losing his God, and his greatest care is of keeping his God. If his box of jewels be safe, then all is safe; but if they are lost, all is lost; and how then is it possible for a Christian to bear up bravely under the loss of all? A man may bear up bravely under the loss of his lumber, and under the loss of his household goods, so long as his jewels are safe and his writings are safe; but if his box of jewels should be lost, and his writings should be burnt, why, then, he wrings his hands, and cries out, Oh, I am undone! I am undone! I am undone! So a Christian can bear up bravely under this worldly loss, and that worldly loss, and the other worldly loss, so long as he enjoys his God; but when he has lost his God, oh then, he cannot but wring his hands, and cry out, I am undone! I am undone! I am undone! I have lost my God, and in losing him, I have lost my life, I have lost my love, I have lost my joy, I have lost my crown, I have lost my heaven, I have lost my happiness, I have lost my all. O Christians! if God be your portion, it will be thus with you upon the loss of your God. But,

(10.) Tenthly, If God be your portion, then you will *set the highest price, value, and esteem upon those that have God for their portion*, Psa. 16:3; Prov. 12:26, 28:6. A man that has God for his portion, never values men for their arts, parts, gifts, gay clothes, gold chains; no, nor by their birth, breeding, high offices, or great places; no, nor by their outward dignities, honours, or riches, but by their interest and propriety in God. A man that has God for his portion, prizes a poor ragged Lazarus that has God for his portion, before a rich Dives that has only gold for his portion. If you have God for your portion, then there is no man in court, city, or country, to that man that has God for his portion; then there is no man in a parish, a country, a kingdom, to him that has God for his portion. A man that has God for his portion, has a higher esteem and a greater respect for a Job, though stripped of all, and sitting upon a dunghill, than he has for a wicked Ahab, though sitting on his royal throne. Paul set a higher price upon Onesimus, though but a servant, a slave, because he had God for his portion, than he did upon Nero, though he was a great and mighty emperor, Philem. 10, 12, 17; 2 Tim. 4:17). And king Ingo valued poor ragged Christians that had God for their portion, above all his glittering pagan nobles that had only the world for their portion, saying, that when all his pagan nobles should, in all their pomp and glory, be turned into hell, those poor Christians, that had God for their portion, should be his consorts and fellow princes in heaven.

Look, as men that have their portion in this world value men according to their worldly portions, so that they that have most gold and silver, and they that have most lordships and lands, they are the best men, the happiest men, the only men in their eyes; so a Christian that has God for his portion, he sets the highest value upon those that have God for their portion, and there are no men in all the world that are so high in his books as they are. A man that has an interest in God loves none, nor likes none, nor honours none, nor delights in none, nor exalts none, nor values none, to those that have God for their portion. Though the men, the great men of this world may sit in the uppermost seats at his table, yet they that have God for their portion, sit in the uppermost rooms of his heart. The Jews say, that those seventy souls that went with Jacob into Egypt, were as much worth as all the seventy nations in the world. And I may say, that one soul that has God for his portion, is more worth than all the souls in the world that have only the world for their portion.

A man that has God for his portion, cannot but set a very high value upon all those that have God for their portion, though in disputable things they may differ from him. A man that has God for his portion, had rather live with those that have God for their portion in a prison, in a dungeon, than live with those that have only the world for their portion in a royal palace; as Algerius, an Italian martyr, was accustomed to say, that he had rather live in prison with Cato than with Caesar in the senate house. And Doctor Taylor, the martyr, rejoiced exceedingly that ever he came into prison, because he came there to have acquaintance with that angel of God, John Bradford, as he calls him. When Joseph was in Egypt, the Scripture says, according to the Hebrew phrase, that 'he tied the princes of Pharaoh's court about his heart,' Psa. 105:22; so a man that has God for his portion, he as it were ties those that have God for their portion about his heart. Oh, he is always best when they are most in his eye, and nearest to his heart. It is his happiness on this side happiness to enjoy communion with them, and it is the greatest unhappiness in this world to be separated from them, Psa. 120:5-7. A man that has God for his portion, values the company of such that have God for their portion above all other company in the world, and he values the favour of such above all other men's favour in the world, and he values the prayers of such above all other men's prayers in the world, and he values the counsels of such above all other men's counsel in the world, and he values the experiences of such above all other men's experiences in the world, and he values the interest of such above all other men's interest in the world, and he values the hopes and expectations of such above all other men's hopes and expectations in the world, and he values the examples of such above the examples of all other men in the world, and he values the displeasure and anger of such above all other men's displeasure and anger in the world. But,

(11.) Eleventhly, If God be your portion, *then you are his portion*. If you have an interest in God, then God has an interest in you; if you have a propriety in God, then God has a propriety in you; if God be truly yours, then you are really his: Song of Sol. 2:16, 'My beloved is mine, and I am his'; Psa. 119:94, 'I am thine, save me'; I am not my own, I am not sin's, I am not Satan's, I am not the world's, I am not friends', I am not relations', but I am yours, save me; I am really yours, I am totally yours, I am solely yours, I am everlastingly yours, save me: Ezek. 16:8, 'I entered into a covenant with thee, and thou becamest mine'; Deut. 32:9, 'For the Lord's portion is his people; Jacob is the lot of his inheritance.'[1] Though God's people are despised of the

---

[1] There are none that have that large interest and propriety in the saints that God has: Zech. 2:12, 'And the Lord shall inherit Judah his portion in the holy land, and shall choose Jerusalem again.'

world, yet they are dear to God, for they are his portion. In these words, 'Jacob is the lot of his inheritance,' he alludes to the division of the land of Canaan, as if the sons of Jacob had fallen to him by lot. The Lord's people are as dear to God, and as near to God, and in as great account with God, as earthly portions and inheritances are or can be among the sons of men: Jer. 12:10, 'Many pastors have destroyed my vineyard, they have trodden my portion under foot, they have made my pleasant portion (or as the Hebrew has it, my portion of desire or of delight) a desolate wilderness.' God's people are not only his portion, but they are his pleasant portion, yea, they are his desirable portion, his delightful portion. If the Lord be your portion, then you are his inheritance, Isa. 19:25; and his peculiar treasure, Exod. 19:5; and his glory, Isa. 46:13; and his ornament, Ezek. 7:20; and his throne, Jer. 17:12; and his diadem, Isa. 62:3; and his jewels, Mal. 3:17. These scriptures speak out plainly and clearly that great propriety and interest that God has in all those that have a propriety and interest in him.

O sirs! look, that as in all God has you have an interest, so in all that you have God has an interest; and look, as what God is, he is for you, so what you are, you are for God; and look, as God is sincerely for you, so you are sincerely for God; and as God is wholly for you, so you are wholly for God; and as God is only for you, so you are only for God; and as God is in all things for you, so you are in all things for God; and as God is at all times for you, so you are at all times for God.

O sirs! There are none under heaven that have that interest in you as God has, if indeed he be your portion. Look what interest the head has in the members, the husband in the wife, the father in the child, the lord in his servant, the general in his soldier, and the prince in his subject, that, all that, and more than that, has God in all those that have an interest in him. There is no man in the world that has such an interest in himself, as God has in him, if indeed God be his portion. Sin cannot say to a man that has God for his portion, You are mine; nor Satan cannot say to a man that has God for his portion, You are mine; nor the world cannot say to a man that has God for his portion, You are mine; nor the creature cannot say to a man that has God for his portion, You are mine. It is only God that can say to such a man, You are mine. As in marriage, none can say, This woman is mine, but the husband; so none can say to a man that has God for his portion, You are mine, but God alone. Look, as no man can truly say, that God is my Lord, and my God, and my father, and my friend, and my wisdom, and my counsel, and my righteousness, and my consolation, and my salvation, and my portion, and my light, and my life, and my love, and my rock, and my fortress, and my deliverer, and my strength, and my buckler, and my high tower, and my help, and my happiness, and my blessedness, and my all in all, but he that has God for his portion; so none but God can look upon a gracious person, and say, This gracious person is mine; he is my bride, my child, my friend, my favourite, my beloved, my darling, my joy, my crown; his heart is set upon me, and his love is inflamed towards me, and his trust and confidence is fixed on me, and his desires and longings are running out after me, and all his joys and delights are terminated in me. But,

(12.) Twelfthly, If God be your portion, then certainly *the least of God is very dear and precious to you*. Oh then the least truth of God will be very precious to you, and the least command of God will be very precious to you, and the least child of God will be very precious to you, and the least concernment of God will be very precious to you. Look, as the least beam of light is precious, and as the least drop of honey is precious, and as the least dust of gold is precious, and as the least degree of health and strength is precious, and as the least measure of liberty is precious; so the very least of God is very precious to that man that has God for his portion. Look, as every little piece and parcel of a worldly man's portion is very dear and precious to him, so every little piece and parcel of God, if I may so speak, is very dear and precious to him that has God for his portion. The least glimpse and manifestations of the love and favour of God, the least taste of the mercies of God, the least anointings of the Spirit of God, the least communications of the grace of God, and the least drops of the consolations of God, are exceedingly sweet and precious to him that has God for his portion. The least good look that a man has from God, and the least good word that a man hears from God, and the least love letter and love token that a man receives from God, is exceedingly precious to that man that has God for his portion, 'One day in thy courts is better than a thousand elsewhere,' Psa. 84:10. He does not say, One year in your courts is better than a thousand elsewhere, but '*One day* in thy courts is better than a thousand elsewhere'; nor does he not say, One quarter of a year in your courts is better than a thousand elsewhere, but '*One day* in thy courts is better than a thousand elsewhere'; nor he does not say, One month in your courts is better than a thousand elsewhere, but '*One day* in thy courts is better than a thousand elsewhere'; to show that the very least of God is exceeding precious to a gracious soul that has God for his portion.

Now by these twelve particulars you may all know whether God be your portion or not, except you are resolved beforehand to put a cheat upon your own immortal souls, and so to make yourselves miserable in both worlds. And let thus much suffice for this use of trial and examination.

Question 2:
How Shall We Show the World that
God Is Our Portion?

Now if, upon trial and examination, any of you shall come to some comfortable satisfaction in your own spirits, that God is your portion, and that you have an undoubted interest and propriety in God, oh then I would upon the knee of my soul entreat and beseech you, I might say, charge and command you, to evidence and declare to all the world your interest and propriety in God.

But you will say, How should we evidence and declare to the world our interest and propriety in God? we are willing to do it, if we did but know how we should do it. Why then, thus:

(1.) First, Evidence and declare your interest and propriety in God, *by your labouring and endeavouring with all your might to draw on others to get an interest and propriety in God.*[1] O sirs! have you been convinced of the necessity and excellency of interest and propriety in God? have you experienced the profit, the sweet, the comfort, and the happiness of propriety and interest in God? and how then can you but strive, as for life, to persuade others to look after their interest and propriety in Christ, as the one thing necessary? When Samson had tasted honey, he gave

[1] Num. 10:29; John 1:39-49; 4:28-30; Acts 10:24-27.

his father and mother some with him, Judg. 14:8, 9. O my brethren, propriety and interest in God is so sweet a morsel, that I cannot see how it is possible for a man to taste of it and not to commend it to others. They that have tasted that the Lord is gracious, cannot but cry out with the psalmist, 'Oh taste and see that the Lord is good,' Psa. 34:8. Propriety and interest in God will never make a man a churl,[1] it will never work a man to make a monopoly of so rare a jewel as that is. Oh the fervent prayers! Oh the burning desires! Oh the vehement wishes! Oh the strong endeavours of such that have an interest and propriety in God, to draw on others to seek after an interest and propriety in God!

All true propriety and interest in God is of a diffusive nature; it is like light, that will spread itself over all; it is like leaven, that will run through all; it is like Mary's box of sweet ointment, that filled all the house with its sweet scent. If you are a minister, evidence your propriety in God in doing all you can to provoke those that are under your charge to secure their propriety in God; other things cannot be secured, but propriety in God may be secured, Acts 26:29. If you are a magistrate that has a propriety in God, evidence it by doing all you can, by your commands, and by your counsel, and by your example, and by your prayers, to persuade and win others over to be restless till they have secured their interest and propriety in God (Josh. 24:15). If you are a father that has interest and propriety in God, oh, then, let your soul be still in travail for your children, till Christ be formed in them, till they are new born, and till they have experienced the power and sweet of propriety and interest in God. But,

[1] [That is, a rude and mean-spirited person.]

(2.) Secondly, Evidence your propriety and interest in God, *by keeping far off from all such sinful courses, practices, and compliances, that may in any way put yourselves or others to question the truth of your propriety and interest in God.* Thus did those worthies, 'of whom this world was not worthy,' in Heb. 11. It is very observable that when the holy things belonging to the sanctuary were to be removed, God commanded Aaron and his sons that there should be a special care had to cover them all over, lest in journeying dust should in any way soil them, Num. 4:5-13. O beloved! it highly concerns you that have an interest and propriety in God, to look narrowly to your hearts, words, works, and ways, and to see that there be such a covering of grace and holiness, such a covering of care, fear, wisdom, watchfulness, and circumspection over your whole man, that no scandalous sins, pollutions, or defilements be found upon you; according to that exhortation of the apostle, in Phil. 2:15, 'That ye may be blameless and harmless, the sons of God, without rebuke, in the midst of a crooked and perverse nation, among whom ye shine (or shine ye) as lights in the world.' Rev. 14:3-5; 3:4.

I have read of the dove, that there is such a native dread of the hawk implanted in her, that she is afraid of every feather that has grown upon a hawk, and that she so detests and abhors the very sight of any such feather that she will fly from it, and keep at the greatest distance imaginable from it. And shall not that divine fear, O Christians! that is planted by the hand of the Spirit in your hearts, be of as great force and prevalency to keep your souls from all those enormities and wicked compliances that may in the least occasion you or others to question your propriety and interest? Remember Francis Spira,[1] and tremble! You know a scrivener[2] may by one great blot at last spoil all that he has done for many days before upon a large patent or lease; so a man may by one foul blot, by one enormous crime, by one wretched act of compliance, dash and obliterate the fairest copy of a virtuous life, and raze out all the visible golden characters of divine graces that once seemed to be printed upon the soul. Look, as one drop of ink colours a whole glass of water, so one gross sin, one shameful action, one hour's compliance with anything of antichrist, will colour and stain all the great things that ever you have suffered, and all the good things that ever you have performed; it will stain and colour all the good prayers that ever you have made, and all the good sermons that ever you have heard, and all the good books that ever you have read, and all the good words that ever you have spoke, and all the good works that ever you have done. And therefore, whatever you do, keep off from sin, and keep off from all sinful compliances, as you would keep off from hell itself. But,

(3.) Thirdly, Declare and evidence your propriety and interest in God, *by maintaining and keeping up the sense*

[1] [An eminent lawyer living near Venice in the Reformation period (16th century). He turned from Romanism, accepted the Protestant faith, but later apostatized and died in despair in 1548. His Life was published in Geneva in 1550, John Calvin supplying a preface. John Bunyan was deeply impressed by what happened to Spira. The man in the iron cage in the Interpreter's House in The Pilgrim's Progress undoubtedly represents him.]

[2] [A scrivener (or scribe) was a person who could read and write or who wrote letters to court and legal documents. Scriveners were people who made their living by writing or copying written material.]

of your interest and propriety in God, in opposition to all other interest whatsoever. Maintain your interest in God in opposition to sin's interest, and in opposition to Satan's interest, and in opposition to the world's interest, and in opposition to antichrist's interest, and in opposition to all carnal and superstitious interests, Psa. 63:1; Rev. 14:1-4: as Moses did, and as Joshua and Caleb did, and as Mordecai and Nehemiah did, and as Daniel and the three young men did, and as the apostles and the primitive Christians did. Certainly the heart of a gracious man cannot but rise, and his anger and indignation cannot but swell, against every thing and every interest that threatens to make a breach upon his interest and propriety in God, Psa. 69:9.

A man that has an interest and propriety in God, in the midst of all oppositions, is like a man made up all of fire, walking in stubble and straw: he overcomes and consumes all oppositions, and all difficulties are but whetstones to his fortitude. He encourages his soul in the face of all oppositions and dangers, as Hezekiah once did his soldiers in 2 Chron. 32:7, 8, 'Be strong and courageous, be not dismayed for the king of Assyria, nor for all the multitude that is with him: for there be more with us than with him. With him is an arm of flesh; but with us is the Lord our God to help us, and to fight our battles. And the people rested themselves upon the words of Hezekiah king of Judah.' He is a fool, we say, that will be laughed out of his coat; but certainly he is a fool in folio that will be laughed out of his skin, nay, out of his soul, out of his profession, out of his eternal salvation; but doubtless such fools as these have never experienced the sweet of propriety and interest in God.

Without a doubt, there were many broad jests and many bitter scoffs broken upon Noah, whilst he was building of his ark. The people laughed at him, and derided him, and thought the poor old man doted and dreamed, not, as we say, of a dry summer, but of a wet winter; but yet Noah's propriety and interest in God being clear, Noah begins his work, and goes on his work, and never ceases till he had finished that work that God had set him about.

Alciat observes in one of his Emblems, that a dog barks most when the moon is at fullest; but whether it be by some special influence that it then works on the dog, or whether it be occasioned by the spots in the moon represented unto him in the form and shape of another dog, I shall not conclude; but yet let the dog bark never so much, the moon will run her course. She will walk her station securely through the heavens, though all the dogs in the town bark never so fiercely at her; so a man that has an interest and propriety in God, and knows it, he is like the moon, he will hold on his course heavenwards and holinesswards, though all the lewd and debauched wicked wretches in city and country should bark at him, and deride him, and oppose him, and speak all manner of evil against him. Propriety and interest in God will make a man set light by all such paper shot, yea, it will carry him through the pikes, not only of evil tongues, but it will also carry him through the most fierce and eager opposition that either Satan himself, or any of his instruments, can possibly raise against him. But,

(4.) Fourthly, Declare and evidence your propriety and interest in God, *by your sweet and noble carriage and deportment towards those that have an interest and propriety in God*. Look, as a child carries it in a different way to his father to what he does to others, so you must carry it in a different way towards those that have an interest and propriety in God, to what you do towards those that have no interest nor propriety at all in God. Though a wife be very kind and courteous to all comers and goers, yet she carries it in a very different way to her husband from what she does to all others; she carries it with a great deal more kindness, and sweetness, and tenderness, and familiarness, and nobleness, *etc.*, towards her husband, than she does towards others, whether they be friends or strangers; and just thus should you carry it towards those that have a propriety and interest in God.

I have not faith enough to believe that such men have any interest and propriety in God, who carry it very strangely, and proudly, and churlishly, and scornfully, and deridingly, and tyrannically, and disdainfully, and enviously, and maliciously, and rigorously, and sourly, and bitterly, towards those that have an interest and propriety in God, and yet carry it at the same time very fairly, and sweetly, and courteously, *etc.*, towards such wretches that have no interest or propriety in God at all, yea, to such that blaspheme his name, and that profane his Sabbaths, and that pollute his ordinances, and that trample upon his mercies, and that despise his warnings, and that are given up to their own hearts' lusts, and that live as if there were neither God, nor heaven, nor hell. But,

(5.) Fifthly, Evidence your interest and propriety in God, *by doing such things for God, which such as have no interest in God cannot do, nor will not do, nor have no heart nor mind to do*. Evidence your interest in God, by doing singular things for God, Matt. 5:44-48; by doing such things for God that are above their reach that have no interest nor propriety in God at all; as by denying yourselves, your sinful selves, your natural selves, and your religious selves; and by keeping a singular guard upon your own hearts, words, and ways; and by stepping over the world's crown to take up Christ's cross, as Moses did, Heb. 11:24; and by lessening yourselves to greaten Christ, as John did, John 3:30-32; and by lifting up of Christ above your lusts, above yourselves, above the world, above outward privileges, above your performances, above your arts, parts, and gifts, as Paul did, Phil. 3:7-9; and by blessing a taking God as well as a giving God, as Job did, Job 1; and by rejoicing and glorying in all the afflictions and sufferings that befall you for Christ's sake and the gospel's sake, as the apostles and primitive Christians did; and by choosing to suffer rather than to sin, as those worthies did 'of whom this world was not worthy'; and by keeping of yourselves from the defilements, pollutions, and abominations of the times, as some in Sardis did, Rev. 3:4; and by following of the Lamb wherever he goes, as those 144,000 did, who had their Father's name written in their foreheads, Rev. 14:1-5. O sirs! it is infinitely better not to challenge any interest or propriety in God at all, than to pretend high as to interest and propriety in God, and yet to do no more for God, nay, it may be not so much, than they that have no interest nor propriety in God at all. But,

(6.) Sixthly and lastly, Evidence your interest and propriety in God, *by falling roundly in with the interest of God, in opposition to all carnal interests in the world*. O sirs! the interest of God will by degrees eat out and swallow up all other interests in the world. Look, as Pharaoh's lean cows ate up the fat, Gen. 41:4, and as Aaron's rod swallowed up the Egyptians' rods, Exod. 7:11, 12, so the interest of God will in time eat up and swallow up all that superstitious carnal worldly antichristian and Satanical interest that men labour now to uphold, with all their might, Isa. 8:9, 10. Dan. 2:35, 'Then was the iron, the clay, the brass, the silver, and the gold, broken to pieces together, and became like the chaff of the summer threshing-floors; and the wind carried them away, that no place was found for them: and the stone that smote the image became a great mountain, and filled the whole earth.' Verse 44, 'And in the days of these kings shall the God of heaven set up a kingdom, which shall never be destroyed: and the kingdom shall not be left to other people, but it shall break in pieces, and consume all these kingdoms, and it shall stand for ever.' And so chapter 7:27, 'And the kingdom and dominion, and the greatness of the kingdom under the whole heaven, shall be given to the people of the saints of the most High, whose kingdom is an everlasting kingdom, and all dominions shall serve and obey him.' Rev. 17:12-14, 'And the ten horns which thou sawest are ten kings, which have received no kingdom as yet; but receive power as kings one hour with the beast. These have one mind, and shall give their power and strength unto the beast. These shall make war with the Lamb, and the Lamb shall overcome them: for he is Lord of lords, and King of kings; and they that are with him are called, and chosen, and faithful.' If these scriptures do not clearly evidence, that the interest of Christ shall swallow up all other interests, I understand nothing.

Now mark, the people of God are the interest of God, and the gospel of God is the interest of God, and the ordinances of God are the interest of God, and the institutions and pure worship of God are the interest of God, *etc.* And therefore, all you that have an interest and propriety in God, evidence it by your ready and resolute falling in with the interest of God. Believe it, they that fall in with the interest of God, shall fall in with the strongest side, and will be sure to carry it against ten thousand worlds. What is the stubble to the flames? what is weakness to strength? what is impotency to omnipotency? what is folly to wisdom? what is emptiness to fulness? No more are all the carnal interests in the world to the interest of God; and therefore thrice happy is that man that falls timely and cordially in with the interest of God.

But now, if upon trial and examination any of you shall find that yet the Lord is not your portion, and this I believe will be the case of many of you, I would exhort all such persons to labour with all their might, yea, to labour as for life, to get the Lord to be their portion. O sirs! this is the one thing necessary, this is the sun among the stars, this is the work of works that lies upon your hands; when this is done, all is done; till this be done, there is nothing done that will do you good in another world. O sirs! your lives lie upon it, your souls lie upon it, eternity lies upon it, your all lies upon it; and therefore you had need be restless till you have gained the Lord to be your portion.

Incitements to See that God Is Our Portion

Now, that I may the more effectually provoke you, and stir you up to this great and glorious, this necessary and weighty work, give me leave to propose these following considerations.

(1.) First, *Consider that your present portion, your present condition, is but miserable and cursed*, Lev. 26:14-39, Deut. 28:15-68. All the earth was cursed upon man's fall, and till fallen man comes to be interested in God, all his earthly enjoyments are cursed unto him; his honours are cursed, and his riches are cursed, and his preferments are cursed, and his pleasures are cursed; the whole portion of his cup is nothing but a little cursed vanity: Job 20:23-29, 'When he is about to fill his belly, God shall cast the fury of his wrath upon him, and shall rain it upon him while he is eating. He shall flee from the iron weapon, and the bow of steel shall strike him through. It is drawn, and cometh out of the body; yea, the glistering sword cometh out of his gall: terrors are upon him. The increase of his house shall depart, and his goods shall flow away in the day of his wrath. This is the portion of a wicked man from God, and the heritage appointed unto him by God.' And so chapter 24:18, 'He is swift as the waters; their portion is cursed in the earth: he beholdeth not the way of the vineyards.' Prov. 3:33, 'The curse of the Lord is in the house of the wicked.' Mal. 2:2, 'If ye will not hear, and if ye will not lay it to heart, to give glory unto my name, saith the Lord of hosts, I will even send a curse upon you, and I will curse your blessings: yea, I have cursed them already, because ye do not lay it to heart.' There is a real curse and a secret curse, an invisible curse and an insensible curse, that lies upon all their souls that have not God for their portion: Gal. 3:10, 'Cursed is every one that continueth not in all things which are written in the book of the law to do them.' And as there is a curse upon all their souls, so there is a curse upon all their comforts, contentments, and enjoyments, that enjoy not God for their portion. Till a man comes to enjoy God for his portion, all his earthly portions are cursed unto him; but when a man comes to enjoy God for his portion, then all his earthly portions are blessed unto him.

O sirs! there is no mitigating of the curse, there is no reversing of the curse, there is no altering of the curse, nor there is no taking of the curse from off your souls, nor from off your earthly portions, but by gaining God to be your portion. O sirs! you will live accursed, and you will die accursed, and you will appear before God accursed, and you will be judged and sentenced by God accursed, and you will be sent to hell accursed, and you will remain to all eternity accursed, if God be not your portion: and therefore oh how should this consideration awaken every sinner to give God no rest till he has given himself as a portion to him. But,

(2.) Secondly, *Consider this, that there is yet a possibility of attaining God to be your portion*, Luke 18:27. All the angels in heaven, and all the men on earth, do not know to the contrary but that God may be your portion, even yours. If you are but heartily willing to be divorced from that wicked trinity, the world, the flesh, and the devil, there is no doubt but that God will be your portion.

O sirs! why has God laid open so clearly and so fully the nature and incomparable excellency of this portion above all other portions before you, but to persuade your hearts, and to draw out your souls to look after this portion, and to make sure this portion, as that in which all your happiness and blessedness lies? Oh that you were wise to consider that now a prize, an opportunity, is put into your hands, that may make you for ever! You have all the ways, and all the means, and all the helps, and all the advantages imaginable for the obtaining of God to be your portion; so that, if God be not your portion, I shall be so bold to tell you that your destruction is from yourselves, Hos. 13:9.

O sirs! though God be a golden mine, yet he is such a mine that may be come at if you will but dig, and sweat, and take pains to purpose, Prov. 2:2-7; though he be a pearl of infinite price, yet Christ can purchase this pearl for you; though he be a matchless and incomparable portion, yet he is such a portion as may be yours, as will be yours, if you are not lacking to your own souls. Why has God sent his ambassadors early and late? 2 Cor. 5:18-20; and why has he, even to a miracle, continued them amongst you to this very day, but that they should acquaint you with his wonderful readiness and willingness to bestow himself as a portion upon you?

O sirs! God is said to be a God of great mercy, and to be rich and plenteous in mercy, and to be abundant in mercy, and to be transcendent and incomparable in mercy; yea, all the mercies of God are sure mercies, they are royal mercies, they are innumerable mercies, they are bottomless mercies, they are unchangeable mercies, and they are everlasting mercies; and therefore there is no reason for any man to despair of obtaining God for his portion.[1] But,

(3.) Thirdly, *Consider that God is a portion-sweetening portion.* God is such a portion as will sweeten all other portions; he is a portion that will make every pleasant portion more pleasant, and that will make every bitter portion sweet. Poverty is one man's portion, and sorrow is another man's portion, and crosses and losses are a third man's portion, and reproaches and sufferings are a fourth man's portion, and sickness and diseases are a fifth man's portion, *etc.* But now God is a portion that will sweeten all these portions. You know the tree that Moses cast into the bitter waters of Marah made them sweet, Exod. 15:23-25. Now this tree was a type of Christ, who will certainly sweeten all our bitterest potions. The church complained in Lam. 3:15, 'that God had filled her with bitterness' (or, as the Hebrew has it, 'with bitternesses'), 'and that he had made her drunken with wormwood': and yet this very consideration, that 'the Lord was her portion,' verse 24, sweetened all. If God be your portion, there is no condition that can make you miserable; if God be not your portion, there is no condition that can make you happy. If God be not your portion, in the midst of your sufficiency you will be in straits; if God be your portion, in the midst of all your straits you shall enjoy an all-sufficiency in an all-sufficient God, Job 20:22. Till God be your portion, O sinner, you will never taste anything but death and bitterness in all your comforts, and in all your contentments, and in all your enjoyments. But,

[1] Psa. 105:8; Eph. 2:4; Psa. 86:15; 1 Pet. 1:1, 3; Psa. 103:11.

(4.) Fourthly, *Consider that all earthly portions are not of that infinite consequence and concernment to you as this portion is.* All earthly portions are but the meat that perishes, John 6:27; they are but motheaten and canker-eaten treasures, Matt. 6:19; James 5:3; they are full of uncertainty, yea, they are all over vanity, Eccles. 1:2; they reach not beyond the line of this mortal life; they can neither suit the soul, nor fill the soul, nor satisfy the soul, nor save the soul; they can neither change the heart, nor reform the heart, nor in the least better the heart; they can neither arm a man against temptations, nor lead a man out of temptations, nor make a man victorious over temptations; they can neither direct the conscience when it is in straits, nor relieve the conscience when it is under distress, nor support the conscience when it is under guilt, nor heal the conscience when it is under wounds; they can neither make our peace with God, nor keep our peace with God, nor augment our peace with God; they can neither bring us to Christ, nor unite us to Christ, nor keep us with Christ, nor transform us into the similitude or likeness of Christ; they can neither bring us to heaven, nor fit us for heaven, nor assure us of heaven. In a word, no earthly portion can free us from death, nor in the least avail us in the day of wrath. By all which it is most evident that all earthly portions are of very little consequence and concernment to the sons of men, to the souls of men.

Oh, but now God is a portion of infinite consequence and concernment to all the sons and souls of men. No man can hear as he should, nor pray as he should, nor live as he should, nor die as he should, till God be his portion; no man is secure from temporal, spiritual, or eternal judgments, till

God be his portion. No man can be happy in this world, or blessed in another world, till God be his portion. O sirs! it is not absolutely necessary that you should have this or that earthly portion, but it is absolutely necessary that you should have God for your portion; for if God be not your portion, all the angels in heaven, nor all the men on earth, cannot prevent your being miserable to all eternity.

(5.) Fifthly, *Consider, that till a man comes, to have God for his portion, he never comes to be temptation-proof.* A man that has God for his portion is temptation-proof; he will say when tempted, as Themistocles did, Give those bracelets to slaves; and as Basil did, who, when he was offered temporary honour, glory, and wealth, *etc.*, answered, Give me glory which abides for ever, and give me riches which will endure for ever; and as he did, who, being tempted with offers of money to desert his religion, gave this excellent answer, Let not any think that he will embrace other men's goods to forsake Christ, who has forsaken his own proper goods to follow Christ;[1] and as that martyr did, who, when he had riches and honours offered him, if he would recant, answered, Do but offer me something that is better than my Lord Jesus Christ, and you shall see what I will say to you; and as Hormisda, a nobleman in the king of Persia's court, did, who, because he would not deny Christ, he was put into ragged clothes, deprived of his honours, and set to keep the camels; after a long time, the king seeing him in that base

[1] When Pyrrhus tempted Fabricius the first day with an elephant, so huge and monstrous a beast, as before he had not seen, and the next day with money and promises of honour, he answered, I fear not your force, and I am too wise for your fraud. If nature could do this, grace can do more.

condition, and remembering his former fortunes, he pitied him, and caused him to be brought into the palace, and to be clothed again like a nobleman, and then persuaded and tempted him afresh to deny Christ, whereupon this noble spirit presently rended his silken clothes, saying, If for these you think to have me deny my faith, take them again; and so he was cast out with scorn a second time. And what was that that made the apostles temptation-proof, and that made those worthies temptation-proof, Heb. 11, and that made the primitive Christians temptation-proof, and that made the martyrs in Queen Mary's days temptation-proof? Certainly, nothing more than this very consideration, that God was their portion.

Ah! sinners, sinners, you will certainly fall, you will readily fall, you will easily fall, you will frequently fall, you will dreadfully fall before temptations, till you come to enjoy God for your portion. Every blast and every wind of temptation will overset and overturn that man that has not God for his portion. Such a man may pray a thousand times over and over, 'Lord, lead me not into temptation,' and yet every day fall before the least temptation, as common experience abundantly evidences; whereas a man that has God for his portion will stand fast like a rock in all storms, yea, in the face of all temptations he will be like mount Zion, that cannot be removed.

Luther counsels every Christian to answer all temptations with this short saying, '*Christianus sum*,' I am a Christian; and I would counsel every Christian to answer all temptations with this short saying, 'The Lord is my portion.' O Christian, when Satan or the world shall tempt you with honours, answer, 'The Lord is my portion'; when they shall tempt you with riches, answer, 'The Lord is my portion'; when they shall tempt you with preferments, answer, 'The Lord is my portion'; and when they shall tempt you with the favours of great ones, answer, 'The Lord is my portion'; yea, and when this persecuting world shall threaten you with the loss of your estate, answer, 'The Lord is my portion'; and when they shall threaten you with the loss of your liberty, answer, 'The Lord is my portion'; and when they shall threaten you with the loss of friends, answer, 'The Lord is my portion'; and when they shall threaten you with the loss of life, answer, 'The Lord is my portion.' O sirs! if Satan should come to you with an apple, as once he did to Eve, tell him that 'The Lord is your portion'; or with a grape, as once he did to Noah, tell him that 'The Lord is your portion'; or with a change of raiment, as once he did to Gehazi, tell him that 'The Lord is your portion'; or with a wedge of gold, as once he did to Achan, tell him that 'The Lord is your portion'; or with a bag of money, as once he did to Judas, tell him that 'The Lord is your portion'; or with a crown, a kingdom, as once he did to Moses, tell him that 'The Lord is your portion.' But,

(6.) Sixthly and lastly, If God *be not your portion, you will be miserable to all eternity.* If God be not your portion, wrath must be your portion, hell must be your portion, everlasting burnings must be your portion, a devouring fire must be your portion, and a separation for ever from the glorious presence of God, Christ, angels, and 'the spirits of just men made perfect,' must be your portion; as you may clearly see by comparing the Scriptures in the margin together.[1] If God be not your portion in this life, you shall

[1] Psa. 11:6; 9:17; Isa. 33:14; Matt. 24:51; 2 Thess. 1:7-10; Heb. 12:22-24.

never have him for your portion in another life; if God be not your portion here, he will never be your portion hereafter. O sirs! if death should surprise you before God is your portion, you will as certainly go to hell, as God is in heaven; and therefore it infinitely concerns you to get God for your portion. There is no way in the world to make the king of terrors to be a king of desires to your soul, O man, but by gaining God for your portion. Of all terribles, death will be most terrible and formidable to that man that has not God for his portion. If you should live and die, O man, without having God for your portion, it had been good for you that you had never been born; and if the day of your birth had been the day of your death, your hell would not have been so hot as now you will certainly find it.

But now, I think, I hear some crying out, O sirs! what shall we do that we may have God for our portion? Oh, had we as many worlds at our disposal as there be stars in heaven, we would give them all that we might have God for our portion. Oh we now see that we can never be happy except God be our portion, yea, we now see that we shall be miserable to all eternity, except God be our portion; and therefore what shall we do that we may have God for our portion?

How to Make God Our Portion

Well then, if you would indeed have God for your portion, let me thus advise you;—

(1.) First, *Labour to be very sensible,*[1] *that by nature you are without God, yea, at enmity with God, and alienated from the life and love of God, and that by nature you are children of wrath and disobedience, and in actual arms and rebellion against the great God.*[2] O sirs, never talk of having God for your portion, till you come to see yourselves without God, and till you come to judge yourselves unworthy of God. Every man in his natural estate is afar off from God three manner of ways (Acts 2:39).

First, In point of opinion and apprehension.

Secondly, In point of fellowship and communion.

Thirdly, In point of grace and conversion.

And till a man comes to be sensible of this, he will never desire God to be his portion. But,

(2.) Secondly, If you would have God for your portion, then *you must trample upon all other portions in comparison of God.*[3] Luther protested that God should not put

[1] [That is, able to sense or feel.]

[2] Eph. 2:12; Rom. 8:7; Eph. 2:1, 2; 4:18.

[3] Augustine prays, Lord, he says, whatever you have given, take it all away, only give my yourself.

him off with the poor things of this world. Oh, go to God, and say, Lord, you have given me a portion in money, but this money is not yourself; you have given me a portion in lands, but these lands are not yourself; you have given me a portion in goods, but these goods are not yourself; you have given me a portion in jewels, but these jewels are not yourself; and therefore give me yourself, and I shall say I have enough. Lord, had I all the world for my portion, yet I should be miserable for ever in that other world, except you bestow yourself as a portion upon my soul. O Lord, give me but yourself, and take away what you please. Oh give me but yourself, and take away all, strip me of all, and I shall with Job sit down and bless a taking God as well as a giving God. Oh go to God, and tell him, with a humble boldness, that though he has given you many good things, yet all those good things will do you no good except he bestow himself upon you as the only good. Oh tell him that he is the first good; tell him that he is the original of all good; tell him that he is the greatest good, the noblest good; tell him that he is a superlative good; tell him that he is a universal good; tell him that he is an unchangeable good; tell him that he is an eternal good; and tell him that he is the most soul-suitable and soul-satisfying good. And therefore tell him that you cannot tell how to live one day without him; yea, that you know not how to be happy one hour without him. But,

(3.) Thirdly, If you would have God for your portion, then *of all precious promises, of all golden promises, plead that most*, Zech. 13:9, 'They shall call upon my name, and I will hear them: I will say, It is my people: and they shall say, The Lord is my God.' O sirs! as ever you would have the great and glorious God for your portion, plead out this noble promise cordially with God; plead it out affectionately, plead it out fervently, plead it out frequently, plead it out believingly, plead it out resolutely, plead it out incessantly. O sirs! This choice promise is a hive full of heavenly honey, it is a paradise full of sweet flowers, it is a breast that is full of the milk of consolation; and therefore be still sucking at this breast, be still pleading of this promise; follow God with this promise early and late, follow him with this promise day and night, follow him with this promise as the importunate widow followed the unjust judge (Luke 18:1-8), and give him no rest till he has made it good to your souls that he is your God, and that he is your portion, and that he is your salvation, and that he is your all in all. Oh tell him that above all things in this world your hearts are set on this, to have God to be your God, to have God to be your portion. Oh tell him that you cannot, tell him that you dare not, tell him that you may not, and tell him that you shall not, be satisfied with anything without God, with anything below God, with anything on this side God, with anything but God; and therefore humbly entreat him, and earnestly beseech him, to be your God, and to be your portion. But,

(4.) Fourthly, If you would have God for your portion, then *you must be willing to be his portion.*[1] God is resolved upon this, that he will be no man's portion that is not willing to be his. You must make a resignation of yourselves to God, if ever you would enjoy an interest in God; you must be as willing to be his people, as you are willing to have him to be your God; you must be as much at God's disposal as

[1] Deut. 32:9; Jer. 12:10; Zech. 2:12.

earthly portions are at your disposal, or else there will be no enjoying of God to be your God. God will engage himself to none that are not willing to engage themselves to him. He that will not give his hand and his heart to God, shall never have any part or portion in God. O sirs! As ever you would have God for your portion, it highly concerns you to give up yourselves to God with highest estimations, and with most vigorous affections, and with utmost endeavours, according to that precious promise, Isa. 44:5, 'One shall say, I am the Lord's; and another shall call himself by the name of Jacob; and another shall subscribe with his hand to the Lord, and surname himself by the name of Israel.' God stands upon nothing so much as the giving up of yourselves to him, nor is he taken with nothing so much as the giving up of yourselves to him.

I have read of Æschines, who, seeing his fellow scholars give great gifts, *viz.* gold, silver, and jewels, to his master Socrates, and he being poor, and having nothing else to bestow, he gave himself, which the philosopher most kindly accepted, esteeming this present above all those rich and costly presents that his scholars had presented to him, and accordingly in love and sweetness he carried it toward him. So there is nothing that God accepts, loves, likes, and esteems, like the giving up of a man's self unto him. This is a present that God prefers above all the gold, silver, and sparkling jewels in the world. Well, sirs, remember this, such as are not as willing to say, Lord, we are yours, as they are to say, Lord, you are ours, such shall never have God for their portion. But,

(5.) Fifthly, If you would have God for your portions, then *you must take up Christ in your arms, and treat with*

God upon the credit of Christ. There is no acquaintance with God, there is no reconciliation to God, there is no union nor communion with God, there is no readmission into the presence and favour of God, without a mediator.[1] God out of Christ is incomprehensible, God out of Christ is exceeding terrible, an absolute God is a consuming fire, Heb. 12:29; and therefore says Luther, *Nolo Deum absolutum,* let me have nothing to do with God himself. The blood of Christ, the blood of the covenant, is that, and only that, that can cement, reunite, and knit God and man together. Themistocles, understanding that king Admetus was highly displeased with him, took up his young son into his arms, and treated with the father, holding his darling in his bosom, and thereby appeased the king's wrath.

O sirs! The King of kings is offended with you, and upon the account of your sins he has a very great controversy with you. Now, there is no way under heaven to pacify his wrath, and turn away his displeasure from you, but by taking up Christ in your arms, and by presenting all your suits in his name. There is no angel in heaven, nor no saint on earth, that can, or that dares, to interpose between an angry God and poor sinners. It is only Christ, the Prince of peace, that can make up a sinner's peace with God, Isa. 9:6. John 14:6, 'Jesus saith unto him, I am the way, the truth, and the life: no man cometh unto the Father, but by me.' There is no way to the Father but by the meritorious blood of the Son; there are none that can stand between everlasting burnings and us but Christ, Isa. 33:14. 'You shall not see my face except you bring your brother Benjamin with you,' said Joseph to his brethren, Gen. 43:3, 5. So says God, Sinners, sinners, you

[1] Eph. 2:16; Heb. 2:17; Col. 1:20; Eph. 1:6, 7.

shall not see my face except you bring Jesus with you, except you bring Christ in your arms; you shall never see my face with joy, you shall never see my face and live. There is a writ of vengeance that is issued out of the court of heaven against poor sinners, and except Christ steps in, they will certainly fall under an eternal arrest, and be thrown into everlasting perdition and destruction. But,

(6.) Sixthly, If you would have God for your portion, then *you must break your league with sin*. You must fall out with sin, if ever you fall in with God. Sin and you must be two, or God and you can never be one. There is no propriety to be had in God, except your hearts rise against that which first disunited and disjointed you from God. Sin and you must part, or God and you can never meet. You shall as soon make an accommodation between light and darkness, heaven and hell, noon and midnight, 2 Cor. 6:14-18, as ever you shall be able to make an accommodation between God and sin. So long as sin remains ours, God will be none of ours. No prince will be one with that subject that lives in the practice of treason and rebellion against him.[1] No prince will be one with him that has killed his only son and heir, and that daringly continues to hold up those bloody weapons in his hands wherewith he has committed that horrid fact. There is no adulteress that can be so shamelessly impudent, or so vainly confident, as to desire pardon of her jealous husband, or to expect a oneness and a sweetness with him, whilst she continues to hold her wanton lovers still in her

---

[1] Pharnaces sent a crown to Caesar at the same time that he rebelled against him, but he returned the crown and this message back: *Faceret imperata prius*, let him return to his obedience first.

arms, and is fully resolved to hold on in her wanton dalliances as in times past.

O sirs! God is that prince that will never admit of peace or union with you till you cease practising treason against him, and till you come to lay down your weapons of rebellion at his feet; he is that jealous husband that will never take you into a oneness, into a nearness and dearness with himself, till you come to abandon all your wanton lovers, and thoroughly to resolve against all wanton dalliances for time to come. If ever you would have God for your portion, you must say to all your wanton lovers, and to all those idols of jealousy that you have set up in your souls, as Ephraim once said to his, 'Get you hence, for what have I any more to do with you?' Hos. 14:8. But,

(7.) Seventhly and lastly, If you would have God for your portion, then *you must wait upon him in the use of all holy means*.[1] In the use of holy means, God makes the clearest, the fullest, and the choicest discoveries of himself; in the use of holy means, poor sinners come to be acquainted with the excellency of God, and with the necessity of having God for their portion; in the use of holy means, poor sinners come to understand the fulness of God, the goodness of God, the graciousness of God, the sweetness of God, and the wonderful freeness, readiness, and willingness of God to give himself as a portion to all such as see their need of him, and that are heartily willing to receive him as their

[1] In my former treatise I have spoken very largely about the use of holy means, especially in my last on 'Holiness,' and therefore a touch here must suffice. [The reference is to his 'Crown of Holiness,' Brooks' largest work, which forms vol. 4 of our (1861–7) edition.—G.]

God and portion; and in the use of holy means God works in poor sinners a readiness, a forwardness, and a blessed willingness to choose God for their portion, to close with God for their portion, to embrace God for their portion, to accept God for their portion, and to own God for their portion. If this question should be put to all the saints in heaven, *viz.*, How God came to be their portion? they would all answer, By waiting upon him in the use of all those holy ways and means that he had appointed for that purpose; and if the same question were put to all the saints on earth that have God for their portion, they would all give the same answer. O sirs! As ever you would have God for your portion, it highly concerns you to wait patiently upon him in the use of all holy means. He that is in the use of holy means is in the way of obtaining God for his portion. But he that casts off the use of the means, he says in effect, I will not have God for my portion, I care not to have God for my portion; let me but have the world for my portion, and let who will take God for their portion.

To prevent mistakes, before I close up this direction, remember that by the use of holy means, I only mean such means that God himself has appointed, commanded, instituted, and ordained. As for those means that are of men's inventing, devising, prescribing, commanding, and ordaining, a man may wait till doomsday in the use of them, before ever he will gain God for his portion; and therefore they are rather to be declined, yea, detested and abhorred, than any way to be owned, minded, or used by any that would have God for their portion. Look, as all the worshippers of Baal got nothing by all their wailing and crying out from morning to night, 'O Baal, hear us! O Baal, hear us!'

1 Kings 18, so they that wait upon God in invented and devised worship will never get anything by all their waiting; no, though they should wait from morning to evening, and from evening to morning, and cut and lance themselves till the blood gush out, as those foolish worshippers of Baal did. And therefore, as ever you would have God for your portion, be sure that you wait upon him only in his own ways, and in the use of his own means. And thus I have done with the use and application of the point.

Objections Answered

So that I have now nothing to do but these two things:

First, To answer a few objections that poor sinners are apt to make against their own souls, and against their enjoying of God for their portion; and,

Secondly, To lay down a few positions that may be of singular use to all such that have God for their portion. I shall begin with the objections.

Obj. 1. I think I hear some poor sinners ready to object and say, O sir! *you have pressed us by many motives to get God for our portion, and we stand convinced in some measure by what you have said, that God is a most excellent, transcendent, glorious portion; but we very much question whether ever God will bestow himself as a portion upon such great, such grievous, such notorious, and such infamous sinners as we are.*

Now to this objection, I shall return these answers.

[1.] First, *God is a free agent, and therefore he may give himself as a portion to whom he pleases.* Men may do with their own as they please, and so may God do with himself as he pleases. Look, as men may give earthly portions to whom they please, so God may give himself as a portion to what sinners he pleases. God is as free to bestow himself upon the greatest of sinners, as he is to bestow himself upon the least of sinners. But,

[2.] Secondly, I answer, *That the Lord has bestowed himself as a portion upon as great and as grievous sinners as you are*, Psa. 68:18. Adam, you know, fell from the highest pinnacle of glory into the greatest gulf of misery, and yet God bestowed himself as a portion upon him, Gen. 3:15. And Manasseh was a sinner of the greatest magnitude, 2 Kings 21, his sins were of a scarlet dye, they reached as high as heaven, and they made his soul as black as hell; for witchcraft, sorcery, cruelty, idolatry, and blood, he was a nonsuch,[1] 2 Chron. 33; he sold himself to work all manner of wickedness with greediness; he did more wickedly than the very heathen, whom the Lord abhorred; in all his actings he seemed to be the firstborn of Satan's strength; and yet the Lord freely bestowed himself as a portion upon him: and so, Ezek. 16:6, 8, 'When I passed by thee, and saw thee polluted in thine own blood, I said unto thee when thou wast in thy blood, Live; yea, I said unto thee, when thou wast in thy blood, Live. Now when I passed by thee, and looked upon thee, behold, thy time was a time of love; and I spread my skirt over thee, and covered thy nakedness: yea, I swore unto thee, and entered into a covenant with thee, saith the Lord God, and thou becamest mine.'

And so, Isa. 46:12, 13, 'Hearken unto me, ye stout-hearted, that are far from righteousness: I bring near my righteousness; it shall not be far off, and my salvation shall not tarry: and I will place salvation in Zion for Israel my glory.' Solomon, Mary Magdalene, Matthew, Zacchaeus, the jailor, and the murderers of Christ, were all very great and grievous sinners, and yet the Lord bestowed himself as a portion upon them; and so God bestowed himself as

[1] [That is, he was unequalled.]

a portion upon those monstrous and prodigious sinners that are mentioned in 1 Cor. 6:9-11, whose souls were red with guilt, and as black as hell with filth. God has been very good to those that have been very bad; and therefore do not despair, O sinner, though thy sins are very great.

I have read a story concerning a great rebel, that had made a great party against one of the Roman emperors, and proclamation being sent abroad, that whoever could bring in the rebel, dead or alive, he should have a great sum of money for his reward; the rebel hearing of it, comes, and presenting himself before the emperor, demands the sum of money proposed: the emperor, thinking to himself, concludes, that if he should put him to death, all the world would be ready to say that he did it to save his money; and so he freely pardoned the rebel, and gave him the money. Here now was light in a dark lantern, here was rare mercy and pity in a very heathen. And shall a heathen do thus, and shall not the great God, who is made up of all loves, of all mercies, of all compassions, of all goodnesses, and of all sweetnesses, do much more? Certainly he will. If the greatest rebels, if the greatest sinners will but come in whilst the white flag of grace and mercy is held forth, they shall find a marvellous readiness and forwardness in God, not only to pardon them, but also to bestow, not only money, but himself as a portion upon them. The greatest sinners should do well to make that great Scripture their greatest companion: Psa. 68:18, 'Thou hast ascended on high,' speaking of Christ, 'thou hast led captivity captive: thou hast received gifts for men; yea, for the rebellious also.' But to what purpose has Christ received gifts, spiritual gifts, gracious gifts, glorious gifts for men, for the rebellious?

Why, it is 'that the Lord God may dwell amongst them.' But,

[3.] Thirdly, I answer, *That God has given out an express promise, that he will make such to be his people which were not his people.* Hos. 2:23, 'I will have mercy upon her that had not obtained mercy; and I will say to them which were not my people, Thou art my people; and they shall say, Thou art my God.' In this precious promise God has engaged himself to have a most sweet harmony, and a most intimate conjunction and communion with such a people as were not his people. But,

[4.] Fourthly, I answer, *That God gains the greatest glory by bestowing himself as a portion upon the greatest sinners.* There is nothing that makes so much for the glory of free grace, and for the exaltation of rich mercy, and for the praise of divine goodness, and for the honour of infinite fulness, as God's bestowing himself upon the greatest of sinners. O sirs! grace appears never so rich, nor never so excellent, nor never so glorious, as when it triumphs over the greatest sins, and when it falls upon the greatest sinners. Grace never shines, nor never sparkles, nor never becomes so exceeding glorious, as it does when it lights upon the hearts of the greatest sinners. The greatest sins most and best set off the freeness and the riches of God's grace. There is nothing that makes heaven and earth to ring and to sound out his praises, so much as the fixing of his love upon those that are most unlovely and uncomely, and as the bestowing of himself upon them that have given away themselves from him.

And it is further observable, that the greatest sinners, when once they are converted, commonly prove the choicest saints, and the rarest instruments of promoting the honour and glory of God in the world. The Canaanites were a wicked and a cursed generation; they were of the race of cursed Ham; they were given over to all whoredom, witchcraft, and cruelty; they offered their sons and daughters to devils; they were the very worst of sinners; they were without God and without the covenant, and counted dogs among the Israelites; and such a one was the Canaanite woman, that you read of in Matt. 15:21-29, till the Lord made it the day of his power upon her soul; but when the Lord had brought her in to himself, ah, what a rare Christian did she prove, for wisdom, zeal, humility, self-denial, love, courage, patience, faith, *etc.*

And so Mary Magdalene was a notorious strumpet, a common whore, among all the harlots none compared to Mary Magdalene,[1] and she was one out of whom Christ cast seven devils (Mark 16:9); and yet when she was changed and converted, oh, with what an inflamed love did she love the Lord Jesus Christ! and with what a burning zeal did she follow after the Lord Jesus! and how abundant was she in her lamenting and mourning after the Lord Jesus Christ! Some report, that after our Saviour's resurrection, she spent thirty years in weeping for her sins in Galba.

And Paul, you know, was a very grievous sinner, but after his conversion, oh what a rare, what an eminent, what a glorious instrument was he in bringing of souls to Christ, and of building up of souls in Christ! Oh what a noble drudge was he for Christ! Oh how frequent! Oh how fervent! Oh how abundant was he in the work of the Lord,

[1] One cannot pass so very strong statements without remarking that there is not the slightest ground for them.—G.

etc. And indeed, in all ages, the greatest sinners, when once they have been converted, they have commonly proved the choicest saints, and the rarest instruments in the hand of God for the advancement of his glory, and the carrying on of his work in the world. I might instance in Luther, and various others, but that I hasten to a close. And therefore,

[5.] Fifthly, I answer, that of all sinners *the greatest sinners undoubtedly stand in the greatest need of having God for their portion.* Look, as they that are most wounded stand in most need of a surgeon, and as they that are most sick stand in most need of a physician, and as they that are in most danger of robbing stand in most need of assistance, and as they that are in most peril of drowning stand in most need of a boat, and as they that are most impoverished stand in most need of relief, so they that are the greatest sinners stand in most need of having God for their portion; for no tongue can express, nor no heart can conceive the greatness of that wrath, of that indignation, of that desolation, of that destruction, and of that damnation that attends and waits upon those great sinners that have not God for their portion, 2 Thess. 2:7-9; and therefore the greater sinner you are, the greater obligation lies upon you to get God to be your God and portion; for till that be done, all your sins, in their full number, weight, guilt, and aggravating circumstances, will abide upon your soul. But,

[6.] Sixthly and lastly, I answer, *that God is a great God, and he loves to do like himself.* Now, there are no works, no actions that are so suitable to God, and so pleasing to God, and so delightful to God, as those that are great; and what greater work, what greater action can the great God do, than to bestow himself as a portion upon the greatest of sinners? It was a great work for God to create the world, and it is a great work for God to govern the world, and it will be a great work for God to dissolve the world, and to raise the dead; and yet doubtless it is a greater work for the great God freely to bestow himself upon the greatest sinners. The love of God is a great love, and the mercies of God are great mercies, and the compassions of God are great compassions, and accordingly God loves to act; and therefore there is ground for the greatest sinners to hope that the Lord may bestow himself as a portion upon them. But,

Obj. 2. Secondly, Others may object and say, *Hereafter we will look after this portion; for the present we are for living in the world, we are for a portion in hand, we are for laying up portions for ourselves, and providing portions for our posterity.* We are first for laying up of earthly treasures, and when we have done that work to purpose, then we will do what we can to obtain this excellent and glorious portion that you have been so long discoursing on, *etc.* Now, to this objection I shall thus answer,

[1.] First, Thus to act is *to run counter-cross to Christ's express commands*: Matt. 6:33, 'But seek ye first the kingdom of God, and his righteousness; and all these things shall be added unto you';[1] and so verses 19, 20, 'Lay not up for yourselves treasures upon earth, where moth and rust doth corrupt, and where thieves break through and steal: but lay up for yourselves treasures in heaven, where neither moth nor rust doth corrupt, and where thieves do not break through nor steal.' And so in John 6:27, 'Labour not for the

---

[1] The Greek word προστιθήσεται *prostithēsetai* signifies a casting in as an overplus, as some overweight, measure, or number.

meat that perisheth, but for the meat which endureth for everlasting life.' O sirs! To act or run cross to God's express commands, though under pretence of revelation from God, is as much as a man's life is worth, as you may see in that sad story, 1 Kings 13:24. O sirs! it is a dangerous thing to neglect one of his commands, who by another is able to command your bodies into the grave, and your souls into hell at his pleasure. Shall the wife make conscience of obeying the commands of her husband? and shall a child make conscience of obeying the commands of his father? and shall the servant make conscience of obeying the commands of his Lord? and shall the soldier make conscience of obeying the commands of his general? and shall the subject make conscience of obeying the commands of his prince, though he be none of his council? and will not you make conscience of obeying his commands that is the prince of the kings of the earth? (Rev. 1:5). But,

[2.] Secondly, *Who but children, madmen, and fools in folio, will pitch upon a less good, when a greater good is offered to them?* What madness and folly is it for men to pitch upon bags of counters, when bags of gold are laid before them! or for men to choose a hundred pounds per annum for life, when rich inheritances and great lordships are freely offered to be made over to them for ever?[1] What were this but, Esau-like, to prefer a mess of pottage before the birth-right? and yet this is the present case of these objectors. God is that rich, that great, that glorious, and that matchless portion that is held out, and freely offered and tendered in the gospel to poor sinners, and they neglect, slight, and reject this blessed offer, and fix their choice, their love,

[1] Children, madmen, and fools, will part with a pearl for a pippin.

their hearts, their affections, upon the perishing vanities of this world. Oh the folly of such, that at a feast feed upon kickshaws,[1] and never taste of those substantial dishes that are for nourishment! Oh the madness of such that prefer the fleshpots of Egypt before the dainties of Canaan! Would not such a merchant, such a tradesman be pointed at, as he goes along the streets, for a fool or a madman, that should neglect such a season, such an opportunity, such an advantage, in which he may be made for ever, as to the world, and all because he is resolved first to secure such a bargain of rags, or such a bargain of old shoes, which will turn out but little to his advantage when he has bought them? Surely yes. Now this is the very case of the objectors, for they neglect the present seasons, the present opportunities of grace and mercy, and of being made happy for ever, by enjoying God for their portion, and all because they are resolved first to secure the treasures, the rags of this world. Certainly, in the great day of account, these will be found the greatest fools that have fooled away such golden opportunities, that were worth more than all the world, and all to secure the rags of the world. But,

[3.] Thirdly and lastly, *How many thousands are now in hell! How many thousands have now their part and their portion in that burning lake, which burns with fire and brimstone for ever and ever! Who thought when they were on earth, that after they had laid up goods for many years with the fool in the Gospel, that then they would look after heavenly treasures, and secure God for their portion; but before they could find time or hearts to set about so noble a work, divine*

---

[1] [That is, a fancy but insubstantial cooked dish, especially one of foreign origin.]

*vengeance has overtaken them, and justice has cut the thread
of their lives, and given them their portion among hypocrites,*
Matt. 7:22, 26, 27, Rev. 21:8. Ah! How many are there that
have died in the time of their earthly projects and designs,
before they ever have set about that great work of securing
God for their portion, Luke 12:15, 22; and how many thousands are there, that God in his just judgment has given up
to insatiable desires of earthly things, Phil. 3:18, 19, and to
a cursed endless covetousness all their days! Some write of
the crocodile, that it always grows, that it has never done
growing; and just so it is with the desires of worldly men,
they always grow, they have never done growing. Now they
are for one thousand, then for ten, then for twenty, then for
forty, then for a hundred thousand; now they are for this
lordship, and then they are for that; now they are for this
good bargain, and then they are for that; their hearts grow
every day fuller and fuller with new desires of further and
greater measures of earthly things; they please themselves
with golden dreams, till they awake with everlasting flames
about their ears, and then they fall, cursing themselves that
they have made gold their confidence, and that they have
neglected those golden seasons and opportunities in which
they might have secured God for their portion. But,

Obj. 3. Thirdly, Others may object and say, *We would
fain*[1] *have God for our portion, and we would willingly apply
ourselves to all those ways and means by which we might
obtain the Lord to be our portion but we are poor unworthy
wretches.* Surely the Lord will never bestow himself as a
portion upon such miserable unworthy ones as we are! We

---

[1] [That is, gladly, willingly.]

are worthy of death, we are worthy of wrath, we are worthy of hell, we are worthy of damnation, but we are in no way worthy of having God for our portion. Did ever the Lord cast an eye of love upon such unlovely and such unworthy sinners, lepers as we are? *etc*. Now to this objection I shall return these answers:

[1.] First, *Though you have no merits, yet God is rich and abundant in mercy*.[1] Your sins, your unworthiness can but reach as high as heaven, but the mercies of God reach above the heavens: Psa. 103:11, 'For as the heaven is high above the earth, so great is his mercy toward them that fear him.' Psa. 108:4, 'For thy mercy is great above the heavens: and thy truth reacheth unto the clouds.' The highest comparisons which the world will afford are not sufficient to express the greatness of God's mercy to poor sinners. Though the heavens are exceeding high above the earth, yet the mercies of God to his poor people are above the heavens. But,

[2.] Secondly, I answer, *that the Lord has never bestowed himself as a portion upon any yet but unworthy ones*. David was as unworthy as Saul, and Job as Joab, and Peter as Judas, and Paul as Simon Magus; and the publicans and harlots that entered into the kingdom of heaven were as unworthy as the publicans and harlots that were shut out of the kingdom of heaven, Matt. 21:31, 32; and the thief that went to paradise was as unworthy as the thief that went to hell. All the saints in heaven, and all the saints on earth, are ready with one joint consent to declare that they were as unworthy as the most unworthiest, when God first bestowed himself as a portion upon them. This objection, I am unworthy, is a very unworthy objection, and therefore away with it. But,

[1] 2 Cor. 4:15; 1 Tim. 1:14; 1 Pet. 1:3.

[3.] Thirdly, I answer, *That God, has nowhere in all the Scripture required any personal worthiness to be in the creature, before he will bestow himself upon the creature.* O sirs! it never came into the thoughts of God, it never entered into the heart of God, to require of men that they should be first worthy of his love before they should enjoy his love, and that they should be first worthy of his mercy before they should taste of his mercy, and that they should be first worthy of his goodness before they should be partakers of his goodness, and that they should be first worthy of himself, before he would bestow himself as a portion upon them. If we should never enjoy God for our portion till we are worthy to enjoy him for our portion, we should never enjoy him. If a man had as many eyes as Argus to search into the Scripture, and as many hands as Briareus to turn over the leaves of Scripture, yet he would never be able to find out one text, one line, yea, one word, in which God requires a personal worthiness in the creature before he gives away himself to the creature. Should God stand upon a personal worthiness to be in the creature before he would look upon the creature, or before he would let out his love to the creature, or before he would extend mercy or pity to the creature, or before he would, in a covenant of free grace, give himself to the creature, no sinner could be saved; man would be forever undone, and it had been good for him that he had never been born. But,

[4.] Fourthly, I answer, *it is not men's unworthiness, but men's unwillingness, that hinders them from having God to be their portion.* Though most men pretend their unworthiness, yet there is in them a secret unwillingness to have God for their God. When they look upon God as a gracious

God, then they are willing to have him to be their God; but when they look upon God as a holy God, then their hearts fly back. When they look upon God as a merciful God, and as a bountiful God, oh then they wish that he were their God; but when they look upon God as a commanding God, and as a ruling and an overruling God, oh then their hearts secretly rise against God. There is a real unwillingness in the hearts of sinners in all respects to close with God, and to have God to be their God: 'Who hath believed our report? and to whom is the arm of the Lord revealed? Isa. 53:1; 'I have spread out my hands all the day unto a rebellious people, which walketh in a way that was not good, after their own thoughts; A people that provoke me to anger continually to my face,' Isa. 65:2, 3; 'How long, ye simple ones, will ye love simplicity? and the scorners delight in scorning, and fools hate knowledge? Turn you at my reproof: behold, I will pour out my Spirit upon you, I will make known my words unto you. Because I have called, and ye refused; I have stretched out my hand, and no man regarded; but ye have set at nought all my counsel, and would none of my reproof; I also will laugh at your calamity; I will mock when your fear cometh,' *etc.* Prov. 1:22-26; 'For thus saith the Lord God, the Holy One of Israel; In returning and rest shall ye be saved; in quietness and in confidence shall be your strength: and ye would not,' Isa. 30:15.

O sirs! Men shall be damned at last, not for *cannots*, but for *will nots*, Matt. 23:37. No man shall be damned because he could not do better, but because he would not do better, Luke 13:34. If there were no will, there would be no hell. At last sinners will find this to be their greatest hell, that they have wilfully destroyed themselves. This is that which will damn with a witness, and this will be that never-dying worm: I might have had Christ and grace, but I would not; I might have been sanctified and saved, but I would not; I might have been holy and happy, but I would not; life and death have been often set before me, and I have chosen death rather than life, Deut. 30:15, 19; heaven and hell have been often set before me, and I have chosen hell rather than heaven; glory and misery have been often set before me, and I have chosen misery rather than glory; and therefore it is but just that I should be miserable to all eternity. No man, no devil, can undo you, O sinner, without yourself; no man can be undone in both worlds but by himself; no man shall be damned for his unworthiness, but for his unwillingness; and therefore never plead this objection more. But,

[5.] Fifthly and lastly, I answer, *that if you will not seek after the Lord to be your portion till you are worthy to enjoy him as your portion, then you will never seek after him, then you will never enjoy him for your God and portion.* Personal worthiness is no flower that grows in nature's garden. No man is born with a worthiness in his heart, as he is born with a tongue in his mouth. It is not the full, but the empty; it is not the rich, but the poor in spirit; it is not the righteous, but the sinner; it is not the worthy, but the unworthy soul, that is the proper object of mercy and pity. The poor publican that cried out, 'Lord, be merciful to me a sinner,' Luke 18:10-15, went home justified, when the thank-God Pharisee returned as proud as he came. The centurion, when he came to Christ, sped well, notwithstanding his personal unworthiness, Matt. 8:5-13. And the prodigal son sped well when he returned to his father, notwithstanding his personal unworthiness; for he was readily accepted, greatly pitied, sweetly embraced, courteously received, and very joyfully and nobly entertained. Witness the best robe that was put upon his back, and the gold ring that was put on his finger, and the shoes that were put on his feet, and the fatted calf that was killed to make the company merry, Luke 15:11-32.

O sirs! If in the face of all your unworthiness you will go to God, and tell him that you are sinners, that you are vile sinners, that you are wretched sinners, that you are very great sinners, yea, that you are the greatest of sinners, and that you have deserved a thousand deaths, a thousand hells, a thousand destructions, and a thousand damnations, and earnestly beseech him to look upon you, and to bestow himself upon you, though not for your worthiness's sake, yet for his name's sake, for his mercy's sake, for his promise's sake, for his covenant's sake, for his oath's sake, and for his Son's sake. Certainly if you shall thus plead with God, all the angels in heaven, and all the men on earth, cannot tell to the contrary, but that you may speed as well as ever the centurion or the prodigal did. I have taken the more pains to answer this objection, that so it may never have a resurrection more in any of your hearts into whose hands this treatise may fall.

I know other objections might be raised, but because I have spoken largely so much in my former writings, I shall pass on to the last thing proposed, and that is, to lay down some positions that may, by the blessing of God, be of singular use to the Christian reader.

Positions that May Be Useful

First Position. As, first, *That it is one thing for a man to have God for his portion, and it is another thing for a man to have an assurance in his own soul that God is his portion.*[1] There are many that have God for their portion who yet are full of fears and doubts that God is not their portion. Thus it was with Asaph in Psalm 77, and thus it was with Heman in Psalm 88, and thus it is with very many Christians in these days. Sometimes God exercises his children with such changeable and such terrible dispensations, as raises many fears and doubts in them about their interest and propriety in God. And sometimes their secret indulging of some bosom idol,[2] their entertainment of some predominant lust, raises strange fears and jealousies in their souls about their interest in God. And sometimes their not closing with the Lord so closely, so fully, so faithfully, so universally, and so sincerely as they should, without any secret reservation, raises many doubts and questions in them whether God be their portion or no. The graces of many Christians are so weak, and their corruptions are so strong, and Satan is so busy with them, and their duties and performances are so weak, so flat, so dull, so sapless, so lifeless, so fruitless, and so inconstant, that they are ready at every turn to say,

[1] Moses' face did shine, and yet he did not see it.
[2] [That is, fondly cherished idol.]

If God be our God, why is it thus with us? If God be our portion, why are our hearts in no better a frame? why have our duties no more spirit, life, and fire in them?

Look, as the sun may shine and yet I not see it; and as the husband may be in the house, and yet the wife not know it; and as the child may have a very great portion, a very fair estate settled upon him, and yet he not understand it; so a Christian may have God for his portion, and yet for the present he may not see it, nor know it, nor understand it: 1 John 5:13, 'These things have I written unto you that believe on the name of the Son of God; that ye may know that ye have eternal life, and that ye may believe on the name of the Son of God.' These precious souls had God and Christ for their portion, and they did believe, and they had eternal life in the seeds and beginnings of it, and in the promise, and in Christ their head, who, as a public person, had taken possession of it in their steads, and yet they had not the assurance of these things in their own souls, Eph. 2:6.

Look, as the babe that has passed the pangs of the first birth does not presently cry out, My father, my father, so the babe of grace, the newborn Christian, does not presently cry out, My God, my God. It is one mercy for God to be my God, and it is another mercy for God to tell me that he is my God; it is one act of grace for God to be my portion, and it is another act of grace for God to tell me that he is my portion. Look, as fire may be hid under ashes for a time, and as bits of gold may be hid in a heap of dust for a time, and as stars may be hid in a dark night for a time, and as a pearl may be hid in a puddle for a time, so God may be a man's portion, and yet this may be hid from him for a time.

Second Position. The second position is this, *That it is one thing for a man to have God for his portion, and another thing for a man clearly and convincingly to make it out to himself or others, that God is his portion.* Doubtless there are many thousands that have God for their portion, who yet, if you would give them a thousand worlds, are not able to make it out to their own or others' satisfaction, that God is their portion.[1] Most Christians attain to but small measures of grace. Now small things, little things, are hardly discerned, they are hardly made out. A little faith is next to no faith, and a little love is next to no love, and a little repentance is next to no repentance, and a little zeal is next to no zeal, and a little hope is next to no hope, and a little holiness is next to no holiness, and a little communion with God is next to no communion with God, and a little conformity to God is next to no conformity to God. Now where there is but a little grace, there it is very difficult for a man to make out the truth of his grace, and so, by consequence to make out the truth of his interest and propriety in the God of grace. It is not grace in truth, but grace in strength that will enable a man to make it out to himself, and to make it out to others, that God is his portion. It is not grace in its sincerity, but grace in its sublimary, in its high and eminent actings, that will enable a man to make it out to himself and others, that God is indeed his God.

---

[1] God sometimes lays such a law of restraint upon the noble faculties of men and women, that they cannot use them at some times as they do at others, as you may clearly see by comparing these scriptures together, Luke 24:14-16, *etc.*; Acts 22:9; Gen. 21:16, 19; John 20:14, 15, *etc.*

Besides, many precious hearts have such weak heads, and such bad logic, and such shallow natural parts,[1] that they are not able rationally nor divinely to argue the case with their own souls, nor to make an improvement of those rules, helps, ways, and means, by which they might be enabled to make it out to themselves and others, that God is their portion. Look, as many persons have often a good title to such and such lands, and to such and such estates and inheritances, though they are not able for the present to clear up their title either to themselves or others; so many of the dear children of God have a good title to God, and a real interest and propriety in God, and yet for the present they are not able to clear up their title to God, nor to clear up their interest and propriety in God, either to themselves or others. And this is so great a truth, that all the faithful ministers of Jesus Christ that deal with poor souls, and that are conversant about souls, are ready from their daily experience to avouch it before all the world. He that shall say, that such have not God for their portion, will certainly condemn the generation of the just.

Third Position. The third position is this, *That where there is a hearty willingness in any man to accept God to be his God, to own God for his God, and to close with God as his God, there God is certainly that man's God*, Isa. 55:1, 2, John 7:37, 38. If there be a cordial willingness in you to take God to be your God, then without all peradventure God is your God. A sincere willingness to accept God to be your God is accepted of God, and is sufficient to enter into a gracious covenant

---

[1] [That is, faculties, capabilities, as in 'a man of many parts,' a man who is capable of doing many things.]

with God. O sirs! a sincere willingness to accept God to be your God, flows from nothing below the good will and pleasure of God. No power below that glorious power that made the world, and that raised Christ from the grave, is able to raise a sincere, a hearty willingness in man to accept God to be his God, and to take God for his God: Psa. 110:3, 'Thy people shall be willing,' or willingnesses, in the abstract and in the plural number, 'in the day of thy power, in the beauties of holiness.' There is no power below the power of the Lord of hosts, that can raise up a willingness in the hearts of sinners. It is not in the power of all the angels in heaven, nor of all the men on earth, to beget a sincere willingness in the heart of man to accept God to be his God. This is work that can only be effected by an omnipotent hand.

Though an emperor may force a woman to marry him that is his slave, because she is his purchase, yet he cannot by all his power force her will; he may force her body to the action, but he cannot force her will to the action. The will is always free, and cannot be forced. But God is that great emperor that has not only a power to marry the soul, which he has redeemed from being Satan's bond-slave, but also a power to make the soul that is unready ready, and that is unwilling willing, to marry him, and to bestow itself freely upon him. If there be in you, O man, O woman, a sincere willingness to take God upon his own terms to be your God, that is, to take him as a holy God, and as a ruling God, and as a commanding God, in one thing as well as another, then he is certainly your God: Rev. 22:17, 'And the Spirit and the bride say, Come. And let him that heareth say, Come. And let him that is athirst, come; and whosoever will, let him take the water of life freely.'

Fourth Position. The fourth position is this, *That it may so fall out, that such a Christian that has God for his portion, that has an interest and a propriety in God, may lose the sight, the sense, the feeling and the evidence of his interest and propriety in God*; and this is evident by comparing the scriptures in the footnote together.[1] Doubtless it is very rare to find a Christian that has had the knowledge, and experience, and evidence of his interest and propriety in God, but that Christian also has experienced what it is to have his interest and propriety in God clouded and darkened. Such Christians that have experienced what the warm beams of the Sun of righteousness mean, have likewise experienced what it is to have their sun set in a cloud; and this truth I might make good, by producing a cloud of witnesses, both from among the martyrs and from among the saints of all ages. But what do I talk of a cloud of witnesses, when the tears that daily drop from many of your eyes, and the sad complaints, and sighs, and groans of many of your souls, sufficiently evidence this sad truth. And therefore let no man conclude that God is not his God, because he has lost the sight and sense of his interest and propriety in God; let no man say, that God is not his portion, because he has lost those evidences, at the present, by which he has formerly proved God to be his portion.

Though a man should lose his writings and evidences that he has to show for such and such an estate, yet his writings and evidences being enrolled in a court of record, his estate remains good, and his title is still good in law; and therefore there is no reason why such a man should sit down, and

[1] Psa. 30:6, 7; 51:13; Job 16:9; 19:10; Job 30:20; Psa. 77; 88; Isa. 8:17; Lam. 3:18.

wring his hands, and cry out, I am undone, I am undone; so though a Christian should lose his writings, his evidences that once he had to show, that once he had to prove God to be his God and portion, and that he had a real interest and propriety in God, yet his writings, his evidences being enrolled in the court of heaven, his title to God, his interest in God remains good; and therefore there is no reason why such a person should sit down dejected, and wring his hands, and cry out, Oh I am undone, I am for ever undone.

Fifth Position. The fifth position is this, *That such that have not, for the present, God for their portion, ought not peremptorily to conclude that they shall never have God for their portion.* Such a person that cannot yet truly say that the Lord is his portion, ought not to despair of ever having God for his portion. The time of a man's life is but a day, and God may bestow himself as a portion upon man in what hour of that day he pleases. In the parable, he bestowed himself as a portion upon some at the first hour, upon others at the third hour, upon others at the sixth hour, upon others at the ninth hour, and upon others at the eleventh hour, Matt. 20:1-17. God is a free agent, and may bestow himself upon whom he pleases, and as he pleases, and when he pleases. There is no sinner, no, not the greatest sinner living under the gospel, that can infallibly determine that God will never be his God.[1] No sinner can conclude that God has peremptorily and absolutely excluded him from mercy, and shut him out among those that he is resolved never to bestow himself upon. For,

---

[1] We except such that have committed the sin against the Holy Ghost.

1. God never made any sinner one of his privy council.

2. In the gospel of grace God has revealed no such thing.

3. Secret things belong only to the Lord (Deut. 29:29).

4. God has bestowed himself as a portion upon as great sinners as any they are that yet have not God for their portion.

5. All the angels in heaven, and all the men on earth, cannot tell to the contrary, but that God may have thoughts of mercy towards you, and that your lot may fall within the purpose of his grace, and that he may bestow himself as a portion upon you before you are cut off from the land of the living. Although a sinner may certainly know at the present that God is not his God, that God is not his portion, yet he does not certainly know that God will never be his God, that God will never be his portion; and therefore no sinner may peremptorily conclude that God will never be his God, because for the present he cannot, he dares not say he is his God.

God gave himself as a portion to Abraham when he was old, when he was a white-headed sinner, Gen. 12:4. And Manasseh was old when he was converted and changed, and when God bestowed himself upon him, 2 Chron. 33:1, 11-13. And Zacchaeus and Nicodemus were called and converted in their old age. When there were but a few steps between them and the grave, between them and eternity, between them and everlasting burnings, then the Lord graciously revealed himself, and bestowed himself as a portion upon them. And if we believe Tertullian, Paul wanted not a prediction of the Holy Spirit in that prophetic blessing of dying Jacob to his youngest son: Gen. 49:27, 'Benjamin shall ravin as a wolf: in the morning he shall devour the prey, and at night he shall divide the spoil.' Paul was of the tribe of Benjamin, in the morning, the fore part of his age, worrying and devouring the flock of Christ, persecuting the church; and in the evening, the declension of his life, dividing the word, a doctor of the nations.[1] And Dionysius tells us that Mary Magdalene, that was so loose and dissolute in her youth, being converted in her old age, she sequestered herself from all worldly pleasures, and lived a most solitary life in the mountains of Gallia, where she spent a full thirty years in meditation, fasting, and prayer. And old godly Similes said that he had been in the world sixty years, but had lived but seven, counting his life, not from his first birth, but from his new birth. And Augustine repented that he had begun to seek, serve, and love God no sooner. By all these instances it is most evident that God may bestow himself as a portion upon sinners, upon very great sinners, yea, upon the greatest of sinners, and that at last cast, when they are stricken in years, and when they are even ready to go out of this world; and therefore let no man despair of having God for his portion, though for the present his soul cannot say, The Lord is my portion.

O sirs! despair is a sin, a very heinous sin, yea, it is that sin that damns with a witness. Despairing Judas perished and was damned, when the very murderers of Christ, believing on Christ, were saved,[2] Acts 2. Despair thrusts God from his mercy seat; it throws disgrace upon the throne of grace; it

---

[1] See my 'Apples of God,' pp. 352-354, two more famous stories of such that were converted in their old age. [See Brooks' *Works*, vol. 1.—G.]

[2] Roger bishop of Salisbury in King Stephen's days was so troubled that he could not live, and dared not die, *etc.*

gives the lie to all the precious promises; it casts reproach upon the nature of God; it tramples under feet the blood of the covenant; it cuts the throat of faith, hope, and repentance; it renders all the means of grace useless and fruitless; it embitters all a man's comforts; it gives a sting to all a man's troubles; it proclaims Satan a conqueror; it raises a hell in the conscience; it makes a man a *Magor-missabib*, a terror to himself and an astonishment to others. In the seventh chapter of Daniel there is mention made of four beasts: the first a lion, the second a bear, the third a leopard, but the fourth, without distinction either of kind, or sex, or name, is said to be very fearful, and terrible, and strong; and such a thing as this fourth beast is desperation, as all have found that have ever been under it. Desperation is a complicated sin; it is a mother sin; it is a breeding sin; it is the complement of all sins; and therefore above all take heed of this sin. O sirs! as you love your souls, and as you would be happy to all eternity, do not despair, nor do not be peremptory in your conclusions, that God will never be your portion, because for the present he is not your portion. Remember the gracious invitations of God, and remember the glorious riches of mercy, and remember the overflowings of infinite grace, and then despond and despair if you can.

Sixth Position. The sixth and last position is this, *That such is the love, care, goodness, and kindness of God to his people, that few or none of them die without some assurance that God is their portion, and that they have an interest and propriety in him.* That here and there a particular Christian, in cases not ordinary, may die doubting, and ascend to heaven in a cloud, as Christ did, Acts 1:9, will, I suppose, be readily granted; and that the generality of Christians shall, first or last, more or less, mediately or immediately, have some comfortable assurance, that God is their God, and that he is their portion, and that they have a real interest and propriety in him, may I suppose be thus evinced.

[1.] First, *Several precious promises that are scattered up and down the Scripture seem to speak out such a thing as this is.* Take these for a taste: Psa. 9:18, 'For the needy shall not always be forgotten: the expectation of the poor shall not perish for ever.' Psa. 22:26, 'The meek shall eat and be satisfied: they shall praise the Lord that seek him: your heart shall live for ever.' Psa. 84:11, 'For the Lord God is a sun and a shield: the Lord will give grace and glory: and no good thing will he withhold from them that walk uprightly.' Hos. 2:23, 'And I will have mercy upon her that had not obtained mercy; and I will say to them which were not my people, Thou art my people; and they shall say, Thou art my God.' Psa. 5:12, 'For thou, Lord, wilt bless the righteous; with favour wilt thou compass him as with a shield.' John 14:21, 23, 'He that hath my commandments, and keepeth them, he it is that loveth me: and he that loveth me shall be loved of my Father, and I will love him, and will manifest myself to him. If any man love me, he will keep my words: and my Father will love him, and we will come unto him, and make our abode with him.'[1]

[2.] Secondly, *The common experiences of the saints, both in the Old and New Testaments, evidence as much.* Song of Sol. 2:16, 'My beloved is mine, and I am his'; Song of Sol. 6:3, 'I am my beloved's, and my beloved is mine'; and Song of Sol. 7:10, 'I am my beloved's, and his desire is towards me.'

[1] Ponder upon that of Ezek. 34:30, 31.

Isa. 63:16, 'Doubtless thou art our father, though Abraham be ignorant of us, and Israel acknowledge us not: thou, O Lord, art our Father, our redeemer; thy name is from everlasting.' Isa. 64:8, 9, 'But now, O Lord, thou art our Father: behold, see, we beseech thee, we are all thy people.' Jer. 3:22, 23, 'Behold, we come unto thee; for thou art the Lord our God. Truly in the Lord our God is the salvation of Israel.' Isa. 25:9, 'And it shall be said in that day, Lo, this is our God; we have waited for him, and he will save us.' I might produce a cloud of witnesses from among the patriarchs and prophets, further to evince this truth; but enough is as good as a feast.

And as the church of God in the Old Testament, so the church of God in the New Testament attained to the same assurance. The believers in Corinth were sealed, and had the earnest of the Spirit in their hearts: 2 Cor. 1:22, 'Who hath also sealed us, and given the earnest of the Spirit in our hearts.' And 2 Cor. 5:1, 5, 'For we know, that if our earthly house of this tabernacle were dissolved, we have a building of God, an house not made with hands, eternal in the heavens. Now he that hath wrought us for the self-same thing is God, who also hath given us the earnest of the Spirit.' And so the believing Ephesians had the like: Eph. 1:13, 'In whom, after ye believed, ye were sealed with the holy Spirit of promise, which is the earnest of our inheritance.' And so Eph. 4:30, 'And grieve not the holy Spirit of God, whereby ye are sealed unto the day of redemption.' And the believing Thessalonians had the same: 1 Thess. 1:4, 5, 'Knowing, brethren beloved, your election of God. For our gospel came not unto you in word only, but also in power, and in the Holy Ghost, and in much assurance.' I might give you many particular instances out of the New Testament to confirm this truth, but these general instances are more convincing and satisfying.

[3.] Thirdly, *If God should not, first or last, sooner or later, mediately or immediately, give his people some comfortable assurance that he is their portion, and that they have a real interest and propriety in him, the spirits, the souls of his people would certainly faint and fail; but this God will never suffer, this God by promise has engaged himself to prevent, as you may see in* Isa. 57:16, 18, 19, 'For I will not contend for ever, neither will I be always wroth: for the spirit should fail before me, and the souls which I have made. I have seen his ways, and will heal him: I will lead him also, and restore comforts unto him, and to his mourners. I create the fruit of the lips; Peace, peace to him that is afar off, and to him that is near, saith the Lord; and I will heal him.' Now, seeing that God has so graciously undertaken for his people, that their spirits shall not faint nor fail, there is no doubt but that, sooner or later, more or less, God will assure his people that he is their portion, and that they have a real interest and propriety in him.

[4.] Fourthly, *The Lord's supper is a sealing ordinance, and was ordained, instituted, and appointed for that very purpose and to that very end, viz.,* to seal up the believer's propriety in God, and to assure him of his interest in God, in Christ, in the everlasting covenant, and in all the benefits of Christ's death, to wit, the favour of God, reconciliation, redemption, and the remission of sins.[1] Now, how can it possibly be imagined, that so glorious an ordinance should be instituted to so great and so glorious an end as to assure believers of their interest and propriety in God,

---

[1] Matt. 26:26-28; 1 Cor. 11:23, 24; Rom. 4:11.

and yet this end should never be effected in them all their days, for whose sake the ordinance was instituted and appointed? Certainly God never appointed any ordinance to accomplish any end, but first or last that ordinance did accomplish that end for which it was appointed and instituted, Isa. 55:10, 11; 45:23. Cyprian shows how the martyrs in the primitive church, when they were to appear before the cruel persecuting tyrants, were wont[1] to receive the Lord's supper, and thereby they were so assured of their interest and propriety in God, and so fired with zeal and fervour, and filled with faith and fortitude, *etc.*, that they made nothing of the greatest torments that those bloody tyrants could inflict upon them. And, says Chrysostom, by the sacrament of the Lord's supper we are so armed against Satan's temptations, that he flees from us, as if we were so many lions that spat fire.

The Jews in the celebration of the passover sang Psalm 113, with the five following Psalms, which they called the great *Hallelujah*, and it was always after that cup of wine, which they called the cup of praise; and thus it should be with the saints. At all times, upon all occasions, in all places, they should sing *Hallelujahs* to God. Oh, but when they are at the Lord's supper, then they should sing the great Hallelujah; but how they will be ever able to sing this great Hallelujah, except first or last, more or less, God gives them some assurance of their interest and propriety in himself, I cannot for my life discern. But,

[5.] Fifthly, *There is in all believers the choice and precious springs of assurance*, as

(i.) *Union and communion with the Father and Son*:

---

[1] [That is, accustomed.]

1 John 1:3, 'That which we have seen and heard declare we unto you, that ye also may have fellowship with us: and truly our fellowship is with the Father, and with his Son Jesus Christ.' Now, that union that is between the foundation and the building, the head and the members, the husband and the wife, the father and the child, the subject and the prince, the body and the soul, is nothing so near a union as that which is between a believer and God. Besides, that union that a Christian has with God is an honourable union, and it is an inseparable union, it is an invincible union, and it is an everlasting union, 1 Cor. 6:16, 17. Now, how is it possible for a man to have such a near and such a glorious union and fellowship with God from the day of his conversion to the day of his dissolution, and yet never come to any assurance of his interest and propriety in God, is a thing not easily imaginable.

(ii.) *Precious faith* is another spring of assurance: 1 Pet. 1:8, 'Whom having not seen, ye love; in whom, though now ye see him not, yet believing, ye rejoice with joy unspeakable and full of glory.' Now, this spring is in all the saints, 2 Pet. 1:1. The faith of expectance will in time rise up into a faith of reliance, and the faith of reliance will in time advance itself into a faith of assurance.

(iii.) *Hope* is another spring of assurance: Col. 1:27, 'Christ in you, the hope of glory'; Heb. 6:19, 'Which hope we have as an anchor of the soul, both sure and stedfast, and which entereth into that within the veil.'

(iv.) A *good conscience* is another spring of assurance, 2 Cor. 1:12.

(v.) Real *love to the saints* is another spring of assurance, 1 John 3:14.

(vi.) And lastly, *the Spirit of God* is another spring of assurance, Rom. 8. Now, that a Christian should have all these choice springs of assurance in his soul, from his new birth to the day of his death, and yet in all that time never come to assurance of his interest and propriety in God, is a thing, I had almost said, beyond all belief. But,

[6.] Sixthly, *There is nothing in all the world that the hearts of the saints are more frequently, more fervently, and more abundantly carried out after, in all their prayers and supplications, than this*, that God would tell them that he is their portion, and that he would clear up their interest and propriety in himself, Psa. 4:6, 7. The constant language of their souls is this: Lord, do but tell us that you are our portion, and then bestow earthly portions upon whom you please; do but clear up our interest and propriety in yourself, and then we shall say, 'Our lot is fallen in a pleasant place, and verily we have a goodly heritage,' Psa. 16:5, 6. Believers know that assurance that God is their portion, and that they have an interest and propriety in him, will ease them of all their sinful cares, fears, terrors, horrors, jealousies, suspicions, and sad apprehensions, which make their lives a very hell. They know that assurance of their interest and propriety in God will make ever bitter sweet, and every sweet more sweet; it will turn a wilderness into a paradise, an Egypt into a Canaan. They know that assurance that God is theirs will raise the truest comforts, the purest comforts, the greatest comforts, the surest comforts, the strongest comforts, the rarest comforts, the sweetest comforts, and the most lasting comforts in their souls, Isa. 40:1, 2. They know that assurance of their interest in God will fit them for the highest duties in Christianity, and for the hardest duties in Christianity, and for the costliest duties in Christianity, and for the most neglected, scorned, and despised duties in Christianity. They know that assurance of their propriety in God will most quicken their graces, and act their graces, and raise their graces, and strengthen their graces, and brighten their graces, and put a lustre and a beauty upon their graces. They know that assurance of their interest in God will wonderfully weaken sin, and effectually crucify their hearts to the world, and sweetly moderate their affections to their nearest and dearest relations, and powerfully arm them both against the world's oppositions and Satan's temptations.

To conclude; they know that assurance of their propriety in God will make death more desirable than terrible, yea, it will make the thoughts of death sweet, and the approaches of death easy, and all the warnings of death pleasant to their souls, and therefore they follow God hard day and night, with strong cries, prayers, tears, sighs, and groans, that he would make it evident to them that he is their portion, and that he would clear up their interest and propriety in him. Now, how can any man that is in his wits imagine that God should always turn a deaf ear to the prayers of his people in this thing especially, considering that their prayers, cries, tears, sighs, and groans are but the products of his own Spirit in them, Rom. 8:26, 27; and considering likewise the several promises, by which he has engaged himself to answer to the prayers of his people? I might tire both you and myself in turning to those particular promises, but that I am resolved against, and therefore take that for all: John 16:23, 24, 'Verily, verily, I say unto you, Whatsoever ye shall ask the Father in my name, he will give it you. Ask, and ye shall receive, that your joy may be full.' This double asseveration, 'Verily, verily,' is never used but in matters of greatest weight and importance; and this gemination,[1] 'Verily, verily,' is a vehement confirmation of the truth of what Christ speaks. Now, from this gracious promise I may safely and clearly infer, that if God the Father will give to believers whatever they ask in the name of Christ, then certainly, at first or last, sooner or later, he will give them assurance that he is their portion, and that they have an undoubted interest and propriety in him; for this is one of the great requests that they are still putting up in the name of Christ, and upon the grant of this request depends the fulness of a Christian's joy. But,

[7.] Seventhly and lastly, *If God should not sooner or later, more or less, assure his people that he is their portion, and that they have an interest and a propriety in him; then he would be a very great loser, if I may so speak*; he would lose many praises, and many thanksgivings; he would lose much of that love, of that honour, and of that delight, and of that admiration, which otherwise he might have from among his children. And it is very observable, that of all the duties of religion there are none that are pressed so closely, so frequently, and so strongly upon Christians, as those of praising God, and rejoicing in God, as all know that know anything of the Scriptures.[2] Now, how it will stand with the holiness of God, and with the wisdom of God, and with the care of God, to be so great a loser in the very things which he has so roundly and earnestly pressed upon his people, when by one sweet word of his mouth he might

[1] [That is, twinning or doubling.]
[2] I might produce above a hundred scriptures to evidence this.

so easily and so happily prevent it, I cannot easily discern. All believers know that there is no such ready, no such effectual way under heaven to draw out their love, their joy, their delight, their praises, and their thanksgiving to God, as God's assuring them that he is their portion, and that they have an unquestionable interest and propriety in him. Certainly that God that loves the praises of his people, and that delights in the rejoicings of his people, and that is so infinitely pleased with the thanksgivings of his people, that God will not always hide himself from his people, that God will sooner or later so manifest himself to his people, that they shall be able to see their interest and propriety in God, and rejoicing to say, 'The Lord is our portion.'

Now, oh you that are the people of the Lord, and that to this very day lie under many fears and doubts about your interest and propriety in God, be not discouraged, do not hang down the head, do not despond, do not despair, for certainly sooner or later God will assure you that he is your portion, and that you have an interest and a propriety in him.

PURITAN 🗝 PAPERBACKS